THE BEST-EVER STEP-BY-STEP

kid's first cookbook

THE BEST-EVER STEP-BY-STEP
kid's first
cookbook

Delicious recipe ideas for 5–12 year olds, from lunch boxes and picnics to quick and easy meals, sweet treats, desserts, drinks, and party food

150 irresistible recipes for kids to cook, with step-by-step instructions and more than 1,000 fantastic photographs

Nancy McDougall

HERMES
HOUSE

This edition is published by Hermes House,
an imprint of Anness Publishing Ltd,
Hermes House, 88–89 Blackfriars Road,
London SE1 8HA
tel. 020 7401 2077; fax 020 7633 9499
www.hermeshouse.com www.annesspublishing.com

If you like the images in this book and would like to investigate
using them for publishing, promotions, or advertising, please visit
our website www.practicalpictures.com for more information.

Publisher: Joanna Lorenz
Senior Editor: Lucy Doncaster
Text Editors: Nancy McDougall and Glynis McGuinness
Designer: Lisa Tai
Photography: William Lingwood
Food Stylists: Lucy McKelvie and Fergal Connolly
Prop Stylist: Helen Trent
Models: Freddie, Cressida, Lucas, Eve, Gus, Kit,
    Scarlett and Lavina
Production Controller: Steve Lang

© Anness Publishing Ltd 2009

Ethical Trading Policy

At Anness Publishing we believe that business should be conducted in an
ethical and ecologically sustainable way, with respect for the environment
and a proper regard to the replacement of the natural resources we employ.

As a publisher, we use a lot of wood pulp to make high-quality paper
for printing, and that wood commonly comes from spruce trees. We are
therefore currently growing more than 750,000 trees in three Scottish
forest plantations: Berrymoss (320 acres/130 hectares), West Touxhill
(305 acres/125 hectares), and Deveron Forest (185 acres/75 hectares).
The forests we manage contain more than 3.5 times the number of
trees employed each year in making paper for the books we manufacture.

Because of this ongoing ecological investment program, you, as our
customer, can have the pleasure and reassurance of knowing that a tree
is being cultivated on your behalf to naturally replace the materials
used to make the book you are holding.

Our forestry program is run in accordance with the UK Woodland
Assurance Scheme (UKWAS) and will be certified by the internationally
recognized Forest Stewardship Council (FSC). The FSC is a nongovernment
organization dedicated to promoting responsible management of
the world's forests. Certification ensures forests are managed in an
environmentally sustainable and socially responsible way. For additional
information about this scheme, go to www.annesspublishing.com/trees

Notes

Standard spoon and cup measures are level.

Electric oven temperatures in this book are for conventional ovens.
When using a fan oven, the temperature will probably need to be
reduced by about 20–40°F/10–20°C. Because ovens vary, check with
your manufacturer's instruction book for guidance.

The nutritional analysis is calculated per portion, for example, a serving
or item), unless otherwise stated. If the recipe gives a range, such as
Serves 4–6, then the analysis will be for the smaller portion size, for
example, 6 servings.

Measurements for sodium do not include salt added to taste.

Large eggs are used unless otherwise stated in the text.

Publisher's Note

Although the advice and information in this book are believed to be
accurate and true at the time of going to press, neither the authors nor
the publisher can accept any legal responsiblity or liability for any errors or
omissions that may be made nor for any inaccuracies nor for any harm or
injury that comes about from following instructions or advice in this book.
All children need to work with adult guidance and supervision and it is the
parent or carer's responsibility to ensure the child is working safely.

Contents

Getting started　　　　　　　6

Safety in the kitchen　　　　　8

Healthy eating　　　　　　　10

Cooking terms explained　　14

Some useful equipment　　　16

Some useful ingredients　　　20

Basic techniques　　　　　　28

Menu ideas　　　　　　　　34

Party ideas　　　　　　　　36

Packed lunches and picnics　38

Snacks and light bites　　64

Quick and easy suppers　86

Main meals　　　　　　118

Desserts and drinks　　154

Weekend treats　　　　188

Party food　　　　　　210

Nutritional notes　　　　　248

Index　　　　　　　　　252

Getting started

Cooking is a lot of fun and very rewarding, whatever your age or previous experience in the kitchen. As with most things, there are some basic guidelines that should be followed, but once these have been learned, you will be able to make a fabulous range of tasty treats.

Making food you can eat and share is plenty of fun, and there is nothing better than seeing your friends or family tuck into the food that you've cooked. What's more, cooking teaches you important skills, such as weighing, measuring, understanding time and counting, which are useful both in and out of the kitchen. Mixing, stirring, sprinkling, and spreading will help your coordination and tasks such as decorating cakes and cookies are a great way to be creative.

Although cakes and cookies aren't the healthiest of foods, homemade ones, made with good quality ingredients and no artificial additives or colorings, are far better for you than most store-bought snacks, and also taste so much better.

Once you have been cooking for a little while you will feel confident enough to try out new foods. You can then start substituting ingredients and creating your own recipes—discovering new combinations of flavors and textures and coming up with some really exciting dishes of your own.

▶ Learning to cook at a young age will stand you in good stead for the rest of your life.

▼ Children of all ages will enjoy helping in the kitchen.

Cooking safely

Children develop at different rates and only parents or guardians will know when their kids are ready to be introduced to using specific tools or are able to help with certain jobs in the kitchen. Working alongside an adult and trying new cooking methods (with close guidance) is a good way for children to learn safe practices and to gain the skills needed for greater independence, although adult supervision is always recommended when children of any age are cooking.

Many of the projects in this book use knives, scissors, graters, electronic equipment, or heat. Adult supervision is always required when using these, no matter how old or experienced the child, and help will be required for younger children. Pictures showing how to do something dangerous, which will require adult help or supervision, have been highlighted with icons, shown below:

(!) = the task being shown uses sharp or dangerous implements or electronic equipment, such as knives, graters, food processors, or blenders. Adult help may be required to do the step or, at the very least, supervise children very carefully.

(✋) = the task being shown involves heat. Adult help may be required to do the step or, at the very least, supervise children very carefully. Oven mitts should be worn when using an oven. Adults should always drain hot foods, such as pasta, and put dishes or pans in the oven and remove them when the food is cooked.

Choosing a project

When selecting a project, first check the colored strip across the top of the page to see how long it might take to make and cook. These don't include any food rising, chilling, resting, or freezing time—instead they are a guide to how long you will need to be in the kitchen for.

In order to help you see how easy or difficult or easy a recipe is we've also added a simple star rating, which works as follows:

★ = the project is "easy as ABC". All children from 5 to 11 should be able to tackle these, with supervision, and there is only a small amount of cutting or electronic equipment use involved. Adults should help with any steps requiring heat or dangerous implements.

★★ = you should "give it a try"! There might be some more cutting or manual dexterity involved. With close parental supervision, most children will be able to enjoy them.

★★★ = the project is "nice and challenging". These are designed for older children and perhaps kids who already have some cooking experience and are ready to try some more advanced techniques. Adult supervision will still always be required for any steps involving dangerous implements or heat.

Getting organized

In addition to the star rating, cooking and preparation times shown in the colored strip at the top of the page, a list of tools is also included on every recipe. It is sensible to check you have everything you need before you start making the recipe, because there is nothing worse than getting halfway through and realizing you can't complete the dish. Child-size equipment should be used where appropriate, and it is important that everything is clean before you start. The same applies to ingredients, and you should make sure you do any preparation listed in the ingredients list, such as chopping or peeling, before you start, so you are completely ready to do the recipe. You could also measure out everything into small bowls, like they do on television, so everything is ready to be combined and you are sure you have all the ingredients.

General rules

1 Always use standard kitchen measuring cups for measuring your dry ingredients. To make sure the top is level, run the flat side of a round-bladed knife across the top. Use a standard measuring cup to measure liquid ingredients.
2 Spoonfuls are all level. Always use proper measuring spoons instead of normal cutlery. They usually come in sets, and measure from a tablespoon down to a quarter of a teaspoon. To make sure the top is level, run the flat side of a round-bladed knife across the top.
3 Ovens should be preheated to the specified temperature at least 10 minutes before you cook the dish. If you are using a fan-assisted oven, follow the manufacturer's instructions for reducing the time and temperature. As a rough guide, reduce the temperature by 68°F or the cooking time by 10 minutes. Try not to open the oven during the cooking time.
4 Although average cooking times are given for some packaged foods, such as pasta and rice, always check the package and follow what is says there, because different brands and different types of ingredients cook in different amounts of time.
5 Always check that meat and fish are completely cooked through before serving. Cooking times can vary slightly depending on how thick the meat or fish is, so it is better to be safe than sorry.
6 Only reheat food once and make sure it's piping hot all the way through before serving.

▲ Younger children should stick to the easier recipes in this book, and should always be supervised by an adult.

Safety in the kitchen

Kitchens can be dangerous places if you are not careful, so it is important that you follow a few basic rules about hygiene and about using equipment, such as sharp knives and ovens, to ensure your cooking experience is both fun and safe.

Before you start
Proper preparation in a kitchen is essential, and if you follow these simple guidelines, then you will not only be safe but the recipes are more likely to work, too.
1 Check with an adult that it's okay for you to cook.
2 Read the recipe all the way through and make sure that you've got enough time to make and cook it without rushing. There's nothing worse than running out of time before you've finished cooking. Ask for help if you need it.
3 Shut pets out of the kitchen before you start to cook. You don't want animal hairs in the food—ugh! And they may get under your feet, which can be dangerous.

▼ Get out any equipment before you start.

4 Get out all the ingredients that you need. Measure the ingredients and put them in bowls. It's much easier to make a recipe if everything is ready to add when you need it, and it means you won't forget to add an ingredient.
   5 Get out all the equipment that you'll need.
   6 Line any cake pans that you will need before making the recipe.

Hygiene in the kitchen
1 Always wash your hands before you start cooking.
2 Tie back long hair.
3 If you handle raw meat or fish, or dirty fruit or vegetables, wash your hands again before you carry on cooking.
4 Use separate cutting boards for raw meat and fish, cooked meat and fish, and fruit and vegetables. If you like, use a different colored board for each type of food. Or wash knives and cutting boards before using them to prepare different types of food.
5 Make sure meat and fish are cooked all the way through before serving. If necessary, cut a piece open in the middle to check.

▶ Tie or clip back long hair securely before you start cooking.

Safety first
general care in the kitchen

✔ If you drop or spill anything on the floor, mop it up immediately. If you leave it until later, you may forget and someone may slip on it.

✔ Handle sharp knives carefully. When chopping and slicing, make sure you keep your fingers well away from the blade. Chop on a board and keep the blade pointing downward. Keep sharp knives out of reach of young children.

✘ Never touch plugs, electrical equipment, outlets, or switches with damp hands—you can get an electric shock.

✔ If particularly young children can't reach the counter easily, stand them on a sturdy chair, making sure it is completely steady. Supervise them closely all the time.

▶ It is really important that you wash your hands thoroughly with hot water and soap before you start cooking. You must also wash them again immediately after touching raw fish or meat, or handling chiles.

Using dangerous implements

1 Adult supervision is always required when you are using dangerous implements.

2 The blades in food processors and blenders are extremely sharp, so never put your hands in to move anything, and ask an adult to help.

3 Always make sure the lid of a blender or the stopper on a processor is firmly on before you press the start button. Adult supervision is required.

4 Let hot soups and sauces cool slightly before putting them in a blender or processor.

5 Keep your fingers well away from the beaters of electric mixers while they are whizzing around. Adult supervision is required.

6 Always make sure the beaters of an electric hand mixer are touching the bottom of the bowl before you switch it on. If you don't, the mixture will fly all over the kitchen when you switch on the mixer.

7 When grating, hold food with your hand away from the cutting edge. Adult supervision is required.

8 Put a damp dish towel under bowls before beating ingredients. This helps to prevent it from slipping.

▲ *Be careful when grating. Hold the grater firmly in one hand, and grip the food with the other hand, away from the cutting edge.*

Safety first
for ovens, stove tops, and microwaves

✔ Turn pan handles to the sides of the stove top, so they can't be accidentally knocked over.

✔ Make sure that the pan you are using is big enough so that the food doesn't boil over or spill over. Only adults only should drain hot foods.

✔ Stir pans carefully, making sure that hot food doesn't slop over the edges. Adult supervision is required.

✔ Always use oven mitts to get food out of the microwave, because although most dishes don't get hot when microwaved, some do. Remove the lid or clear plastic wrap covering the food carefully to avoid being burned by steam. Adult supervision is required.

✔ Ask an adult, wearing oven mitts, to take bowls and pans out of the oven.

✔ Make sure you turn off the stove top as soon as you've finished using it. If you leave it on, you may touch it or put something onto a hot ring that will break or melt with the heat.

◀ *Adults should remove hot pans and dishes from the oven, wearing oven mitts.*

✔ Be careful when frying and NEVER leave a hot skillet unattended. Stir-frying and shallow-frying should be done only by older children. Deep-frying must be done only by adults.

✔ Food must be dry before it comes into contact with hot fat—otherwise, the fat can spit out and burn. If food seems damp, pat it dry with paper towels. Stand back from the pan and lower the food in gently, one piece at a time. Adult supervision is required.

✔ Steam can burn really badly, so keep your hands away from steaming kettles and pans and be careful when removing the lid from a pan containing boiling water.

✘ Never put aluminum foil, metal dishes, or dishes or cups with metal paint rims in the microwave.

Healthy eating

Cooking at home is a really fun way to find out about ingredients and try out a wide range of different foods that you may not have had before. Making meals from scratch is also much healthier and tastier than eating TV dinners and take-out foods.

Cooking is the perfect way to learn why we need to eat a healthy diet, what certain foods do for our bodies, and how to judge if food is fresh, ripe, and good quality. Ask a lot of questions, such as why certain foods are good for you.

Mealtimes are the best opportunity to show off your new skills, so whenever possible try to gather everyone together around the table. Weekends are often the best time to try more complex dishes because there is generally more time to cook.

▼ *This diagram illustrates how much of each type of food you should try to eat during a day.*

▶ *Cooking your own food encourages you to try new things, such as this fresh homemade pasta.*

A balanced diet

Children of all ages need a balanced diet with at least five portions of fruit and vegetables a day, plus two to three portions of protein (meat, fish, eggs, nuts, or legumes) and two to three portions of dairy produce (milk, yogurt, and cheese). They also need some starchy carbohydrates (bread, rice, pasta, breakfast cereals, and potatoes) with each meal.

FOOD WHEEL

Carbohydrates, such as bread, potatoes, pasta, and rice

Fresh fruit, vegetables, and salads

Protein, such as meat, poultry, fish, eggs, dairy, nuts, and legumes

Natural fats, such as oily fish, avocados, and nuts

Eat only a small amount of fatty or sugary foods, such as cakes, cookies, potato chips, and candy

▲ *Eating a rainbow of different colored fruit and vegetables every day ensures you get all the vitamins and minerals you need.*

Maximum vitality

In order to get the best from the food you eat, lightly cook vegetables or serve them raw in salads (overcooking destroys many of the nutrients, especially vitamin C). Sticks of raw carrot, celery, red bell pepper, and cucumber are great served with a dip, and grated raw carrot mixed with golden raisins and roasted cashew nuts makes a tasty snack.

Menu essentials

Although everyone needs to eat a balanced diet, children do have a few special requirements. The following should be included on a weekly basis:

1 Calcium-rich foods are necessary for strong teeth and bones, so foods such as milk, cheese, yogurt, soybeans, tofu, and nuts are very important. Fortified breakfast cereals, margarine, and oily fish contain dietary vitamin D, which ensures a good supply of calcium in the blood.
2 Vitamin A, found in milk, margarine, butter, leafy green vegetables, carrots, and apricots, promotes good vision and healthy skin. Although carrots may not make you see in the dark, they will help you have eagle eyes!
3 Iron is important for healthy blood and energy levels. Good sources include red meat, liver, fish, beans, lentils, green vegetables, and fortified breakfast cereals.
4 In order to be able to absorb all that iron, your body needs vitamin C. As well as being found in citrus fruit, such as oranges and lemons, it is also present in tomatoes and potatoes.
5 Oily fish, such as mackerels and sardines, are a good source of protein, vitamins, and minerals, and they also contain omega 3 fatty acids, which have heart-friendly properties. Omega 3 is also found in seeds and walnuts, as well as in some products that have been enriched with the fats, such as milk and eggs.

◀ *Dairy and eggs are high in calcium and packed with vitamins.*

An easy way to check you are eating the right balance of foods over a day is to imagine a dinner plate and divide it into several sections. One third should be filled by carbohydrates, one third with fresh fruit, vegetables, or salad, and the remaining third divided into three smaller sections containing protein, natural fats, and a very small amount of added fat or sugar, such as potato chips, chocolate, or cookies. This is often called a food wheel, and it is illustrated by the diagram opposite.

It is also extremely important that you eat three meals a day, because children require a lot of energy for rushing around and for growing. Breakfast is especially vital for enabling concentration at school and providing energy to see you through until lunch. It also provides a good opportunity to eat high-fiber fortified breakfast cereals and a dose of vitamin C in the form of a glass of orange juice.

In order to ensure you eat a good range of foods during a week, sit down and plan your meals. This not only gives you the chance to have your say about what you eat, but it also means you can plan ahead and check you have all the ingredients.

Five a day

Children and adults need at least five portions of fruit and vegetables a day, of which half should be vegetables and half should be fruit. These should be as varied in color as possible—think of the foods as a rainbow and have five different colors each day. A medium apple, orange, banana, pear, or peach is one portion. Fruit juice counts as only one portion of fruit. If you don't like eating large pieces of fruit, you can make them into smoothies or cut them into bite-size pieces.

Eat your greens!

Small children are often choosy about their food. If they refuse a few foods but still eat a balanced diet, it's probably best not to make a fuss about it. No one food is essential. So if, for instance, they won't eat Brussels sprouts and cooked cabbage but will eat raw cabbage in homemade coleslaw, then it's best not to nag them. Food should be a pleasure not a battle. Just keep encouraging them to try a tiny amount of new foods—experts say that sometimes it takes up to eight tries before a small child will accept something different. However, if a child will eat only a very small range of foods, and these are mostly unhealthy, then you will need to resort to disguising healthy food in soups and sauces. Vegetables are one of the most common foods that children are fussy about.

Making homemade vegetable soup is a good way of encouraging children to eat more vegetables—butternut squash and carrot soup always seem popular. You can also add chopped vegetables to casseroles and curries and pasta sauces. If it is meat that they won't eat, you can blend cooked chicken into a vegetable soup. If older children have made a decision to become vegetarian, however, you should try to respect their choice and make sure that they get adequate protein from other sources.

Going foraging or picking fruit is another good way of encouraging them to try new foods, as well as teaching them where it comes from. If they select and handle the food themselves, they will be more inclined to try it.

▶ *Fresh vegetables can be used in many dishes.*

Special diets

Food allergies and intolerance are on the increase, especially in children under five. The most common foods that can cause an adverse reaction are cow's milk, eggs, peanuts and other nuts, soybeans, and wheat. Allergic reactions are also known to have been caused by citrus fruit, chicken, goat milk, sesame and other seeds, and exotic fruit, such as mango.

After the age of five many, but not all, children outgrow their allergies, so it is worth consulting your doctor and, if so advised, trying them with a very small amount of the food. Some children, however, have a severe, immediate reaction to certain foods, called anaphylaxis, which can be lethal. Peanuts are the most common cause of this, so you need to be careful to avoid exposing children to any food that may have been in contact with nuts. If you are cooking for other children or giving a children's party, it is best to ask the parents well in advance if any of the children have special requirements.

▲ *Picking fresh fruit is loads of fun and will teach you a lot about where different foods, such as apples, come from.*

▲ *Many children are intolerant or allergic to foods such as eggs, dairy products, and nuts, so check before feeding other children.*

Staying healthy

There is an ever-increasing problem with childhood obesity in the Western world and we need to make sure that children have a healthy diet and don't eat too much sugar and fat in the form of candy and fatty snacks, such as potato chips. However, that needs to be balanced by making sure that growing youngsters have enough calories to give them energy, especially when they are going through a growing spurt or doing a lot of exercise. Energetic, growing teenagers need more calories than their parents.

All children are different, even in the same family, so you need to watch them and treat the diet of each one individually. If you think a child is becoming obese, gently encourage him or her to cut out some of the treats and replace them with healthy snacks, such as fruit and low-fat, low-sugar yogurts. However, be tactful and don't make an issue of it—the last thing you want to do is make the child self-conscious and anxious. If a child is growing, it's best to keep his or her weight even and let the child "grow into it" instead of try to lose weight.

Encourage children to drink more water and cut out sugary drinks—this alone can make a huge difference. Sugar in commercial beverages is empty calories that have no nutritional value and don't help to satisfy the appetite. Water is best, but if they won't drink plain water, give them low-calorie drinks. Avoid drinking a lot of fruit juice as a thirst quencher. A glass of freshly squeezed orange juice a day is a good source of vitamin C, but if they drink several glasses, the calories will mount up.

◀ Homemade fruit smoothies are a much healthier choice than carbonated drinks or milkshakes.

Milkshakes made with anything other than fruit and milk should be enjoyed only on special occasions. These are very fattening and because they're drinks, they slip down without really being considered as food. Don't cut out milk altogether (unless they have a dairy allergy) because it's a valuable source of calcium and protein. Children under five should have whole milk. Older children can have semi-skimmed milk.

Many experts think the main cause of childhood obesity is lack of exercise, so encourage your children to walk more and do more sports. Take them swimming, or go for country walks and cycle rides—it will do you good, too.

▲ Low-fat yogurt served with homemade fruit puree and topped with granola makes a tasty dessert or snack.

▲ Milk makes a delicious and nutritious drink, and is very important for the development of strong, healthy bones.

Cooking terms explained

Although some cooking terms, such as rinse or chop, may be familiar, there are some words that may be new to you. This easy-to-use directory explains some of the basic terms that will appear in the recipes and should make them easier to follow.

▶ Most cooking techniques, such as kneading dough, are easy once you know how.

Bake To cook food in the oven.

Beat To mix and soften ingredients with a spoon, whisk, fork, or electric mixer (adult supervision is required).

Blend To mix ingredients until the mixture looks smooth. This is done in a bowl with a whisk, spoon, or electric mixer, or in a blender. Adult supervision is required when using electrical equipment.

Brown To fry meat in a hot pan until it turns brown. Adult supervision is required.

Chop To cut food into pieces. Use a sharp knife and a cutting board. Adult supervision is required.

Drain To pour off the water. This is often done by pouring it through a colander or strainer. To drain fried food, lift it using a spatula or slotted spoon and transfer it to a plate lined with paper towels. Adults should drain anything hot.

Drizzle To sprinkle drops of liquid onto food.

Flake To break drained, cooked, or canned fish into pieces using a knife and fork. As you do it, remove any bones carefully with your fingers.

Fold To carefully mix flour or other ingredients into a cake mixture. Always use a metal spoon and be careful not to knock the air out of the mixture.

Fry To cook food in hot oil or fat. Frying is only for older children and adults must always supervise. There are different types of frying:
- **Deep-frying** is done in a pan or a deep-fat fryer so that the food is completely submerged in oil. Only adults should do this.
- **Shallow-frying** is done in a skillet, usually in about ¼ inch of oil.
- **Stir-frying** is best done in a wok. The food is cut into even, small pieces and is constantly moved around the pan as it cooks over a high heat.
- **Dry-frying** is done in a nonstick skillet without added fat. The fat in the food melts and comes out as it cooks, so the food cooks in its own fat.

Garnish To decorate dishes with food, such as herbs, slices of lemon, grated chocolate, or berries.

▲ Cake ingredients are often beaten together.

▲ There are many different ways of chopping food.

▲ Tuna and other fish can be easily flaked with a fork.

▲ Olive oil is often drizzled over foods before or after cooking.

▲ Shallow-frying is usually done in a skillet.

▲ Cream is often whipped until it is really stiff.

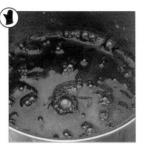

▲ When a liquid is simmering you will see small bubbles.

▲ Sifting flour or other dry ingredients removes any lumps.

Grate To shred food by sliding it from the top to the bottom of a grater. Most graters have holes of different sizes on each side. Use the biggest ones for foods such as cheese and the smallest ones for lemon zest (see zest) and nutmeg. Adult supervision is required.

Grease To brush or rub a baking pan or a bowl with oil or butter so that food doesn't stick during cooking.

Knead To make dough smooth by working the mixture with your hands on a floured surface. Bread dough must be kneaded vigorously for at least 5 minutes, but cookie and pastry dough should be handled gently, just until the dough forms a smooth ball, or it will become tough.

Line To put nonstick parchment paper in the bottom or bottom and sides of a cake pan so that the mixture doesn't stick to it. For small cakes or muffins, put a paper cake liner or paper muffin liner in each hole of a muffin pan.

Melt To heat a solid food, such as butter or chocolate, and make it liquid. Chocolate needs to be melted slowly in a heatproof bowl set over a pan containing a small amount of barely simmering water (known as a *bain marie*). The water should not touch the bottom of the bowl, or the chocolate can burn. Adult supervision is required.

Mash To pulp foods such as cooked potatoes or bananas until they form a smooth paste. This can be done with a potato masher or a fork.

Puree To squash fruit or cooked vegetables to make them smooth and saucelike. Use a blender or food processor (adult supervision is required), or put the food in a strainer set over a bowl and push it through with a wooden spoon.

Sift To push foods such as flour and confectioners' sugar through a strainer into a bowl to remove lumps.

Simmer To cook liquid so slowly that small bubbles just come to the surface. Adult supervision is required.

Whisk or whip To beat food using an electric mixer (adult supervision is required) or a whisk until it becomes stiff, in the case of cream or egg whites, or free of lumps, in the case of sauces.

▲ Kneading should be done on a lightly floured surface.

▲ Take your time when melting chocolate.

▲ Line muffin pans with colorful paper liners.

▲ Pushing fruit through a strainer creates a puree.

Some useful equipment

There is an almost endless selection of gadgets and gizmos available for the kitchen, but many of these are not actually necessary for making the recipes in this book. This directory lists those that are most useful and will help you understand their uses.

▶ *Tools such as graters are vital for many recipes.*

Scales and cups

Large quantities of fresh fruit and vegetables are often weighed in scales at the supermarket before they are purchased. If helping with the shopping, you will find spring-loaded scales in the produce section. They will have a large bowl to put the food in and a dial that goes around as you add food. Add the food to the bowl until the pointer reaches the correct weight you need

▲ *Spring-loaded weighing scales*

and is steady. If you purchase meat from a butcher or fish dealer, he or she will weigh the meat for you. Scales are also used by professional bakery chefs because they are more accurate than measuring in cups.

In most homes, many dry ingredients, such as flour, sugar, and rice, as well as smaller produce, such as peas, raisins, or chopped mushrooms or celery, are measured in standard measuring cups. These come in a set of ¼ cup, ⅓ cup, ½ cup, and 1 cup. To measure ingredients in a cup, use the back edge of a knife with a rounded blade to level off the ingredients.

Measuring cup

Used for measuring liquids accurately, a heatproof glass cup is better than a plastic one because it can hold hot liquids. A 2½-cup measuring cup is the most useful size. To measure a liquid ingredient,

▼ *Measuring cup*

put the cup on a counter and crouch down so that your eyes are level with it, then pour in the liquid until you have the right amount. If you look from above the cup when measuring, you'll end up with the wrong amount.

Measuring spoons

These are used for measuring small amounts accurately, especially baking powder and spices. Spoonfuls in recipes are always level. To measure a level

▲ *Measuring spoons*

teaspoon accurately, fill it and then run your finger or the back of a blunt knife across the top.

Bowls

▲ *Mixing bowls*

You need bowls in several sizes, including a large bowl, for mixing cakes and doughs, plus a medium one and a small one. Before you start a recipe, make sure your bowl is large enough to mix all the ingredients easily, without spilling food over the edge. This is important

for mixing cakes and batters. Ovenproof glass bowls are good because they are heatproof and sturdy and you can see through them. The best bowls have rounded bottoms so that you can get to every bit of the mixture with your whisk, spatula, or spoon.

Strainer

For sauces and purees, you can use a strainer to make them smooth, or use it to drain small ingredients, such as rice or peas. You can use it for sifting dry ingredients, such as flour and confectioners' sugar, to remove any lumps and introduce air into the mixture (which helps to make cakes lighter). You can also use a sifter.

▲ *Strainer*

Colander

This is essentially a large bowl with holes in it used for draining foods, such as pasta or cooked vegetables, or for rinsing fruit and vegetables. Only adults should strain hot liquids. Always remember to put the colander in the sink or over a bowl or pan before you pour liquid through it.

▲ Colander

Cutting boards

It's best to have several plastic cutting boards in different colors so that you can use different ones for each type of food. This means that any bacteria that is in raw meat or fish, or any strong odors, don't get passed onto other foods, such as fruit. There's nothing worse than a fruit salad tasting of onion! Ideally, you should have a separate board for each of the following: raw meat, raw fish, cooked meats, and cheeses, vegetables, and fruit. Plus you need a wooden bread board for cutting bread and cakes. Always wash boards really thoroughly, especially after using them for raw meat or fish. Never cut food, using sharp knives, directly on a table or counter because you'll cut and ruin it.

▲ Cutting boards

Knives

If you're old enough to use sharp knives, you will need at least two: a medium one, called a cook's knife, for chopping—about 10 inches long with a 6-inch blade—and a small one with a serrated edge for cutting foods with smooth skins, such as tomatoes and cucumber. Always handle knives very, very carefully with an adult present. Ask an adult to sharpen them if they are blunt. It's actually safer to use a sharp knife than a blunt one because it will cut through food easily, so that you won't have to press hard before it will cut, and it won't slip.

▲ Sharp knives

Peeler

Use a peeler to peel vegetables, such as carrots and potatoes, and fruit, such as apples and pears. They are great for removing just the thin peel and not a thick layer of the fruit or vegetable. There are two main types of peeler: straight ones and Y-shape ones. Most people find the Y-shape type easier to use. Ask an adult to show you how to use the one in your kitchen, but remember to always hold the piece of fruit or vegetable in one hand and peel with the other, making sure you keep your fingers well away from the sharp edge. You can peel away from you or toward you. Adult supervision is required.

▲ Y-shape peeler

Grater

Most graters have at least two cutting surfaces, but some special ones, called microplanes, only have one. Use the side with big holes for grating cheese and carrots and the side with fine holes for lemon zest, ginger, and nutmeg. It's easiest to use a box grater, which has a handle on top and sits on a cutting board, so that it doesn't slide about as you grate. Graters can cut fingers as well, so keep your fingers away from the edge. Adult supervision is required.

▼ Box grater

Garlic press

A really handy tool for crushing garlic cloves without using sharp knives or getting your hands smelly, a garlic press is easy to use—simply put a peeled clove of garlic in the space in the press and press the handles together so the garlic comes out through the holes.

▲ Garlic press

Cookie cutters

These metal or plastic shapes are used for cutting out cookies. You need at least one round cutter to make cookies but if you have a lot of shapes and sizes you can make different shapes. They are also useful for cutting shapes out of slices of bread.

▲ Cookie cutters

Rolling pin

A long, smooth, round, heavy bar, usually made of wood, a rolling pin is used for rolling out pastry or cookie dough, as well as for bashing cookies to crumbs and flattening meat.

▲ Rolling pin

Wooden spoons

Use a wooden spoon to stir food in pans and for beating cake mixtures. You will need two or three different sizes, so that you can use a small one in a small pan or bowl and a long one in a large pan or bowl. Some spoons have one straight edge, which is useful for getting right into the corners of pans when you're making sauces that get thicker as they cook.

▲ Wooden spoons

Slotted spoon

A large metal spoon with holes in it, a slotted spoon is used to lift pieces of solid food out of pans, leaving the liquid behind in the pan.

Ladle

A big spoon with a deep bowl and a long handle, a ladle is used for scooping soup, stews, or sauces out of a pan or bowl.

▲ Slotted spoon and ladle

Spatulas

This thin, flat tool has a flat metal end with holes in it and a long rigid handle. It is used for lifting things off baking sheets and out of skillets and roasting pans, so that any fat in the pan drains off through the holes. They are available in several different shapes and sizes.

◄ Spatulas

Flexible spatula

Bendy rubber or plastic spatulas are used for scraping the sides of a mixing bowl to make sure you get all the mixture out and don't waste any. They are also useful for pushing food down into blenders.

▲ Flexible spatula

Tongs

Useful for turning pieces of food or removing them from a skillet or from under the broiler, tongs have long handles to keep your hands away from spitting fat. The easiest ones to use have scalloped edges on the gripping heads, which grip food well and means you can hold them safely.

▲ Tongs

Wire whisk

There are two types of wire whisk: a balloon whisk, where the wires make a round shape, and a coil whisk, which has a sturdy wire shaped into a loop at the end, with a fine wire coiled all the way around it. Use for whisking eggs, cream, or other liquids.

◄ Balloon whisk

Citrus juicer

There are different types of juicers. The easiest one to use has a bowl underneath to collect the juice and a filter with holes in to catch the seeds. They can be glass or plastic. You can also get a wooden juicer on the end of a short handle. You insert the squeezer end into the halved fruit and twist so the juice flows out into a bowl underneath.

▼ Lemon juicer

Cooling rack

A large, flat wire rack on short legs, this is used to cool cakes and cookies.

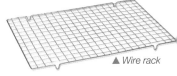

▲ Wire rack

With cakes, remove the lining paper before you put it on the rack, or it can be hard to remove. You can get cooling racks that stack on top each other, which are useful in a small kitchen or if you have more than one tray of food to cool.

Timer

This device is a great help because it's easy to forget how long things have been cooking when you're having fun in the kitchen. Always set the timer when a recipe gives a specific time. It counts backward and pings when the time is up.

▲ Timer

Food processor

This multifunctional machine has a main bowl with a lid and a variety of attachments, some of which are supplied with the original purchase, while others can be bought separately. It is very useful for finely chopping raw ingredients, such as onions, as well as for quickly combining ingredients. Adult supervision is required.

▲ *Food processor*

Blender

This has a plastic or glass pitcher placed on top of a motorized base, which powers blades inside the pitcher. It is sometimes part of a food processor, but is also available on its own. Blenders can be used to puree fruits and cooked food. Adult supervision is required.

▲ *Blender*

Electric mixer

Extremely useful for mixing cakes or whisking cream or eggs, handheld electric mixers usually come with detachable beaters and several different speed settings. Adult supervision is required.

▲ *Electric mixer*

Cake pans

There are many different types and sizes of cake pans. Spring-loaded cake pans have a clip on the side and a removable bottom, while sandwich pans are shallower and in one whole piece.

▲ *Different types of cake pans and a muffin pan.*

Muffin pans

These are baking trays with dents in them. Muffin pans with deeper holes are used for baking muffins. Those with shallow holes are useful for cooking cupcakes and tarts. You can line both types with paper liners. They are mostly metal, but you can also get bendy silicone ones.

Skillets

Nonstick skillets are best because food doesn't stick to them. You need a small skillet, about 6¼ inches across at the bottom, for making omelets or pancakes and a large one for frying foods, such as vegetables and eggs. Always check with an adult that the tools you use for turning food won't damage the surface. Adult supervision is required when using heat.

◀ *Skillets*

Wok

A large, deep pan with rounded edges, this pan is used for stir-frying vegetables, meat, and fish. A wok must be large so that there's plenty of room to move the food about. A flat bottom is best so that it will sit safely on the stove top without moving around. Adult supervision is required.

▲ *Wok*

Grills or grill pans

A flat, heavy metal plate that is part of some stove tops, sometimes with a ridged bottom, is called a grill. A grill pan is a heavy skillet with a ridged bottom. Flat grills can be used for some recipes, such as biscuits, while ridge ones are for cooking fish or steaks, chops, or hamburgers. Adult supervision is required.

▲ *Grill pan*

Pans

Used for heating and cooking all kinds of foods, pans are available in many sizes and materials. Ones with lids are best, because they let you control how quickly the food cooks and how much water evaporates during cooking. Adult supervision is required.

▲ *Pan with a lid*

Some useful ingredients

There is an almost endless range of foods available in supermarkets and grocery stores. When buying ingredients for a recipe, it is important that you get exactly the right thing, so it is worth making a list. This directory covers some of the more commonly used foods.

Fruit

There are loads of different types of fruits available in supermarkets, some of which you can buy all year, while others, such as strawberries, are available at only certain times of the year. Most are delicious simply chopped up and eaten raw, or they can be used to make a wide range of mouthwatering cakes, desserts, and other scrummy treats.

▶ *Chopping up fresh vegetables and fruit for different dishes is very satisfying.*

PEELING AND CORING AN APPLE

1 Hold the apple in one hand and peel it with the other hand, using a vegetable peeler, starting from the stem end and peeling all the way around. Adult supervision is required.

2 Put the apple on a cutting board, position a sharp knife in the middle, and cut in half. Put each half on the board, cut-side down, and cut in half again. Adult supervision is required.

3 Turn each quarter, flat-side down, and carefully slice away the core. Cut each quarter into three or four slices or into bite-size cubes, depending on what the recipe says.

Apples There are many types of apples and you probably have your own favorite, but for cooking purposes all-purpose apples are usually suitable. All-purpose apples are often eaten raw but are also used in cooking, especially where you want the pieces to stay whole when they're cooked. Some of the nicest varieties of all-purpose apples are Cortland, Golden Delicious, Pink Lady, Granny Smith, McIntosh, and Jonagold. Rome Beauty is a good choice if you want an apple for baking, as are Gravenstein, Gala, and Braeburn. Some apples used for cooking have a sharp flavor, so you may need to add a little sugar.

▲ *Granny Smiths*

Bananas As bananas ripen they turn from green to yellow and eventually get small brown spots on the skin. If you want to make a banana cake, let them sit in the fruit bowl until they've got a lot of little brown spots on the skin. This will mean that they're riper, softer, sweeter, and have a stronger banana flavor.

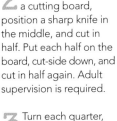

▲ *Bananas*

Berries From strawberries, raspberries, and blackberries to blueberries and gooseberries, berries can be used in all kinds of dishes. Eat them mixed with yogurt or on cereal, or you can stir them into hot oatmeal. They're also great added to muffins, crumbles, or pies. You can often buy dried or frozen berries if you can't find fresh ones.

▼ *Raspberries*

Cherries Sweet and juicy, there are many different varieties of cherry, which vary in color from yellow to bright red to dark red. They're at their best eaten raw, but they're also good in cooking.

▲ Red cherries

You can buy a special gadget to remove pits from cherries easily or you can use a small, sharp knife—although this is fussy and messy work. So if you don't have this gadget, it's easiest to cook the cherries whole and let everyone spit the pits out. For cooking, you can also buy frozen or canned pitted cherries.

Other pitted fruits Apricots, peaches, nectarines, and plums are a real seasonal treat. These sweet fruits have a wonderful flavor and scent and are yummy eaten as they are, made into fruit salads, or baked on their own or as pies and tarts. The best way to remove the pits is to cut the fruit in half, twist to separate, and then pull out the pit. When fresh ones are out of season, you can buy dried varieties. These can be nibbled for a healthy snack or cut into pieces and added to cakes and other bakes. They can also be poached until soft in a little apple juice or syrup, then pureed.

▲ Peaches and nectarines

Citrus fruits From tangy lemons and sour limes to juicy oranges and aromatic grapefruits, citrus fruit is really useful in the kitchen. Lemons and limes are especially good, because the juice can be used for flavoring sweet and savory dishes, for making salad dressings, and for marinating meat and fish. The juice also stops chopped fruit, such as apples and pears, from turning brown.

The zest (the colored part of the rind) of lemons, limes, and oranges contains oils that are full of flavor and can be used in cakes, puddings, and marinades. Grate it off the fruit using the finest side of a grater. Unwaxed fruit is best if you're going to use the zest.

▲ Lemon

▲ Kiwis

Kiwis About the size and shape of an egg, kiwis have a rough, hairy, skin. Inside, the sweet, soft flesh is a bright green color flecked with little black seeds, which you eat.

Lychees This tropical fruit has a rough, pink, papery skin that you can't eat. Peel it off and inside you'll find a shiny, silky white fruit with delicious, exotic smelling flesh. Inside that is a large black pit that you can't eat.

▲ Lychees

Mangoes Juicy, large oval fruit with a big pit in the middle, mangoes are widely available. They are delicious in fruit salads or made into fools and ice creams, and they're also great added to savory salads, especially with chicken or shrimp. The skin color varies with the type of mango—they can be green or orange with a pink blush. The flesh is a deep orange color. To test if a mango is ripe, hold it in the palm of your hand and squeeze it gently. If it gives slightly, it is ripe.

▲ Mango

PREPARING MANGOES

1 Put the mango on a cutting board, on its side. Using a sharp knife, cut from top to bottom, either side of the pit, so that you have two halves. Adult supervision is required.

2 Put one half on a board, cut-side up, and cut parallel lines, about ½ inch apart, cutting almost all the way through the flesh. Make similar cuts the other way to make little squares.

3 Holding the half in both hands, push the skin side upward so the mango flesh opens up. Cut the flesh off the skin and it will come away in cubes. Repeat with the other half.

Passion fruits This tropical fruit has an egglike shape with a hard, inedible skin. Cut it in half and scoop out the pretty, delicious seeds and scented juicy flesh—it's delicious served on ice cream or stirred into plain yogurt. Passion fruit is ripe and ready to eat when the skin is wrinkled.

▲ *Passion fruit*

Pineapples To test if a pineapple is ripe, smell it—if it smells sweet and fruity, it will taste good. If it doesn't smell, it won't have much taste and may be a little dry. Alternatively, try plucking out one of the spiky leaves—if it comes out easily, it is ripe. To prepare a pineapple, ask an adult to help you cut off the skin and core because you need a large, sharp knife.
▲ *Pineapple*   It is delicious raw or sliced and barbecued.

Vegetables

Wonderfully versatile, tasty, and healthy, there is a huge range of vegetables just waiting to be transformed into delectable dishes. Many, such as potatoes and carrots, will be familiar to you, while others, such as eggplants, may be new.

Potatoes Filling and cheap, potatoes can be cooked in many ways. If you are going to bake or boil them in their skins, ensure that you first scrub them well with a brush. They can also be peeled and

▲ *Potatoes*
boiled, mashed, chipped, roasted, sautéed, or used to thicken soups. There are a lot of different varieties, and it usually says on the package what they are suitable for. Waxy ones are best for salads, while fluffy types are best for mashing, roasting, and baking.

Squashes These vegetables come in many shapes and sizes and include zucchini, and butternut, acorn, and spaghetti squashes and pumpkins. With the exception of summer squashes, such as zucchini, all need peeling and their seeds removing before use. They can be cut up, baked or

▲ *Pumpkin*   boiled, or used to make soups or pies.

CHOPPING AN ONION

1 Put the onion on a cutting board and cut it in half, from the top down to the hairy root end. Peel off the skin with your fingers. Cut off the root end. Adult supervision is required.

2 Put one half on the board, cut-side down, and make parallel cuts, close together, right through to the board, going almost all the way to the top end, but leaving the top intact.

3 Turn the onion around and cut across these cuts in parallel lines all the way along the length, so that the onion is cut into small cubes. Repeat with the other half of the onion.

Onions One of the cornerstones of cooking, onions are infinitely versatile in the kitchen and crop up in a whole range of dishes, from soups, salads, and pickles, to casseroles and sauces. There are a lot of types available, including small, sweet shallots, standard white onions, red onions, tender leeks, long, mild scallions, and thin green chives.

▲ *Red, yellow, and white onions*

Garlic Famous for its strong smell and flavor, garlic is one of the most frequently used flavorings in cooking. It can be roasted whole, or peeled and finely chopped or grated to be added raw to dips or cooked in other dishes.
▼ *Garlic*

Broccoli Bright green, tasty, and very good for you, broccoli can be eaten in a number of ways—lightly steamed, raw and chopped in salads, or cooked and blended with a range of ingredients, such as cream or cheese, to make a nourishing soup.

▲ Broccoli

Cabbage There are many different types of cabbage, from small Brussels sprouts and mild white cabbage to leafy savoy cabbage, vibrant red cabbage, and Chinese pak choy. All can be steamed, stir-fried, or boiled. The white and red types are ideal for shredding and eating raw, while the softer, green-leafed types are best cooked.

▲ Brussels sprouts

Carrots Young carrots don't need peeling—just scrub them with a vegetable brush. Old carrots are best peeled with a vegetable peeler. To cook carrots, cut them into thin sticks or slices and cook in a small amount of boiling water in a covered pan for about 5 minutes, until just tender. Baby carrots can be cooked whole. Raw carrots can be grated and added to salads or cut into short sticks and served with dips.

▲ Carrots

Celery Crunchy and flavorsome, celery is one of the vegetables that is used as the base for many stews, casseroles, and soups. It is also tasty eaten raw with dips, such as hummus, for a healthy snack.

▶ Celery

Peas One of the few vegetables that is often better from frozen, green peas make an ideal accompaniment to most main dishes, or can be added to favorites, such as chicken pot pie or lasagne, for extra flavor. Sugar snaps and snow peas can be eaten whole and raw, or lightly steamed for just a minute.

▲ Snow peas, sugar snaps, and peas

Beans There are many different types of beans, including green beans, string beans, and fava beans. They are best eaten as fresh as possible.

▲ Fava beans

Bell peppers Available in jewel-bright colors that make food look good, bell peppers are also tasty. Red, yellow, and orange bell peppers have a sweeter flavor than green ones, so they're the nicest to use in most recipes. Bell peppers are good eaten raw, in salads, or with dips, or cooked in stir-fries, casseroles, and sauces. To prepare them, cut them in half lengthwise and cut out any white pith and all the little white seeds.

▼ Assorted bell peppers

▲ Eggplants

Eggplants Large, oval, glossy dark purple vegetables with cream colored flesh, these are always eaten cooked. They are good halved, stuffed, and baked; sliced and then grilled, broiled, or fried; or cut into chunks, drizzled with oil, and baked.

MASHING POTATOES

1 Ask an adult to drain cooked potatoes, then return to the pan over a low heat for 30 seconds to help burn off any excess water. Remove from the heat and mash the potatoes with a potato masher by firmly moving it up and down. Make sure all the potatoes are mashed.

2 Add a little milk and keep mashing until you have wonderful, fluffy mashed potatoes. Season to taste with salt and ground black pepper. For a change, you can also add a heaped teaspoon of mustard, some grated cheddar cheese, or some chopped chives.

Spinach If you're using spinach in a recipe, you'll be surprised by how much the recipe says you need. This is because a large amount of fresh spinach reduces to a really small amount when it's cooked. Fresh spinach needs to be washed well before you cook it. Put it in a large bowl of cold water and swirl it around with your hands to rinse it. Then lift it out and put it in your largest pan. Don't add any water—you can cook it with just the water that clings to the leaves. Put the lid on the pan, cook for 2 minutes, then give it a stir and cook for another 2 minutes, or until it's wilted and soft. Baby leaf spinach is wonderful in salads. You can buy it in bags already washed.

▲ *Spinach*

PEELING TOMATOES

Put the tomatoes in a large heatproof bowl and ask an adult to cover with boiling water. Let stand for exactly one minute (count to 60), then lift out of the water and pierce the skin of each tomato with a small sharp knife. You should be able to peel off the skin easily.

Salad greens There are many salad greens, including different types of lettuce, arugula, watercress, and Asian leaves, such as mizuna. They make wonderful salads or can be added to sandwiches for extra color and crunch.

▲ *Arugula and lamb's lettuce*

Herbs

All kinds of herbs can be used in recipes. Among the most commonly used are rosemary, thyme, sage, mint, oregano, cilantro, parsley, and basil. Some, such as rosemary and sage, need to be cooked in a dish, while others, especially basil, are delicious raw in salads or scattered on top of pizzas.

▲ *Basil*

Spices

It is difficult to have every spice on hand, but some, such as black pepper, cumin seeds, coriander seeds, paprika, ground allspice, nutmeg, ground ginger, and cinnamon are essential for any cook. In order to prolong their flavor, keep them in airtight containers.

▲ *Cinnamon sticks and ground allspice*

▲ *Clockwise from left: beef tomatoes, vine-ripened tomatoes, cherry tomatoes, and standard tomatoes*

Tomatoes There are many types of tomatoes—tiny, medium, and huge ones, round ones, and oval ones. You can even get yellow tomatoes, as well the usual red ones. For most of the recipes in this book, you can use whatever tomatoes you happen to have.

Cherry tomatoes are tiny and sweet and make a great snack. Vine-ripened tomatoes have the best flavor. Plum tomatoes are the oval-shape ones, which are wonderful for cooking because they have less seeds and juice than other tomatoes and loads of flavor. Beef tomatoes are the huge round ones—they're great sliced in salads or hollowed out, stuffed, and baked.

Canned tomatoes are cheap and very versatile, and because they're picked and canned when they're ripe, they often have a better flavor than fresh ones. For cooking, it's easiest to buy canned tomatoes, either chopped or whole.

Meat, poultry, and fish

There are too many types of meat, poultry, and fish available to list them all here, but in general it is important that you use the type specified in the recipe because the cooking time will have been calculated for that variety. It is worth paying a little extra for good-quality foods, because both the flavor and the texture will be better.

▼ *Selection of fish and large shrimp.*

Dairy and eggs

There are many types of milk, cream, yogurt, and eggs available, and they are used in all kinds of recipes.

Milk, cream, and yogurt These everyday ingredients are widely used in sweet and savory dishes, adding a rich, creamy taste and texture. Organic types usually taste better than standard ones, although if you are cooking with them, then it won't matter too much which you use. Whole-fat versions will be creamiest, although semi-skimmed or low-fat types are perfectly acceptable for cooking. There are three main types of cream: light cream, for pouring; whipping cream, for whipping; and heavy cream, for pouring or whipping. Use whichever is listed in the ingredients.

▲ *Clockwise from left: milk, whipped cream, and light cream*

Butter There are two main types of butter—salted and unsalted. Unsalted butter is usually better for making cakes and cookies, while the salted type is better for spreading.

▲ *Butter*

Cheese From hard, strong varieties, such as Cheddar and Parmesan, to soft, mild ones, such as brie or creamy marscarpone, cheese can be used in all kinds of savory and sweet dishes. Some, such as Cheddar or mozzarella, are perfect for melting, while others, such as feta or halloumi, are better crumbled or sliced and served raw or just lightly cooked. Use whichever type is recommended in the recipe.

▲ *Parmesan cheese*

Eggs Boiled, poached, fried, scrambled, baked, or beaten and used in all kinds of recipes, eggs are a mainstay of every kitchen. Most of the recipes in this book use large hen's eggs, but duck and quail eggs are also delicious, especially when hard-cooked and used in salads.

▲ *Quail's eggs*

Nuts

From cashew nuts, peanuts, pine nuts, and walnuts to brazil nuts, hazelnuts, almonds, and macadamia nuts, most types of nuts are delicious eaten raw as a healthy snack, or they can be chopped up and incorporated in a wide range of sweet and savory dishes, including stir-fries, crumbles, brownies, and cereal bars.

▲ *Pine nuts and hazelnuts*

Seeds

A great addition to breakfast cereals, cookies, salads, stir-fries, and breads, there is a wide range of seeds that can be used in the kitchen. Common types include sunflower seeds, pumpkin seeds, poppy seeds, and sesame seeds.

▲ *Sunflower seeds*

Noodles

Made from either egg and wheat (egg noodles) or rice flour (rice noodles) and available fresh or dried, noodles are a great accompaniment to stir-fries or can be added to soups for extra texture. There are various thicknesses available, as well as whole-wheat types, but all are quick and easy to cook. Simply follow the method in the recipe and read the package instructions.

▲ *Different types of egg noodles*

Pasta

▲ *Dried penne*

One of the quickest and easiest things to cook, there are two main types of pasta—fresh and dried—and these can be standard or wholewheat. They come in many shapes and sizes, from small macaroni to large conchigliette. Most fresh pasta is made with egg yolks, making it richer, so you need less. Cook all types according to the package instructions, in a large pan of lightly salted boiling water. Then simply add your favorite sauce and eat!

Rice

There are several different types of rice, including long-grain rice, converted rice, brown rice, basmati rice, paella rice, risotto rice, jasmine rice, and short-grain rice. It's important to use the one mentioned in the recipe, because they look, taste, and feel different when cooked, and also take different amounts of time to cook. If in doubt, read the package information—it will tell you what the rice is best for.

▲ *Jasmine rice*

Flour

There are four main types of flour and it's important when you're making a dish to use the correct type. All-purpose white flour is generally used for making unsweetened pastry, cookies, sauces, muffins, batter, and some cakes.

White bread flour is made from wheat that has a high gluten (a protein found in wheat) content. This means that when it's mixed with water and kneaded it becomes stretchy and elastic, which makes it ideal for making bread, pizza bases, yeast rolls, and puff pastry.

Self-rising flour is all-purpose white flour with a raising agent (such as baking powder) added. The proportion of rising agent is the same in all brands of self-rising flour, and is the correct amount to make many types of cakes, such as cupcakes and sponge cake. If a recipe needs more or less rising agent, it will use all-purpose flour and baking powder or self-rising flour with added baking powder.

Whole-wheat flour is made from the whole grains of wheat, and is brown, higher in fiber, and healthier than white flour. It is used to make bread, biscuits, and cakes.

▲ *Whole-wheat flour*

Rising agents

Baking powder is a rising agent that is added to cakes with the flour to make them rise well. It is made of an alkali (usually baking soda) and an acid-reacting chemical (such as cream of tartar), plus some dried starch or flour to make it more bulky. When it is mixed with liquid and heated in the oven it forms tiny air bubbles, which make the cake mixture expand and rise. You need only tiny amounts, so it's vitally important to measure it accurately. Some recipes call for baking soda and cream of tartar instead of baking powder, or in addition to it.

▲ *Baking powder and baking soda*

Sweet things

There are a lot of different types of sugar. They all sweeten food, but taste different, and the way they mix into recipes and react to cooking varies, so make sure you use the correct type.

White sugar There are three main types of white sugar: granulated, superfine, and confectioners' sugar. Granulated sugar is the type that you add to tea and coffee. In cooking, it's used for making syrups and in recipes where it is dissolved in hot water. You can use unbleached or white granulated sugar.

▲ *Granulated and superfine sugars*

Superfine sugar has finer grains that dissolve more easily in mixtures than the coarser grains of granulated sugar. It is used in cakes, cookies, and other desserts. You can use unbleached superfine sugar or ordinary white superfine sugar in these recipes.

Confectioners' sugar, or powdered sugar, is ground to a fine powder and used to make frostings.

Brown sugars Unrefined brown sugars have fine grains and a caramel flavor. They can be light or dark brown sugar, molasses sugar, or raw sugar. Dark brown sugar has a stronger flavor than light brown sugar. If you don't have this type, replace it with superfine sugar. Molasses sugar is considered to have the best flavor, while raw sugar, with its large crystals, is used to make a crunchy topping.

▲ *Muscovado and demerara sugars*

Honey The world's oldest sweetener, honey is a totally natural product, made by bees. Clear honey is best for cooking because it mixes in more easily. Cloudy, crystallized honey is best for spreading on bread because it is thicker. You can buy a

▲ *Honey* huge range of special honeys, such as heather honey and orange blossom honey. These are named after the flowers from which the bees collected the nectar and each one has its own special flavor. For cooking, it's a waste to buy expensive honey—any clear honey is fine.

Light corn syrup and maple syrup
Sweet, light corn syrup is a by-product from sugar manufacture. Maple syrup is made from the sap of the sugar maple tree. Both are used as sweeteners on   ▲ *Corn syrup*
oatmeal, pancakes, and ice cream, as well as in some recipes, such as oat bars and gingerbread.

Molasses Dark, thick molasses is another by-product of sugar manufacturing. It has a stronger flavor and a dark, almost black color. It is used in gingerbread
▲ *Molasses* and rich fruit cakes.

Chocolate The ultimate treat for those with a sweet tooth, chocolate can be used to make many luscious desserts, tarts, cakes, and cookies. It is worth using the best-quality you can find, because it will taste much better.   ▲ *White, milk, and*
If using bittersweet chocolate,   *bittersweet chocolates*
look for packages that say "70% cocoa solids," because it will have the best flavor. Milk chocolate is less strong and tends to be creamier. White chocolate is very sweet. All are available in blocks or as drops, and can be melted and used in recipes.

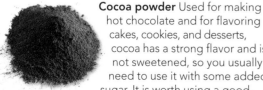

Cocoa powder Used for making hot chocolate and for flavoring cakes, cookies, and desserts, cocoa has a strong flavor and is not sweetened, so you usually need to use it with some added sugar. It is worth using a good-
▲ *Cocoa powder* quality type to get the best flavor.

MELTING CHOCOLATE

1 Break the chocolate into squares and put into a heatproof bowl that is the right size to sit on top of a pan.

2 Fill one fourth of the pan with water and put the bowl on top.

3 Heat gently until simmering. The water should never touch the bottom of the bowl. Stir occasionally until the chocolate has just melted. Immediately remove the bowl from the pan. Adult supervision is required.

Oils
Used for most types of frying, drizzling, and in salad dressings, oil is a key ingredient in the kitchen. Olive oil has a strong flavor that is great for salad dressings and for cooking dishes from Mediterranean countries. Some types are very expensive. These are called virgin and extra virgin olive oils, and they are made from the first pressing of the olives. For most of the recipes in this book, ordinary olive oil is fine.

Sunflower and vegetable oils are all-purpose oils without much flavor. They are great for some dishes, such as roast potatoes.   ▲ *Olive oil*

Sesame oil has a strong flavor that is good in Asian cooking, while walnut oil has a nutty flavor that is wonderful for salad dressings.

Vinegar
Besides the all-purpose white vinegar, there are a lot of different types of vinegars, including cider, red wine, white wine, balsamic, and flavored ones, which are used for salad dressings, and there are also
▲ *Rice and*   rice vinegar and sherry vinegar,
malt vinegars widely used in Asian cooking.

Basic techniques

A range of skills are required in the kitchen. Most of these are easy, and all of them will become easier as you practice. This section explains how to do some of the most useful techniques, helping you to make a range of delectable treats!

Measuring fluids

Accurate measuring is essential for really successful cooking, especially with baking. For tiny amounts use proper measuring spoons—you can buy them cheaply from supermarkets or department stores. They come in a set and should have spoons that measure out ¼ teaspoon, ½ teaspoon, 1 teaspoon, and 1 tablespoon.

To measure large amounts of liquids, use a see-through measuring cup, which can be made from plastic or a special heatproof glass. To measure accurately, you need to make sure the cup is on a level surface, then squat down until your eye is level with the markings on the side and pour in the liquid slowly until it reaches the right level. If you pour it in and look down into the cup, you'll find that a measurement that looks right from above is different when you look at it from eye level. Try this with some water and see for yourself! You can also now get special sloped measuring cups that give you accurate readings from above, and these are even easier to use.

▲ *Measuring cup and spoons*

▶ *Knowing how to do simple tasks, such as beating, will enable you to make all kinds of dishes.*

Measuring dry ingredients

Some professional chefs use scales to measure dry ingredients, such as flour and sugar, because this is a more accurate way to measure ingredients. For most cooks, however, dry ingredients are measured using standard kitchen measuring cups. These are very easy to use. Simply scoop up the dry ingredient and shake until the surface is roughly level, then run the straight back edge of a blunt knife across the surface of the ingredient to level it completely. Brown sugar should be packed into the cup.

Small amounts, such as spices and baking powder, need to be measured with measuring spoons. Unless a recipe says otherwise, the spoonfuls must be level. Run the blunt side of a knife along the top to level it. If you do this over a piece of paper towel it will be easy to tip any excess back into the jar.

▲ *Measuring cups and spoons*

MEASURING SPOONFULS

Fill the correct size measuring spoon right to the top. For sticky things, such as corn syrup, you can first lightly grease the spoon with a little butter. Then the syrup or honey will just slide off.

USING SCALES

Make sure the pointer is at zero when the pan is empty—there will be a screw or dial that you can use to adjust it. Then add the food to the pan until the pointer reaches the correct place and is steady.

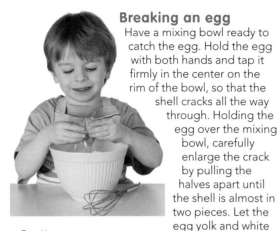

Breaking an egg

Have a mixing bowl ready to catch the egg. Hold the egg with both hands and tap it firmly in the center on the rim of the bowl, so that the shell cracks all the way through. Holding the egg over the mixing bowl, carefully enlarge the crack by pulling the halves apart until the shell is almost in two pieces. Let the egg yolk and white fall into the bowl positioned below and discard the egg shell. Repeat the process with more eggs as many times as necessary.

▲ *Breaking an egg is easy once you know how, and is an invaluable skill in the kitchen.*

Whipping cream

The only creams that you can whip successfully are heavy cream and whipping cream. Light cream won't whip. Make sure the cream and the bowl are chilled before you start. Use a balloon or coil whisk or an electric handheld mixer (on the slowest speed and with adult supervision) and whip until the cream is just floppy and holds its shape. Don't whip too much or the cream will start to separate and look grainy, and if you keep over-whipping you'll end up with butter!

Grinding in a pestle and mortar

Put the ingredients in the mortar (bowl) and grind by pressing and rolling firmly with the pestle (stick), until you have a coarse powder. If you don't have a proper pestle and mortar, you can cheat by putting the spices in a small bowl and grinding them with the end of rolling pin.

▲ *Pestle and mortar*

SEPARATING AN EGG

1 Have two mixing bowls ready. Carefully tap the egg on the side of a bowl and gently pull the two halves apart over the bowl, so that just the egg white starts to fall into the bowl.

2 Tip the yolk from one half of the egg shell to the other several times, so that the yolk stays whole and all of the white falls into the bowl. Pour the yolk into the other bowl.

Top tip: If you're separating more than one egg, you need three bowls. One for the yolks, one for the separated whites, and one to break the egg over. This way if the yolk breaks and you get some yolk in the white, you only ruin one egg (you can use it for scrambled egg). Egg whites won't whisk successfully if they have any yolk in with them.

WHISKING EGG WHITES

1 Put the egg whites in a spotlessly clean, completely dry, large bowl and make sure the whisk is clean and dry as well. Holding the bowl firmly with one hand, tilt the bowl slightly and start whisking, using a circular motion, with the other hand.

2 Whisk the whites until they form stiff peaks. If using an electric mixer, start at slow speed for the first minute, then increase the speed to high. If you're brave, you can test if they are done by turning the bowl upsidedown. If they're whisked enough, they'll stay in the bowl.

Top tip: You can use a balloon whisk, a rotary egg beater, or an electric mixer, but if you're whisking more than two egg whites, it's best to use an electric mixer, in which case adult supervision is required

Zesting a lemon, lime, or orange

The zest is the colored part of the rind of the lemons, limes, and oranges and it's full of flavor. To remove the zest, wash the fruit under cold running water and then dry it thoroughly with paper towels. Grate it on the finest side of a grater, being careful to remove only the colored zest and not the white pith below it, which tastes slightly bitter. Sharp graters grate flesh as well as food, so be careful to keep your fingers away from the cutting edge! Adult supervision is required.

Sometimes a recipe mentions a strip of zest. This is usually added to syrups while they are simmering to flavor them and then taken out before eating. To peel off a strip of zest, run a vegetable peeler along the length of the fruit, using just enough pressure to remove the colored zest. Adult supervision is required.

Creaming butter and sugar

It's important that butter or margarine is soft before you start. Put them in a large bowl and beat together with a wooden spoon or electric mixer, until the mixture is smooth with a soft, light, creamy texture. A wooden spoon is fine for small amounts, but for large amounts it will be hard work and it's it's easier with an electric mixer. Adult supervision is required.

When you cream a mixture really well, the sugar grains will look smaller and the mixture will become much lighter in color. If you use superfine sugar, it will make the mixture change from yellow to a pale cream color. This is because there will be a lot of tiny air bubbles trapped in it. These little air bubbles expand as the cake cooks and help to make the cake light.

Keep stopping and scraping down the sides of a bowl with a spatula, so any mixture that gets stuck on the sides of the bowl goes back into the main mixture and it gets creamed together evenly.

▶ Creaming can be done with a spoon or an electric mixer.

RUBBING IN FLOUR AND BUTTER

1 First sift the flour and salt into a large mixing bowl, holding the strainer above the bowl. This lets air get into the flour.

2 Make sure the butter or margarine is the right temperature—it should be cold but not too hard, and a knife should cut through it without pressing hard. Cut the butter or margarine into cubes and add to the flour.

3 Lift a little flour and butter out of the bowl and rub between the tips of your fingers and thumbs, letting it fall back into the bowl. Keep doing this until the pieces of butter get smaller and smaller and look like crumbs.

Top tip: You need cold hands to rub in well. If your hands are warm, put them under cold running water for 1 minute.

Folding in ingredients

Always use a large metal spoon (tablespoon size) to fold in. You need to gently cut the spoon down through the mixture and then bring it back to the top, folding it over as you do. Be as gentle as possible so you don't knock out the air in the mixture. Stop as soon as it's evenly mixed.

All-in-one cakes

You can make great cupcakes, sponge cakes, and light fruitcakes using a very easy all-in-one method. First, sift the flour and baking powder into a large bowl, holding the strainer or sifter above the bowl. This ensures the flour and baking powder are evenly mixed and adds air to the flour. Add all the other ingredients (butter or margarine, sugar, and eggs plus any flavoring, such as vanilla, if used) and beat with a wooden spoon or an electric mixer (adult supervision is required), on slow speed, until everything is thoroughly mixed, then press STOP.

GATHERING PASTRY DOUGH TOGETHER

1 After rubbing the flour and fat together, sprinkle a little cold water evenly over the surface and mix with a round bladed knife until it starts to come together in clumps.

2 Add approximately 1–1½ tablespoons of ice cold water for every 1 cup of flour. Start by adding 1 tablespoon and then add a tiny bit more if necessary.

3 Gather the dough together with your fingertips and thumb—you should have a firm dough that leaves the sides of the bowl clean. Shape into a smooth ball.

4 Wrap the dough in plastic wrap and, if you have time, chill it in the refrigerator for at least 30 minutes. This isn't essential if you're in a hurry, but it makes the dough easier to roll.

KNEADING DOUGH

1 Put the dough on a lightly floured counter and lightly dust your hands and the surface of the dough with flour. Flatten the dough slightly, then fold it over toward you.

2 Press the heels of your hands into the dough and push it away from you to stretch it. Turn the dough a quarter of the way around and push and stretch again.

3 Turn it another quarter way around and repeat again. Keep doing this, dusting the counter with a little more flour if necessary, for 5–10 minutes, until the dough feels elastic and smooth.

4 Depending on what type of dough you are making, you may need to let it rise, shape it into balls, or roll it out with a rolling pin.

Rolling out dough

Lightly dust a clean, dry counter and a rolling pin with flour or, if rolling out a fondant icing, use confectioners' sugar. Put the ball of dough or icing on the counter and flatten it slightly with the rolling pin. Roll the pin over the dough away from you, pressing just enough to make the dough longer, but not to squash it. Then give the dough a quarter turn and roll it away from you again.

Carry on doing this, lightly dusting the counter and rolling pin with more flour or confectioners' sugar when necessary, until the dough is slightly thicker than a coin. By turning the dough a quarter way around between rolls, you should end up with a round shape.

If you want a square shape, pat the dough into a square with your hands before you start rolling. For an oblong, pat it into a square and then roll twice away from you, turn, and roll once, then turn again and roll twice.

▶ Rolling out pastry, cookie dough, or fondant icing is easy if you know how.

LINING A PIE PLATE

1 Roll out the dough to the correct thickness and until it is about 2 inches larger than the plate you want to line. Check by placing the plate on top of the dough occasionally as you roll.

2 Put the rolling pin in the middle of the circle, then gently lift one end of the dough and fold it over the rolling pin. Move it on the rolling pin to fit over the top of the plate.

3 Using your fingers, press the dough into the plate to line the bottom and the sides, easing it right into the corners. Let any excess hang over the edge. Roll the rolling pin over the top to cut off the excess.

4 Prick the bottom of the dough with a fork. To help prevent it from shrinking during cooking, cover it with plastic wrap and chill for 20 minutes. Preheat the oven to 400°F.

5 Cut out a large piece of parchment paper and place it on top of the pastry. Cover with dried beans, pasta, or rice and bake for 10 minutes. Uncover the pastry and return to the oven for another 5 minutes.

▶ Try to stamp out as many shapes as you can from a piece of rolled-out pastry or dough, then reroll the leftovers and stamp out more shapes.

Stamping out pastry and cookie shapes

Once you have rolled out your pastry or cookie dough, you may want to stamp out different shapes. To do this, dip the chosen cutter into flour, tap to knock off any excess, then position the cutter on the rolled-out dough. Press down firmly with the palm of your hand, but do not twist or move the cutter if you can help it. Lift up the cutter, remove the shape, and place it on a baking sheet. Repeat all over the dough, stamping out as many shapes as possible. Gather the remaining dough together, then roll it out again and stamp out more shapes. Continue until you have used all the dough.

Greasing and lining a pan

If the recipe just says to grease a pan, you simply need to smear the inside with butter or oil. You can use a small piece of parchment paper, a pastry brush, or your fingers. Make sure you go right into the corners.

To line the bottom and sides of a cake pan, cut a strip of parchment paper a little wider than the height of the pan. It needs to be long enough to go all the way around the pan. Make a fold all the way along the long side, ½ inch in, then make small cuts all the way along the folded part, about ½ inch apart, like a pleat. Put the pan on a sheet of parchment paper and draw around the outside with a pencil. Cut out with scissors. Lightly grease the inside of the pan. Put the strip of paper inside the edge to line the sides, with the pleat at the bottom and the fold in the corner. Put the paper bottom shape in to cover the snipped bit.

Piping frosting

Once you have cooked your cookies or your cake, you may want to decorate the top with frosting. You can buy special pens from cake decorating stores, but it is also very easy to make your own frosting and use a piping bag, which you can either buy or make. Whichever you use, you will need special nozzles, which fit into the smaller pointed end of the piping bag. Ensure these are securely in place before you start.

Spoon a few tablespoons of frosting into the bag, gently squeezing the open end until the frosting is pushed down to the nozzle end. Over a piece of parchment paper, gently squeeze a bit harder until some of the frosting comes out. Practice squeezing out the frosting on the paper before you start decorating, then pipe squiggles, lines, words, flowers, or whatever you like onto the surface. Refill the bag as and when needed.

▼ *Let your imagination run wild when decorating cookies and cakes.*

LINING THE BOTTOM OF A CAKE PAN

1 Put a small pat of butter in the pan and, using either a piece of scrunched up parchment paper or your fingers, rub it all over the inside surface of the pan to coat it.

2 Put the pan on a piece of parchment paper and draw around the outside edge with a pencil to mark the shape. Carefully cut out the parchment circle with scissors.

3 Place the parchment circle in the bottom of the pan, pushing it down well and right into the edge so that the bottom is covered and there are no gaps. Pour in the cake mixture.

MAKING A PAPER PIPING BAG

1 Cut a square piece of nonstick parchment paper 9 inches x 9 inches. Fold in half diagonally. With adult supervision, cut along the fold so that you have two triangular pieces.

2 Place a triangle flat with the longest side facing you. Mark the center of the longest side by pinching the paper. Take one corner edge of the longest side up to fit onto the top corner.

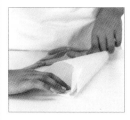

3 Hold it there while you do the same with the other corner, wrapping it right around. You will now have a cone shape with a narrow end. Secure with tape. Slip the icing nozzle into the cone.

Menu ideas

Whether you want a quick bite after school or to try your hand at creating a feast for your family, there is a recipe in this book to suit the occasion. These sample menus show what kind of recipes may go together to make up a tasty meal, but you can easily adapt them yourself.

Winter warmer

* Tomato and bread soup
* Fish and cheese pies
* Rice pudding
* Vanilla milkshake

▲Tomato and bread soup p. 123

▲ Fish and cheese pies p. 137

▲ Rice pudding p. 157

Light summer meal

* Hummus
* Tuna pasta salad
* Banana and toffee ice cream
* Ruby red soda

▲ Hummus p. 40

▲ Tuna pasta salad p. 85

▲ Banana and toffee ice cream p. 162

After-school fast feast

* Ham and pineapple pizza
* Chunky veggie salad
* Baked bananas
* Totally tropical

▲ Ham and pineapple pizza p. 95

▲ Chunky veggie salad p. 82

▲ Baked bananas p. 161

Picnic

* Ciabatta sandwich
* Speedy sausage rolls
* Apricot and pecan bars
* Banana muffins
* Fresh orange fizz

◄ Speedy sausage rolls
p. 41

◄ Banana muffins
p. 194

► Ciabatta sandwich
p. 67

► Fresh orange fizz
p. 176

Barbecue

* Thai pork burgers
* Cheesy burgers
* Colorful chicken kebabs
* Lemony couscous salad
* Pineapple sorbet on sticks
* Fruit punch

◄ Cheesy burgers
p. 153

◄ Lemony couscous salad
p. 55

► Colorful chicken kebabs
p. 108

► Pineapple sorbet on sticks
p. 163

School cake sale

* Gingerbread people
* Stripy cookies
* Peanut and jelly cookies
* Luscious lemon cake
* Pecan squares
* Creamy fudge

◄ Gingerbread people
pp. 226–27

◄ Luscious lemon cake
p. 201

► Stripy cookies
p. 241

► Pecan squares
p. 204

Party ideas

One of the best things about parties is that it gives you a good excuse to indulge in all your favorite treats. Instead of making all the food yourself, you can ask a few of your friends to come around and help you—getting the party going early!

Birthday bonanza

* Crazy rainbow popcorn
* Sandwich shapes
* Mini ciabatta pizzas
* Wobbly gelatins
* Balloon cake
* Rainbow juice and fruit slush

BIRTHDAY PARTY THEMES
- Wild animals
- Clowns
- Pirates
- Fairies
- Witches and wizards
- Dragons and monsters

◄ Sandwich shapes p. 215

▲ Crazy rainbow popcorn pp. 212–13

◄ Balloon cake pp. 234–35

◄ Mini ciabatta pizzas p. 218

► Wobbly gelatins p. 230

COOK'S TIPS

► It is always best to write down your party ideas well in advance and talk them through with a parent or guardian. That way you can ensure you have all the right ingredients ready.

► Cut food up really small so that everyone can try a bit of each food and less gets wasted.
► Pack up any leftovers and put them into goody bags.
► Decorate paper tablecloths yourself, following the theme of the party.

Halloween

* Tortilla squares
* Chicken mini rolls
* Spooky cookies
* Chocolate witchy apples
* Jack-o'-lantern cake
* What a smoothie

◀ Tortilla squares p. 219

◀ Spooky cookies p. 236

▶ Chocolate witchy apples p. 237

▶ Jack-o'-lantern cake pp. 238–39

Midnight feast

* Cheese and ham tarts
* Eggstra special sandwich selection
* Sweet toast toppers
* Butterscotch brownies
* Strawberry shake

◀ Cheese and ham tarts p. 46

◀ Eggstra special sandwich seletion pp. 42–43

▶ Butterscotch brownies p. 60

▶ Strawberry shake p. 185

Breakfast party

* Cantaloupe melon salad
* Ham and tomato scramble
* Buttermilk pancakes
* French toast
* Strawberry and apple cooler

▶ Cantaloupe melon salad p. 171

▶ Ham and tomato scramble p. 75

◀ French toast p. 193

◀ Strawberry and apple cooler p. 181

Packed lunches and picnics

Whether you are at school, going on a day trip, or simply want something delicious to enjoy outside in the park, portable food should be easy to eat, tasty, and able to withstand travel. This selection of savory and sweet treats will provide you with plenty of inspiration, so roll up your sleeves and get cooking!

Hummus

Originally from the Middle East, hummus is perfect for a packed lunch or picnic, served with pita, crusty bread (which you can toast in advance), or vegetable sticks.

serves **4**

ingredients
- **canned chickpeas**, 14 ounces, drained
- **garlic cloves**, 2
- **sea salt**, a pinch
- **tahini** (*see* Cook's Tip) or **smooth peanut butter**, 2 tablespoons
- **olive oil**, 4 tablespoons
- **lemon**, juice of 1
- **cayenne pepper**, ½ teaspoon, plus a little extra for sprinkling
- **sesame seeds**, 1 tablespoon

tools
- ✱ **Colander or strainer**
- ✱ **Blender or food processor**
- ✱ **Spoon or spatula**
- ✱ **Small nonstick skillet**

1 Put the chickpeas in a colander or strainer and rinse under cold water.

2 Put the chickpeas in a blender or food processor with the garlic and a pinch of salt. Blend until almost a paste. Adult supervision is required.

3 Add the tahini or peanut butter and blend until quite smooth. Very carefully, with the motor running, pour in the oil and lemon juice. Adult supervision is required.

4 Stir in the cayenne pepper. If the mixture is too thick, stir in a little water.

5 With adult supervision, heat a skillet.

6 Add the sesame seeds. Cook for 2–3 minutes, shaking the skillet, until golden. Adult supervision is required. Sprinkle some cayenne over the hummus. Serve, or spoon into a plastic container.

COOK'S TIPS
▶ The hummus will keep fresh in a sealed plastic container in the refrigerator for 2–3 days.

▶ Tahini is a paste made from sesame seeds traditionally used in hummus. It has a thick, creamy texture very similar to peanut butter.

tahini

Speedy sausage rolls

These sausage rolls are wrapped in slices of bread, brushed with butter, then baked until crispy. They will make perfect picnic food.

makes 18

ingredients
- **multigrain white bread**, 8 slices
- **cocktail sausages**, 8 ounces
- **butter** or **margarine**, 3 tablespoons
- **carrot** and **cucumber sticks**, to serve

tools
- ✳ **Cutting board**
- ✳ **Large serrated knife**
- ✳ **Nonstick baking sheet**
- ✳ **Small pan**
- ✳ **Pastry brush**
- ✳ **Oven mitts**

COOK'S TIPS
▶ You can spread a a little ketchup or mild mustard over the slices of bread before wrapping them around the sausages to add a little flavor.
▶ Melt butter in the microwave on Full Power (100%) for 30 seconds. Adult supervision is required.

1 Preheat the oven to 375°F.

2 On a cutting board, trim the crusts off the bread. Cut into slices that are a little shorter across the width than the length of the cocktail sausages. Adult supervision is required.

3 Wrap each piece of bread around a sausage, with the ends of the sausage sticking out. Place on a baking sheet.

4 Put the butter or margarine in a pan and heat gently until just melted. Adult supervision is required.

5 Brush the melted butter or margarine over the sausage rolls.

6 Bake in the oven for 15 minutes, until the bread has browned and the sausages are cooked through. Ask an adult to remove them from the oven.

7 Cool, then serve with some carrot and cucumber sticks, or pack into a sealable plastic container to transport.

Eggstra special sandwich selection

A delicious sandwich makes a convenient and quick packed lunch, picnic, or after-school snack. Egg is always a favorite, so why not learn the basics with these two great fillings.

serves **6**

ingredients
- **white** or **whole-wheat bread**, 12 thin slices
- **butter**, 4 tablespoons, at room temperature

for the egg and cress filling
- **small eggs**, 2
- **mayonnaise**, 2 tablespoons
- **garden cress** or **watercress**, ½ carton
- **salt** and **ground black pepper**

for the egg and tuna filling
- **small eggs**, 2
- **canned tuna in oil**, 3 ounces, drained
- **paprika**, 1 teaspoon
- **lemon juice**, a squeeze
- **salt** and **ground black pepper**
- **peeled and thinly sliced cucumber**, ¼ cup

eggs

garden cress carton

COOK'S TIP
▶ Garden cress, such as upland cress, is easy to grow and is great to add to any sandwich filling. Look for upland cress seeds (or if you prefer a peppery flavor, mustard or watercress seeds) in garden centers. Sprinkle the seeds onto wet paper towels and let stand in a light, warm place. They will sprout within a couple of days.

tools
- ✳ Large pan
- ✳ Large metal spoon
- ✳ Cutting board
- ✳ Large sharp knife
- ✳ 2 mixing bowls
- ✳ Wooden spoon
- ✳ Fork
- ✳ Serrated bread knife
- ✳ Butter knife

1 To make the egg and cress filling, fill a pan with water and bring up to the boil. Carefully lower the eggs into the water on a large draining spoon. Bring the water back up to the boil and boil the eggs for 8 minutes. Adult supervision is required.

2 Ask an adult to place the pan under cold running water for a few minutes, until the eggs are cool.

3 Remove from the water and let stand until cold, then tap on a hard surface to crack the shell and peel it away.

4 Put the eggs on a chopping board and use a large knife to finely chop the eggs. Adult supervision is required.

5 Place the eggs in a bowl and add the mayonnaise, cress, and salt and pepper. Mix well.

6 To make the egg and tuna filling, cook the eggs in the same way as for the egg and cress filling.

7 Put the tuna in a bowl and flake with a fork. Mix the chopped eggs with the tuna, paprika, lemon juice, salt, and pepper.

8 **To make the sandwiches**, remove the crusts from the bread using a serrated knife on a cutting board. You can keep the crusts on, if you like. Adult supervision is required. Spread the butter over the bread, then lay half of the slices on the board.

9 Spread the egg and cress filling over one half of the bread slices and the egg and tuna filling over the other half, topping with the cucumber. Top with the remaining bread slices and press down gently. Cut into triangles. Adult supervision is required.

10 If eating immediately, arrange all the sandwiches on a plate and garnish with tomato wedges and parsley. Alternatively, if you have made them for a lunch box or picnic, wrap the sandwiches tightly in plastic wrap and chill in the refrigerator until required. The sandwiches will keep fresh for 4–5 hours.

Ham and mozzarella calzone

serves **2**

A calzone is a kind of "inside-out" pizza—the dough is on the outside and the filling on the inside. It's a great way of making pizzas for picnics or packed lunches. They travel well wrapped in paper or plastic wrap.

ingredients
- **pizza dough mix**, 1 package
- **ricotta cheese**, ½ cup
- **freshly grated Parmesan cheese**, 2 tablespoons
- **egg yolk**, 1
- **chopped fresh basil**, 2 tablespoons
- **salt** and **ground black pepper**
- **mozzarella cheese**, 3 ounces, cut into small cubes
- **cooked ham**, 3 ounces, finely chopped
- **olive oil**, for brushing

tools
- ✳ **2 nonstick baking sheets**
- ✳ **2 mixing bowls**
- ✳ **Wooden spoon**
- ✳ **Rolling pin**
- ✳ **Metal spoon**
- ✳ **Pastry brush**
- ✳ **Small knife**
- ✳ **Oven mitts**
- ✳ **Spatula**
- ✳ **Wire rack**

1 Preheat the oven to 425°F. Lightly brush two nonstick baking sheets with oil.

2 Make the dough according to the package instructions. Knead briefly until smooth on a lightly floured surface, then shape into a ball.

3 Divide the dough in half and place on a floured surface. Using a rolling pin, roll out each piece to a 7-inch circle.

4 Mix together the ricotta and Parmesan cheeses, egg yolk, basil, salt, and pepper in a large bowl with a spoon.

5 Spread the cheese mixture over half of each circle, leaving a 1-inch border. Sprinkle the mozzarella and ham on top.

6 Brush the edges of the dough with water and fold the uncovered dough over the filling.

7 Press the edges to seal. Carefully lift onto baking sheets. Brush with oil and make a small hole in the top of each. Bake for 15–20 minutes, until golden.

8 Ask an adult to remove the calzone from the oven and lift it on to a wire rack with a spatula. Serve warm, or let stand until cold and wrap in plastic wrap to transport.

basil leaves

Tomato and cheese pizza

This yummy pizza is easy and a lot of fun to make. It is delicious warm or cold, making it a great choice for a tasty, portable packed lunch.

serves **2–3**

ingredients

- **pizza crust**, 1, about 10–12 inches in diameter
- **olive oil**, 2 tablespoons
- **mozzarella**, 5 ounces, thinly sliced
- **ripe tomatoes**, 2, thinly sliced
- **fresh basil leaves**, 6–8
- **freshly grated Parmesan cheese**, 2 tablespoons
- **ground black pepper**

for the tomato sauce

- **olive oil**, 1 teaspoon
- **onion**, 1, finely chopped
- **garlic cloves**, 2, peeled and finely chopped
- **canned chopped tomatoes**, 14 ounces
- **tomato paste**, 1 tablespoon
- **chopped fresh herbs**, such as **oregano, parsley, thyme**, or **basil**, 1 tablespoon
- **sugar**, a pinch
- **salt** and **ground black pepper**

mozzarella

tools
- ✳ Cutting board
- ✳ Medium knife
- ✳ Large pan
- ✳ Wooden spoon
- ✳ Nonstick baking sheet
- ✳ Pastry brush
- ✳ Oven mitts

1 **To make the tomato sauce**, heat the oil in a large pan, add the onion and garlic, and fry for 5 minutes. Add the tomatoes, tomato paste, herbs, sugar, and seasoning. Stir to combine, then simmer for 15–20 minutes, until thick. Remove from the heat. Adult supervision is required.

2 Preheat the oven to 400°F. Place the pizza crust on a baking sheet and brush with 1 tablespoon of the oil.

3 Spread over the tomato sauce, leaving a small gap around the edge. Put the mozzarella and tomato on top.

4 Roughly tear the basil leaves and sprinkle over the pizza with the grated Parmesan cheese. Drizzle over the remaining olive oil and season with plenty of black pepper.

5 Bake in the oven for 15 minutes, until crisp and golden.

6 Ask an adult to remove the pizza from the oven. Let cool slightly, then cut into wedges. Eat warm or let stand to cool completely, then wrap in plastic wrap or put in a plastic container to transport.

COOK'S TIP
▶ Make double the quantity of the sauce and freeze it.

Cheese and ham tarts

These tasty little tarts are a clever twist on ham and cheese sandwiches, and will make a welcome change.

makes **12**

ingredients
for the pastry
- **all-purpose flour**, 1 cup
- **chilled margarine**, 4 tablespoons, cubed

for the filling
- **mild cheese**, ½ cup
- **ham**, 2 thin slices, chopped
- **frozen corn**, ½ cup
- **egg**, 1
- **milk**, ½ cup
- **salt** and **ground black pepper**
- **paprika**, a pinch
- **carrot** and **cucumber sticks**, to serve

tools
- ✴ **Mixing bowl**
- ✴ **Palette knife** or **wooden spoon**
- ✴ **Rolling pin**
- ✴ **3-inch round fluted cookie cutter**
- ✴ **12-hole nonstick muffin pan**
- ✴ **Grater**
- ✴ **Whisk or fork**
- ✴ **Oven mitts**

1 **To make the pastry,** place the flour in a bowl and add the margarine. Using your fingertips, rub the margarine into the flour until the mixture resembles bread crumbs. Gradually add 4 teaspoons of cold water and mix to a smooth dough with a palette knife or wooden spoon.

2 Form the dough into a ball, then wrap in plastic wrap and chill in the refrigerator for 20 minutes.

3 Preheat the oven to 400°F. Put the dough onto a floured surface and lightly knead. Using a rolling pin, roll out the dough until thin.

4 Stamp out 12 circles with a cookie cutter, rerolling the dough trimmings as necessary. Press into the holes of a muffin pan. Chill for 30 minutes.

5 **To make the filling,** grate the cheese. Adult supervision is required. Mix with the ham and corn.

6 Divide the cheese mixture among all the tarts. Beat together the egg, milk, and seasoning with a whisk or fork. Pour into the tarts and sprinkle the tops with paprika.

7 Cook in the oven for 12–15 minutes, until risen and browned. Ask an adult to remove from the oven and cool slightly before loosening and sliding out with a palette knife.

8 Serve warm or cold with carrot and cucumber sticks, or wrap in plastic wrap to transport.

(!) = Watch out! Sharp or electrical tool in use. (🖐) = Watch out! Heat is involved.

Spicy sausage tortilla

This chunky Spanish omelet is a meal in one pan and is delicious eaten warm or cold. Colorful and filling, it is perfect for a lunchtime treat.

serves **4–6**

ingredients

- **chorizo** or **spicy sausages**, 6 ounces
- **olive oil**, 5 tablespoons
- **potatoes**, 1½ pounds, peeled
- **onions**, 10 ounces, peeled and halved
- **eggs**, 4
- **chopped fresh parsley**, 2 tablespoons
- **grated Cheddar cheese**, 1 cup
- **salt** and **ground black pepper**
- **chopped tomatoes** and **basil**, to serve (optional)

tools

- ✳ **Cutting board**
- ✳ **Medium sharp knife**
- ✳ **8-inch nonstick skillet with an ovenproof handle**
- ✳ **Draining spoon**
- ✳ **Mixing bowl**
- ✳ **Fork**
- ✳ **Spoon**
- ✳ **Palette knife**
- ✳ **Oven mitts**

Cheddar cheese

1 Thinly slice the sausages on a cutting board. Heat 1 tablespoon of the oil in the skillet. Add the sausage to the skillet and fry until brown and cooked through. Adult supervision is required.

2 Lift out with a draining spoon, drain on paper towels, and set aside.

3 Thinly slice the potatoes and onions. Adult supervision is required.

4 Add 2 tablespoons of oil to the skillet. Fry the potatoes and onions for 2–3 minutes, turning often. Cover. Cook for 30 minutes, turning occasionally, until softened. Adult supervision is required.

5 In a mixing bowl, beat the eggs with a fork, then mix in the parsley, cheese, sausage, and seasoning. Gently stir in the potatoes and onions.

6 Wipe out the skillet with paper towels, then add the remaining 2 tablespoons of oil and heat on high. Add the potato-and-egg mixture and cook over a low heat, until the egg begins to set. Adult supervision is required.

7 Meanwhile, ask an adult to preheat the broiler to hot.

8 When the bottom of the tortilla has set (check by lifting up one side), ask an adult to place under the broiler for 2 minutes, until golden.

9 Cut into wedges and serve with tomatoes and basil. Or, cool and wrap in plastic wrap to transport.

Popeye's pie

Popeye was a famous cartoon character who ate a lot of spinach to make him really strong. Serve yourself this crunchy layered pie at lunchtime and you too can have bulging muscles!

serves 4

ingredients
- **oil**, for greasing
- **fresh spinach**, 2 pounds (see Fact File)
- **butter**, ½ cup
- **grated sharp Cheddar cheese**, ½ cup
- **feta cheese**, ⅔ cup, drained
- **salt** and **ground black pepper**
- **phyllo pastry**, 10 ounces
- **mixed ground cinnamon, ground nutmeg**, and **ground black pepper**, 2 teaspoons of each

FACT FILE

SPINACH
As well as large, slightly tough spinach leaves, supermarkets now sell a tender, young leaf variety that is ideal for eating raw in salads. Spinach is nutritious (especially when it is eaten raw because none of the nutrients will be destroyed, as they are by cooking) and it contains a lot of important vitamins and minerals. It is very easy to prepare and doesn't take long to cook, and in this recipe you get to squash it in your hands.

spinach leaves

tools
- ✳ Small, deep-sided roasting pan
- ✳ Colander
- ✳ Large, deep skillet with lid
- ✳ 2 mixing bowls
- ✳ Grater
- ✳ Small pan
- ✳ Pastry brush
- ✳ Clean, damp dish towel
- ✳ Fork
- ✳ Oven mitts

1 Preheat the oven to 325°F. Brush the inside of a roasting pan with a little oil. Remove the tough stalks from the spinach. Put the spinach in a colander and wash. Drain. Melt 2 tablespoons of the butter in a skillet.

2 Add the spinach. Season. Cover and cook for 5 minutes, until wilted. Adult supervision is required.

3 Ask an adult to drain the spinach, then squeeze to remove as much liquid as possible.

4 Put the grated cheese in a large bowl, then crumble the feta cheese over it. Add the salt and ground pepper and stir to mix. Gently melt the remaining butter in a small pan. Remove from the heat. Adult supervision is required.

5 Unfold the pastry so the sheets are flat. Peel off a sheet and use to line part of the bottom of the pan.

6 Brush the pastry with melted butter. Keep the remaining sheets covered with a damp dish towel.

7 Continue to lay phyllo pastry sheets across the bottom and up the sides of the pan, brushing each time with butter, until two thirds of the pastry has been used. Don't worry if the sheets flop over the top edges—they will be tidied up later.

8 Put the cool, squeezed spinach in the mixing bowl and break up any clumps with a fork. Add to the bowl containing the cheeses and mix to combine thoroughly.

9 Spoon the mixture into the pastry-lined pan and spread out. Fold the pastry edges over the filling.

10 Crumple up the remaining sheets of pastry and arrange them over the top of the filling.

11 Brush the pastry with the remaining melted butter and sprinkle the mixed spices over the top.

12 Put in the oven and bake for 45 minutes. Raise the temperature to 400°F. Cook for 10–15 minutes more. Ask an adult to remove from the oven and let stand in the pan for 5 minutes to let it cool. Cut into squares and serve, or let cool and wrap up to transport.

Tomato and pasta salad

Pasta salads are great for packed lunches, because they are portable and filling. This one contains roasted tomatoes and arugula for a colorful taste sensation.

serves 4

ingredients

- **ripe baby Italian plum tomatoes**, 1 pound, halved lengthwise
- **extra virgin olive oil**, 5 tablespoons
- **garlic cloves**, 2, cut into thin slivers
- **salt**, a pinch
- **dried pasta shapes**, such as **shells**, **butterflies**, or **spirals**, 2 cups
- **balsamic vinegar**, 2 tablespoons
- **sun-dried tomatoes in olive oil**, 2 pieces, drained and chopped
- **sugar**, a large pinch
- **arugula**, 1 handful, about 2½ ounces
- **salt** and **ground black pepper**

tools

- ✳ **Cutting board**
- ✳ **Small sharp knife**
- ✳ **Roasting pan**
- ✳ **Large pan**
- ✳ **Colander**
- ✳ **Large mixing bowl**
- ✳ **Large spoon or whisk**

1 Cut the tomatoes in half. Adult supervision is required. Arrange them, cut-side up, in a roasting pan. Drizzle 2 tablespoons of the olive oil over them and sprinkle with the slivers of garlic. Season.

2 Preheat the oven to 375°F.

3 Place in the preheated oven and roast for about 20 minutes, turning once, until the tomatoes are soft and the skin is turning golden. Ask an adult to remove from the oven and set aside to cool.

4 Meanwhile, halfway through the cooking time, fill two-thirds of a large pan with water and a pinch of salt. Bring to a boil. Add the pasta and bring back to a boil. Cook for 8–10 minutes, or according to package instructions, until just tender (al dente). Adult supervision is required.

5 Put the remaining oil in a bowl with the vinegar, sun-dried tomatoes, sugar, and a little salt and pepper to taste. Stir to mix.

6 Ask an adult to drain the pasta, add it to the bowl of dressing, and toss to mix. Add the roasted tomatoes and mix gently.

7 Before serving, add the arugula leaves and toss gently to combine. Serve warm or let stand until cool, then chill. To transport, pack into a sealable plastic container.

COOK'S TIP

▶ If you are in a hurry, you can make the salad with halved raw tomatoes instead.

Chicken pasta salad

Packed with colorful, crunchy vegetables and juicy chunks of cold roast chicken, this scrummy salad is perfect for using up Sunday's leftover chicken.

serves **4**

ingredients

- **salt**, a pinch
- **short pasta**, such as **mezze rigatoni, fusilli**, or **penne**, 12 ounces
- **olive oil**, 3 tablespoons
- **cold cooked chicken**, 8 ounces (see Cook's Tip)
- **small red** or **yellow bell peppers**, 2 (about 7 ounces)
- **scallions**, 4
- **pitted green olives**, ½ cup
- **mayonnaise**, 3 tablespoons
- **Worcestershire sauce**, 1 teaspoon
- **wine vinegar**, 1 tablespoon
- **salt** and **ground black pepper**
- **fresh basil leaves**, a few, to garnish

tools

- ✳ Large pan
- ✳ Colander
- ✳ Mixing bowl
- ✳ Wooden spoon
- ✳ 2 cutting boards
- ✳ Medium knife

1 Fill two-thirds of a large pan with water and a pinch of salt. Bring to a boil. Add the pasta and bring back to a boil. Cook for 8–10 minutes, or according to package instructions, until just tender (al dente). Drain and rinse. Adult supervision is required. Put in the bowl. Toss with the olive oil.

2 Meanwhile, cut the chicken into bite-size pieces using a knife. Adult supervision is required. Remove any bones, skin, or fat. Add to the bowl.

3 On another board, cut the bell peppers in half. Remove and discard the seeds and membranes.

4 Chop the bell peppers into bite-size pieces. Trim the scallions and slice. Adult supervision is required.

5 Add, along with all the remaining ingredients to the bowl, season, and mix. Garnish with basil to serve, or pack into a sealable plastic container to transport.

COOK'S TIP

▶ If you don't have any leftover cooked chicken you can buy some or cook some from raw. With adult supervision, place the chicken in a pan and cover with water. Bring to a boil, reduce the heat and simmer for 15–20 minutes or until cooked through.

Mozzarella and avocado salad

serves **2**

This colorful salad is an Italian favorite and it's very quick to make. It can easily be packed in a sealed plastic container, making it great for picnics and packed lunches.

ingredients
- **mozzarella cheese**, 5 ounces
- **ripe plum tomatoes**, 4 large
- **salt**, to taste
- **ripe avocado**, 1 large (*see* Cook's Tip)
- **fresh basil leaves**, 12, or **fresh Italian parsley**, a small handful
- **extra virgin olive oil**, 3–4 tablespoons
- **ground black pepper**

tools
- ✳ **Cutting board**
- ✳ **Large knife**
- ✳ **Teaspoon**

COOK'S TIP
▶ If you are planning to take this salad on a picnic or in a packed lunch, don't slice the avocado until as late as possible because it can turn brown after a while. To avoid this, just sprinkle the avocado with a little lemon juice.

avocado

1 Thinly slice the mozzarella and tomatoes. Adult supervision is required. Arrange the cheese and tomatoes on a plate and sprinkle over a little salt.

2 Cut the avocado in half along its length. Adult supervision is required. Hold each half and twist in opposite directions to separate.

3 Carefully lift out the pit from the middle of one half of the avocado. (You may need to do this by digging under it a little with a teaspoon).

4 Gently peel away the skin with your fingers. If the avocado is ripe enough, the skin should come away easily.

5 Slice crossways into half moons. Adult supervision is required.

6 Arrange on the tomatoes, then sprinkle over the basil or parsley. Drizzle over the oil, and add some pepper. Serve immediately, or, to transport, pack into a sealable plastic container.

(!) = Watch out! Sharp or electrical tool in use. = Watch out! Heat is involved.

Tuna and bean salad

It's always worth keeping a couple of cans of beans and tuna handy in your pantry to throw together this fantastic salad for a last-minute picnic. Juicy chunks of tomato and flecks of parsley add color and extra flavor.

serves **4–6**

ingredients
- **canned cannellini** or **borlotti beans**, 28 ounces (*see Variations*)
- **canned tuna fish**, 14 ounces, drained
- **extra virgin olive oil**, 4 tablespoons
- **lemon juice**, 2 tablespoons
- **chopped fresh parsley**, 1 tablespoon
- **ripe tomatoes**, 4, cut into chunks
- **scallions**, 3 (optional)
- **salt** and **ground black pepper**
- **fresh parsley**, chopped, to garnish

tools
- ✳ **Strainer or colander**
- ✳ **Large serving dish**
- ✳ **Medium bowl**
- ✳ **Fork**
- ✳ **Small bowl**
- ✳ **Spoon**
- ✳ **Cutting board**
- ✳ **Small knife**

canned tuna

1 Pour the canned beans into a strainer or colander and rinse well under plenty of cold running water. Drain well. Place in large serving dish.

2 Put the tuna in a medium bowl and break into large flakes with a fork. Arrange over the beans in the dish.

3 Make the dressing by combining the oil with the lemon juice in a small bowl. Season with salt and pepper, and stir in the parsley. Mix well.

4 Pour the dressing over the beans and tuna in the bowl and toss gently with a fork. Add the chunks of tomato.

5 If using, thinly slice the scallions. Adult supervision is required. Scatter them over the salad and toss well to combine everything.

6 Garnish with parsley, if using, and serve or chill until ready to use. To transport, pack into a sealable plastic container.

VARIATIONS
- You can use any beans you might have handy in your pantry, including mixed beans, chickpeas, lima beans, or kidney beans, or a mixture of two or three different types.
- You can replace the tuna with any other canned fish, such as salmon, mackerel, or sardines.

Confetti salad

This salad gets its name from the little pieces of brightly colored chopped vegetables that are mixed in with cold rice. Perfect for a tasty meal on the go.

serves **6**

ingredients
- **long-grain rice**, 1½ cups
- **ripe tomatoes**, 2 small (about 8 ounces)
- **green bell pepper**, 1
- **yellow bell pepper**, 1
- **scallions**, 1 bunch
- chopped, **fresh Italian parsley** or **cilantro**, 2 tablespoons

for the dressing
- **olive oil**, 5 tablespoons
- **sherry vinegar**, 1 tablespoon
- **strong Dijon mustard**, 1 teaspoon
- **salt** and **ground black pepper**

tools
- ✳ **Large pan**
- ✳ **Strainer**
- ✳ **Large heatproof bowl**
- ✳ **Small sharp knife**
- ✳ **Colander**
- ✳ **Cutting board**
- ✳ **Medium sharp knife**
- ✳ **Whisk**
- ✳ **Small bowl**

1 Place the rice in a pan and cover with water. Bring to a boil and cook for 10–12 minutes, or according to the package instructions, until just tender. Adult supervision is required.

2 Ask an adult to drain the rice in a strainer, rinse, and drain again. Let cool.

3 Meanwhile, place the tomatoes in a heatproof bowl and ask an adult to pour boiling water from a kettle over them to cover. Let stand for 5 minutes, until the skins soften and start to split (if they don't split, pierce them with the tip of a sharp knife and they should start to split).

4 Ask an adult to drain them in a colander. Let cool slightly, then peel away the skin with your fingers.

5 On a cutting board, cut the tomatoes into quarters. Carefully cut out the seeds and discard. Chop into chunks. Adult supervision is required.

6 Cut the bell peppers in half and cut out the seeds and membranes; discard. Dice the peppers. Trim and slice the scallions. Adult supervision is required.

7 To make the dressing, whisk all the ingredients together in a small bowl.

8 Transfer the rice to a large serving bowl with the tomatoes, bell peppers, and scallions. Add the herbs and the dressing, season, and mix well. Serve or chill until required. To transport, pack into a sealable plastic container.

Lemony couscous salad

Couscous is a lovely light and fluffy grain that is perfect for making salads because it absorbs all of the delicious flavors. It makes a really quick lunch box treat.

serves 4

ingredients
- **vegetable stock**, scant 2 cups
- **couscous**, 1⅔ cups
- **zucchini**, 2 small
- **black olives**, 16–20
- **slivered almonds**, ¼ cup, toasted (optional)

for the dressing
- **olive oil**, 4 tablespoons
- **lemon juice**, 1 tablespoon
- **chopped fresh cilantro**, 1 tablespoon
- **chopped fresh parsley**, 1 tablespoon
- **ground cumin**, a pinch
- **cayenne pepper**, a pinch

tools
- ✳ **Small pan or heatproof pitcher**
- ✳ **Large heatproof bowl**
- ✳ **Fork**
- ✳ **Cutting board**
- ✳ **Medium sharp knife**
- ✳ **Wooden skewer**
- ✳ **Whisk**
- ✳ **Small bowl**

1 With adult supervision, put the stock into a pan and bring to a boil. Or, put it in a heatproof pitcher and heat in the microwave for 90 seconds, or until boiling.

2 Meanwhile, place the couscous in a large heatproof bowl. Ask an adult to pour over the stock.

3 Stir the couscous with a fork, then set aside for 10 minutes, until the stock has been absorbed and the couscous has fluffed up.

4 Meanwhile, trim the zucchini and cut them into pieces about 1 inch long. Slice into thin strips. Adult supervision is required.

5 If the black olives have pits in them, push them out with a skewer. Cut the olives in half. Adult supervision is required.

6 Fluff up the couscous with a fork, then mix in the zucchini strips, pitted black olives, and slivered almonds, if using.

7 To make the dressing, whisk the olive oil, lemon juice, cilantro, parsley, cumin, and cayenne together in a small bowl. Stir into the salad and toss gently. Serve immediately or chill until required. To transport, pack into a sealable plastic container.

black olives

Fabulous fruit salad

Tropical fruit is perfect for picnic and packed lunch fruit salads because it stays firm and fresh for a long time and always has a tasty refreshing flavor.

serves 4

ingredients
- **pineapple**, 1 small
- **kiwis**, 2
- **ripe mango**, 1
- **watermelon**, 1 slice
- **peaches**, 2
- **bananas**, 2
- **tropical fruit juice**, 4 tablespoons

kiwi

tools
* **Cutting board**
* **Large sharp knife**
* **Small sharp knife**
* **Mixing bowl**
* **Vegetable peeler**

(!) **1** Ask an adult to help you slice the bottom and top off the pineapple. Stand upright. Cut away the skin by "sawing" down. Using the tip of a small, sharp knife, cut out the "eyes" (dark round pieces). Cut the pineapple in half lengthwise, then cut out the core. Chop into bitesize pieces. Put them in a bowl.

2 Use a vegetable peeler to remove the skin from the kiwis. Cut in half lengthwise, then into wedges. Add to the bowl.

(!) **3** Peel the mango with the peeler, then stand on a board and cut down to create slices. Cut these into smaller pieces. Adult supervision is required.

(!) **4** Cut the watermelon into slices, then cut off the skin; discard. Cut the flesh into chunks, then remove the seeds. Adult supervision is required.

5 Cut the peaches in half, remove the pits, and cut into wedges. Peel and slice the bananas. Adult supervision is required.

COOK'S TIP
▶ To make a coconut cream to serve with the salad, you can add toasted, dry shredded coconut to softly whipped cream.

6 Add all the fruits to the bowl and gently stir in the fruit juice. Cover tightly with plastic wrap and chill in the refrigerator for about 30 minutes before serving. To transport, pack into a sealable plastic container.

Yogurt cups

Spoon some yogurt into a suitable container, then create your favorite topping to stir in at school. Make a batch of each so you can mix and match!

serves **2**

ingredients
- **plain yogurt**, ⅔ cup
- **a topping of your choice**

for the raspberry and apple puree
- **apple**, 1, peeled and chopped
- **raspberries**, ⅔ cup

for the apricot compote
- **dried apricots**, 3, chopped
- **apple**, 1, peeled and chopped
- **large nectarine**, 1, pitted and chopped

for the granola
- **rolled oats**, 1 cup
- **sunflower seeds**, 2 tablespoons
- **sesame seeds**, 2 tablespoons
- **hazelnuts**, 2 tablespoons
- **almonds**, ¼ cup, roughly chopped
- **sunflower oil**, 2 tablespoons
- **honey**, 2 tablespoons
- **raisins**, 2 tablespoons
- **dried sweetened cranberries**, 2 tablespoons

tools
- ✳ Peeler
- ✳ Cutting board
- ✳ Sharp knife
- ✳ 2 small pans
- ✳ Wooden spoon
- ✳ Blender or food processor
- ✳ 2 mixing bowls
- ✳ Medium pan
- ✳ 2 nonstick baking sheets
- ✳ Oven mitts

1 To make the raspberry and apple puree, put the apple in a pan with the raspberries and a little water. Cook over a low heat for 5 minutes, stirring until soft. Adult supervision is required.

2 Put in a blender or food processor and blend until smooth. Adult supervision is required. Chill.

3 To make the compote, put the apricots, apple, and nectarine in a pan with a little water.

4 Bring to a boil, reduce the heat, and simmer for 10 minutes, until soft. Put in the blender or food processor and blend until smooth. Adult supervision is required. Chill.

5 To make the granola, preheat the oven to 275°F. Mix together the oats, seeds, and nuts in a mixing bowl.

6 Heat the oil and honey in a pan until combined. Add to the oat mixture and stir, then spread out on the baking sheets. Adult supervision is required.

7 Bake the granola for 50 minutes, until crisp, tossing so the mixture does not stick. Ask an adult to remove from the oven.

8 Pour into a clean bowl and stir in the raisins and cranberries. Cool, then store in an airtight container. Serve the yogurt with a topping of your choice.

Apricot and pecan bars

A tried-and-tested favorite made even more delicious by the addition of maple syrup, fruit, and nuts, these juicy bites are a real energy booster at any time of day.

makes **10**

ingredients
- **unsalted butter**, ⅔ cup, diced
- **light Barbados** or **brown sugar**, ⅔ cup
- **maple syrup**, 2 tablespoons
- **rolled oats**, 2 cups
- **pecan nuts**, ½ cup, chopped
- **dried apricots**, ¼ cup, chopped

tools
- ✳ **7-inch square, shallow baking pan**
- ✳ **Parchment paper**
- ✳ **Large heavy pan**
- ✳ **Wooden spoon**
- ✳ **Medium sharp knife**
- ✳ **Oven mitts**
- ✳ **Cutting board**

1 Preheat the oven to 325°F. Lightly grease and line a baking pan with parchment paper.

3 Remove the pan from the heat and stir in the oats, nuts, and apricots until well combined.

2 Put the butter, sugar, and maple syrup in a large heavy pan and heat gently, stirring occasionally, until the butter has melted. Adult supervision is required.

4 Spread the mixture evenly in the prepared pan and, using a knife, score lines in the mixture to make ten bars. Bake for 25–30 minutes, until golden.

5 Ask an adult to remove the pan from the oven and cut through the scored lines with the knife.

6 Let cool, then turn out onto a board, and cut into pieces along the scored lines. Adult supervision is required. To transport, wrap in foil or plastic wrap.

VARIATIONS
- Substitute the pecans with walnuts, brazil nuts, pine nuts, hazelnuts, or almonds.
- Omit the nuts and replace with the same amount of chocolate chips, chewy banana chips, or even dry shredded coconut.

walnuts

Date slices

These are packed with fruit and seeds, which makes them a healthy choice for lunch boxes.

makes **12–16**

ingredients
- **light Barbados** or **brown sugar**, ¾ cup
- **dried dates**, 1 cup, chopped
- **self-rising flour**, 1 cup
- **muesli**, ½ cup
- **sunflower seeds**, 2 tablespoons
- **poppy seeds**, 1 tablespoon
- **golden raisins**, 2 tablespoons
- **plain low-fat yogurt**, ⅔ cup
- **egg**, 1, beaten

for the topping
- **confectioners' sugar**, 1¾ cups, sifted
- **lemon juice**, 1–2 tablespoons
- **pumpkin seeds**, 1–2 tablespoons

tools
- ✳ **11 x 7-inch shallow baking pan**
- ✳ **Parchment paper**
- ✳ **Large mixing bowl**
- ✳ **2 wooden spoons**
- ✳ **Oven mitts**
- ✳ **Small mixing bowl**
- ✳ **Medium sharp knife**

1 Preheat the oven to 350°F. Line a 11 x 7-inch baking pan with parchment paper.

3 Spread in the pan and bake for 25 minutes, until golden brown. Ask an adult to remove from the oven and let cool.

5 Spread the lemon frosting over the cooled mixture and sprinkle the top with pumpkin seeds.

2 In a large mixing bowl, stir together all the ingredients, except the confectioners' sugar, lemon juice, and pumpkin seeds, with a wooden spoon.

4 **To make the topping,** put the confectioners' sugar in a small bowl and stir in enough lemon juice so it can be spread.

6 Let set before cutting into squares or bars with the knife. Adult supervision is required. To transport, wrap in aluminum foil or plastic wrap.

VARIATION
• As an alternative, try substituting the dates with chopped apricots, figs, pear, or soft mango, or try a mixture of your favorites. Instead of golden raisins, you can use dried blueberries or cranberries.

Butterscotch brownies

These gorgeous treats are delicious served warm with whipped cream or vanilla ice cream as a dessert or they make irresistible picnic food.

makes **12**

ingredients
- **white chocolate chips**, 1 pound
- **unsalted butter**, 6 tablespoons
- **eggs**, 3
- **light Barbados** or **brown sugar**, ¾ cup
- **self-rising flour**, 1½ cups
- **walnuts**, 1½ cups, chopped (see Variations)
- **vanilla extract**, 1 teaspoon

tools
- ✳ 11 x 7-inch shallow baking pan
- ✳ Parchment paper
- ✳ Small heatproof bowl
- ✳ Small pan
- ✳ Wooden spoon
- ✳ Large mixing bowl
- ✳ Electric mixer or whisk
- ✳ Large metal spoon
- ✳ Strainer
- ✳ Palette knife
- ✳ Oven mitts
- ✳ Medium sharp knife

1 Preheat the oven to 1375°F. Grease and line the bottom of a 11 x 7-inch baking pan with parchment paper. Lightly grease the sides of the pan.

2 Place about a quarter of the chocolate chips with the butter in a heatproof bowl. Ask an adult to fill a pan about halfway with boiling water. Place the bowl over the pan, making sure the water doesn't touch the bottom of the bowl. Let stand until the chocolate and butter melt. Stir gently, remove from the heat, and let cool slightly.

3 Place the eggs and sugar in a large bowl and beat until light and foamy. Whisk in the melted chocolate mixture.

4 Sift over the flour and fold in with the metal spoon with the walnuts, vanilla extract, and the remaining chocolate chips.

5 Spread out the mixture in the pan with a palette knife and bake for 30 minutes, or until risen and brown.

6 Ask an adult to remove from the oven and leave to cool. Cut into 12 bars. Adult supervision is required. To transport, wrap in plastic wrap.

VARIATIONS
- If you prefer not to use nuts, then why not try adding the same quantity of milk or semisweet chocolate chips to make double chocolate brownies.
- Alternatively, you can add raisins, golden raisins, or banana chips.

Chocolate thumbprint cookies

makes **16**

Chunky, chocolatey, and gooey all at the same time, these cookies are filled with a spoonful of chocolate spread after baking—perfect for a mid-morning snack!

cocoa powder

ingredients
- **unsalted butter**, ½ cup, at room temperature, diced
- **light Barbados** or **brown sugar**, ½ cup
- **egg**, 1
- **all-purpose flour**, ⅔ cup
- **cocoa powder**, ¼ cup
- **baking soda**, ½ teaspoon
- **rolled oats**, generous 1 cup
- **chocolate spread**, 5–6 tablespoons

tools
- ✳ Large nonstick baking sheet
- ✳ Large mixing bowl
- ✳ Wooden spoon or electric mixer
- ✳ Oven mitts
- ✳ Wire rack
- ✳ Palette knife
- ✳ Teaspoon

1 Preheat the oven to 350°F. Grease a large baking sheet.

3 Add the egg, flour, cocoa powder, baking soda, and oats and mix well.

5 Dip a thumb in the flour. Press into the center of each cookie, making an dip.

2 In a large mixing bowl, beat together the butter and sugar for about 10 minutes with a wooden spoon or an electric mixer (with adult supervision) until pale and creamy.

4 Using your hands, roll spoonfuls of the mixture into balls. Place these on the baking sheet, spacing them well apart so there is room for spreading. Flatten slightly.

6 Bake for 10 minutes. Let cool for 2 minutes, then transfer to a wire rack to cool more. Adult supervision is required. Spoon a little chocolate spread into the center of each.

COOK'S TIP
▶ If you like, freeze half of the cookies for another time. Simply thaw, then return to the oven for a few minutes before serving. Alternatively, freeze half of the raw cookie dough, then simply thaw at room temperature and continue to cook as in the recipe.

Peanut butter cookies

These sweet, nutty cookies are an all-time favorite, especially served with a glass of milk. Try sandwiching two cookies together with strawberry jelly for a real treat.

makes 24

ingredients

- **butter**, ½ cup, allowed to reach room temperature, diced
- **light brown sugar**, ¾ cup
- **egg**, 1
- **vanilla extract**, 1 teaspoon
- **crunchy peanut butter**, 1 cup
- **all-purpose flour**, 1 cup
- **baking soda**, ½ teaspoon
- **salt**, a pinch

tools

- ✳ Large mixing bowl
- ✳ Electric mixer or wooden spoon
- ✳ Small mixing bowl
- ✳ 2 forks
- ✳ Strainer
- ✳ 2 nonstick baking sheets
- ✳ 2 metal teaspoons
- ✳ Oven mitts
- ✳ Palette knife

1 Put the butter and sugar in a large bowl. Beat with a wooden spoon or electric mixer (with adult supervision) until pale and creamy.

2 In a small bowl, mix the egg and vanilla extract, then gradually beat into the butter mixture, beating well after each addition.

3 Mix in the peanut butter. Sift together the flour, baking soda, and salt and stir into the mixture to form a soft dough. Wrap in plastic wrap and chill for 30 minutes.

4 Preheat the oven to 350°F. Grease two baking sheets.

5 Spoon out rounded teaspoonfuls of the dough and roll into balls. Place the balls on the baking sheets.

6 Press flat with a fork into circles 2½ inches in diameter. Create a crisscross pattern by pushing down with the fork.

7 Bake the cookies for about 12 minutes, or until pale golden brown.

8 Ask an adult to remove them from the oven. Cool for a few minutes, then lift off with the palette knife and cool on a wire rack. To transport, wrap in plastic wrap.

Blueberry and lemon muffins

makes 12

This great American favorite makes good use of blueberries, which give a tangy contrast to the sweet muffin mixture. They make a fantastic break-time snack.

ingredients
- **all-purpose flour**, 1¼ cups
- **superfine sugar**, scant ½ cup
- **baking powder**, 2 teaspoons
- **salt**, a pinch
- **butter**, 4 tablespoons
- **eggs**, 2
- **milk**, ¾ cup
- **vanilla extract**, 1 teaspoon
- **grated lemon rind**, 1 teaspoon
- **fresh blueberries**, 1¼ cups

tools
- ✳ 2 6-hole muffin pans
- ✳ Paper muffin liners (optional)
- ✳ Strainer
- ✳ 2 large mixing bowls
- ✳ Medium pan
- ✳ Fork or whisk
- ✳ Wooden spoon
- ✳ Large metal spoon
- ✳ Oven mitts
- ✳ Wire rack

1 Preheat the oven to 400°F. Lightly grease two muffin pans, or you can use paper liners to line them. Colored ones will look best.

3 Gently melt the butter in a pan. Remove and cool for 5 minutes. Adult supervision is required.

2 Sift the flour, sugar, baking powder, and salt into a large glass bowl and set aside.

4 In a different bowl, whisk the eggs until blended. Add the melted butter, milk, vanilla extract, and lemon rind and stir well until thoroughly combined.

5 Make a well in the dry ingredients and pour in the egg-and-butter mixture. Using a large metal spoon, stir until the flour is just moistened and incorporated. It is important not to overmix the mixture until it is smooth—it should look a little lumpy.

6 Fold the blueberries into the mixture with a metal spoon. Spoon into the pans or paper liners.

7 Bake for 20–25 minutes, until golden. Ask an adult to remove from the oven. Transfer to a wire rack to cool. To transport, wrap in plastic wrap.

Snacks and light bites

You are bound to be hungry when you come home after school or a busy day out and about, and this is when quick snacks come into their own. Whether you want something satisfyingly savory or a sweet energy boost, this chapter provides a wide range of tempting bites that are sure to hit the spot.

Frankfurter sandwich

This scrummy sandwich is a twist on a normal hot dog and fries, combining the frankfurter and potatoes with mayonnaise and onions between two slices of bread.

makes **2**

ingredients
- **potato**, 1 medium (about 5 ounces)
- **mayonnaise**, 2–3 tablespoons
- **scallions**, 2, chopped
- **salt** and **ground black pepper**
- **butter**, 2 tablespoons, softened
- **whole-wheat bread**, 4 slices
- **frankfurters**, 4
- **tomatoes**, 2, sliced

scallions

tools
- ✳ Peeler
- ✳ Medium sharp knife
- ✳ Cutting board
- ✳ Small pan
- ✳ Colander
- ✳ Small bowl
- ✳ Butter knife
- ✳ Large serrated knife

(!) **3** Ask an adult to drain the potatoes in a colander. Let stand until completely cold, then mix with the mayonnaise and scallions. Season.

1 Peel the potatoes, then cut into small cubes. Adult supervision is required.

2 Put the potatoes in the pan and cover with water. Cover and bring up to the boil. Cook, uncovered, for about 5 minutes, until the potatoes are soft. Adult supervision is required.

4 Butter the bread and divide the potato salad equally between two slices, spreading it to the edges.

(!) **5** Slice the frankfurters into bite-size pieces. Adult supervision is required. Arrange over the potato salad with the tomato slices.

6 Sandwich with the remaining bread, press together lightly, and then cut the sandwich in half diagonally.

VARIATIONS
- For a super-speedy sandwich, you can simply replace the homemade potato salad with 2 cups of store-bought potato salad.
- Replace the frankfurters with leftover sausages.

(!) = Watch out! Sharp or electrical tool in use. = Watch out! Heat is involved.

Ciabatta sandwich

If you can find a ciabatta flavored with sun-dried tomatoes, it makes the sandwich even tastier. Prosciutto is the Italian name for Parma ham.

makes **3**

ingredients
- **mayonnaise**, 4 tablespoons
- **pesto**, 2 tablespoons
- **ciabatta loaf**, 1
- **mozzarella cheese**, 4 ounces, sliced
- **plum tomatoes**, 4, sliced
- **prosciutto**, 3 ounces, thinly sliced
- **fresh basil leaves**, 6–8, torn

tools
- ✳ Small bowl
- ✳ Wooden spoon
- ✳ Cutting board
- ✳ Large serrated knife
- ✳ Butter knife
- ✳ Medium sharp knife

3 Spread the cut side of both halves with the pesto mayonnaise.

1 Stir together the mayonnaise and pesto in a small bowl with a wooden spoon until they are thoroughly mixed.

2 On a cutting board, carefully cut the ciabatta in half horizontally with a serrated knife. Adult supervision is required.

4 Slice the cheese and tomatoes. Adult supervision is required. Lay the cheese on half of the ciabatta. Cut or tear the prosciutto into strips and arrange over the top.

5 Cover the prosciutto strips with the sliced tomatoes and plenty of torn basil leaves.

6 Top with the other half loaf and press down. Carefully cut into pieces with the serrated knife. Adult supervision is required. Serve.

VARIATIONS
- For an intense tomatoey flavor, replace the fresh tomatoes with sunblush or sun-dried ones.
- Replace the green pesto with whole-grain or smooth Dijon mustard, if desired.
- This sandwich is also delicious warm. Wrap in aluminum foil and place on a baking sheet. Cook in an oven preheated to 350°F for 10–15 minutes, until the cheese has melted completely.

Toasted bacon sandwich

Everyone's favorite, bacon sandwiches are the ultimate in after-school comfort food. It is worth using good-quality bacon to make the snack, and it is a good idea to remove the rind once the bacon is cooked because this makes it easier to eat.

each serves **2**

ingredients
* **vegetable oil**, 1 tablespoon
* **smoked** or **unsmoked lean bacon**, 4 strips, or **fatty bacon**, 8 strips
* **whole-wheat** or **white bread**, 4 slices
* **butter**, for spreading
* **mayonnaise**, 2 tablespoons
* **ketchup**, to serve (optional)

tools
* **Large nonstick skillet**
* **Spatula**
* **Bread board**
* **Butter knife**
* **Small sharp knife** (optional)
* **Large serrated knife**

1 With adult supervision, put the oil in a skillet and heat until sizzling.

2 Add the bacon and cook for 2–3 minutes, depending on how crispy you like it, then turn over and cook for an additional 2 minutes. Transfer to paper towels to drain. Adult supervision is required.

3 Toast the bread on both sides, either in a toaster or under a preheated broiler, until golden. Adult supervision is required.

4 Spread half the toast with butter, and the other half with mayonnaise. If you are using ketchup, spread this on top of the butter, or dot over the toast.

5 Using your fingers or a small sharp knife, pull or cut away the bacon rind from the drained, slightly cooled bacon, if desired.

6 Place two strips of lean bacon or four strips of fatty bacon on each of the pieces of toast spread with butter. Add ketchup on top of the bacon, if desired.

7 Top with the pieces of bread spread with mayonnaise and press down firmly to secure. With adult supervision, carefully cut in half with a serrated knife and serve.

VARIATION
• Everyone likes bacon sandwiches done in a particular way. Additions can include sliced tomatoes and lettuce to make a toasted BLT, or mustard or a spicy tomato relish.

lettuce

(!) = Watch out! Sharp or electrical tool in use. 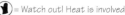 = Watch out! Heat is involved.

Cheesy treats

Croque monsieur, a French snack that literally means "crunch gentleman," makes a tasty alternative to normal ham and cheese sandwiches. Welsh rarebit is a special recipe of cheese served on toast with mustard and a dash of paprika or cayenne pepper.

each serves **2**

ingredients
for the croque monsieur
- **Gruyère** or **Cheddar cheese**, 3 ounces
- **butter**, for spreading
- **country-style bread**, 4 slices
- **lean honey roast ham**, 2 slices
- **ground black pepper**
- **fresh Italian parsley**, to garnish (optional)

for the Welsh rarebit
- **bread**, 2 thick slices
- **butter**, for spreading
- **spicy** or **mild mustard**, 2 teaspoons
- **Cheddar cheese**, 3¾ ounces, sliced
- **paprika** or **cayenne pepper**, a pinch
- **ground black pepper**

tools
- ✳ **Cutting board**
- ✳ **Medium knife**
- ✳ **Butter knife**
- ✳ **Oven mitts**

Cheddar cheese

1   **To make the croque monsieur**, ask an adult to preheat a sandwich toaster or a broiler to high.

2   With adult supervision, slice the cheese on a cutting board. Butter the bread. Place the cheese and ham on two slices. Top with the other slices of bread and press together.

3   Cook in a sandwich toaster or under the broiler, until browned on both sides. Adult supervision is required. Serve garnished with parsley, if using.

4   **To make the Welsh rarebit**, preheat the broiler to high and toast the bread on both sides. Adult supervision is required.

5   Spread the toast with butter and a thin layer of mustard, then top with the cheese. Cook under the broiler until the cheese melts and starts to brown. Adult supervision is required.

6   Sprinkle a little paprika or cayenne pepper on the cheese. Season with pepper and serve.

COOK'S TIP
▶ Bread can quickly become too brown or even burn when cooked under a broiler, so it is very important that you ask an adult for help and keep a close watch on the bread while it is cooking.

Cheese toasts

Melted cheese on toast makes a yummy, after-school snack to keep you going until dinner time, and these tasty variations are sure to please your stomach.

VARIATIONS
- Cut the bread into funny shapes with novelty cookie cutters. Small children might enjoy animal shapes or people (to make families) or simple circles, squares, or triangles. You can theme the cheese toasts for special occasions, such as Halloween, Valentine's Day, or Easter. Or, why not try increasing the quantities and stamping out names (one slice of bread per letter) or messages, such as "happy birthday" or "happy anniversary."
- To make edible tic, tac, toe games, use square pieces of bread and top with cheese as in the recipe. Using thin strips of red bell pepper, divide the toasts into nine squares. Use strips of scallions to make the crosses and slices of pepperoni or sliced, pitted black olives to make the circles.

red bell pepper and scallions

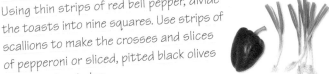

each serves 4

ingredients
- **Cheddar cheese**, 6–8 ounces
- **eggs**, 2
- **whole-grain mustard**, 1–2 teaspoons
- **butter**, 4 tablespoons, softened
- **bread**, 4 slices
- **tomatoes**, 2–4, halved (optional)
- **ground black pepper**
- **watercress** or **fresh parsley**, to serve (optional)

stripy toasts
- **butter**, 4 tablespoons, softened
- **bread**, 4 slices
- **white Cheddar cheese**, 4 ounces, sliced
- **orange-colored hard cheese**, 4 ounces, sliced

tools
✱ Grater
✱ Mixing bowl
✱ Whisk
✱ Wooden spoon
✱ Shallow casserole
✱ Butter knife
✱ Nonstick baking sheet
✱ Oven mitts
✱ Spatula

1 Preheat the oven to 450°F. Grate the Cheddar cheese. Place the eggs in a mixing bowl and whisk lightly. Stir in the grated cheese, whole-grain mustard, and black pepper.

2 Grease the inside of an ovenproof bowl with some of the butter.

3 Spread the remaining butter on the bread. Lay it, buttered-side down, in the casserole.

4 Divide and spread the cheese mixture among the slices of bread.

5 With adult supervision, bake in the oven for 10–15 minutes, or until well risen and golden brown.

6 Meanwhile, place the tomatoes (if using) on a nonstick baking sheet. Put the tomatoes in the oven for the last 5 minutes of the toasts' cooking time, until soft. Adult supervision is required.

7 Ask an adult to remove the casserole from the oven. Lift the toasts out with a spatula and serve immediately with the tomatoes. Garnish with sprigs of watercress or parsley (if using).

8 **To make the stripy toast**, grease the inside of a casserole with some of the butter. Spread the remaining butter on the bread. Lay the bread, buttered-side down, in the dish.

9 Arrange alternate slices of white and orange cheeses on each of the pieces of bread to make stripes. Bake for 10–15 minutes, until bubbly and golden brown. Adult supervision is required. ⓘ

Sweet toast toppers

These tasty bites make a great weekend snack or after-school energy booster. They are also good as part of a special breakfast in bed for your mom and dad!

each serves **2–4**

ingredients
jelly toast
- **butter**, 6 tablespoons, at room temperature
- **vanilla extract**, a few drops
- **bread**, 4 slices
- **jelly**, 4 teaspoons

cinnamon toast
- **butter**, 6 tablespoons, at room temperature
- **ground cinnamon**, 2 teaspoons
- **superfine sugar**, 2 tablespoons
- **bread**, 4 slices
- **fresh fruit**, (optional)

tools
- ✳ **Small bowl**
- ✳ **Wooden spoon**
- ✳ **Butter knife**

raspberry jelly

bread

3 Spread the toast thickly on one side with the flavored butter and the jelly. Serve immediately.

1 **To make the jelly toast**, mix the butter with the vanilla extract in the small bowl with the wooden spoon, until soft and smooth.

2 Toast the bread on both sides in a toaster or under a preheated broiler. Adult supervision is required.

4 **To make the cinnamon toast**, mix the butter with the cinnamon and half the sugar in the small bowl with the wooden spoon, until soft and smooth.

5 Toast the bread on both sides, either in a toaster or under a preheated broiler. Adult supervision is required. Spread the toast with the cinnamon butter.

6 Sprinkle with the remaining sugar. Serve at once, with pieces of fresh fruit, if desired.

VARIATION
• To make different-flavored butters, try adding 2 teaspoons orange or lemon juice and a little finely grated orange or lemon rind, almond or coffee extract, allspice, or honey to the butter.

orange rind

(!) = Watch out! Sharp or electrical tool in use.   (🥄) = Watch out! Heat is involved.

Eggtastic

These two classic egg recipes are simple, but are worth knowing because they can be eaten for breakfast, lunch, or as a healthy snack at any time of the day.

each serves **1**

ingredients

boiled egg with toast sticks

- **egg**, 1
- **bread**, 4 thin slices
- **butter**, a little, for spreading
- **salt**, to taste

poached egg on toast

- **eggs**, 2
- **lemon juice** or **vinegar**, 1 teaspoon
- **bread**, 2 thin slices
- **butter**, for spreading
- **salt** and **ground black pepper**

tools

- ✳ Small pan
- ✳ Slotted spoon
- ✳ Bread board
- ✳ Large serrated knife
- ✳ Butter knife
- ✳ Large, deep skillet
- ✳ Egg poaching rings (optional)
- ✳ Knife

1 **To make the boiled egg with toast sticks**, place the egg in a pan and ask an adult to pour in hot water to cover. Bring to a boil and cook for about 3 minutes for a soft egg or 4 minutes for a soft yolk and firm white.

3 Meanwhile, make the toast sticks. Toast the bread, spread with butter, then cut it into slices. Serve the boiled egg with the toast sticks and salt on the side to sprinkle over.

2 Remove with a slotted spoon and place in an egg cup. Ask an adult for help.

4 **For the poached eggs on toast**, ask an adult to fill three-fourths of a skillet with hot water.

5 Heat gently until just simmering. If you have egg poaching rings, then add them to the pan.

6 Carefully crack open the eggs, and place into the skillet or rings. Cook for 2–3 minutes, until the eggs have turned white and set. Adult supervision is required.

7 Meanwhile, lightly toast the bread and spread with butter.

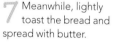

8 Carefully remove the poached eggs from the skillet with a slotted spoon, being careful not to break the yolks. Adult supervision is required. Arrange on the toast, season to taste, and serve.

Egg-stuffed tomatoes

You will enjoy slipping the slices of hard-boiled egg into the tomatoes when you make this tasty lunch, but not as much as you will enjoy eating them!

serves **4**

ingredients

- **eggs**, 4
- **mayonnaise**, ¼ cup
- **chopped fresh chives**, 2 tablespoons
- **chopped fresh basil**, 2 tablespoons
- **chopped fresh parsley**, 2 tablespoons
- **ripe tomatoes**, 4
- **ground black pepper**
- **salad greens**, to serve

eggs

tools

- ✳ Medium pan
- ✳ Slotted spoon
- ✳ Small bowl
- ✳ Spoon
- ✳ Egg slicer or sharp knife
- ✳ Medium sharp knife
- ✳ Cutting board

1 Ask an adult to fill a pan with hot water and bring to a boil. Carefully place the eggs onto a slotted spoon and lower into the water. Boil for 8 minutes.

2 Ask an adult to place the pan under a cold tap until the water is cool. Let the eggs stand until cold. Peel.

3 Mix together the mayonnaise and herbs in a small bowl with a spoon. Set aside.

4 With an egg slicer or sharp knife, cut the peeled, hard-cooked eggs into slices, being careful to keep the slices intact. Adult supervision is required.

5 Using a sharp knife, make deep cuts in the tomatoes to ½ inch from the bottom of each tomato. Do not cut right through the bottom. Adult supervision is required. There should be the same number of cuts in each tomato as there are slices of each hard-cooked egg.

6 Gently fan open the tomatoes and sprinkle with a little black pepper.

7 Carefully place an egg slice into each slit. Place each stuffed tomato on a plate with a few salad greens and serve immediately with the herb mayonnaise.

 = Watch out! Sharp or electrical tool in use.   🖐 = Watch out! Heat is involved.

Ham and tomato scramble

serves **2**

Scrambled egg isn't just for breakfast—it makes a delicious and easy lunch or snack. Watch the timings or you can end up with overcooked, rubbery eggs.

ingredients
- **ham**, 2 slices
- **tomato**, 1
- **red bell pepper**, ¼, seeded
- **eggs**, 2
- **milk**, 1 tablespoon
- **butter**, 3 tablespoons
- **bread**, 2 slices

tools
* Medium sharp knife
* Cutting board
* Mixing bowl
* Fork
* Nonstick skillet
* Wooden spatula
* Butter knife
* Small novelty-shaped cookie cutters (optional)

1 Finely chop the ham on a cutting board. Halve the tomato, scoop out and discard the seeds, then chop finely. Finely chop the pieces of bell pepper. Adult supervision is required.

2 Put the eggs and milk in a bowl and whisk lightly with a fork.

3 Heat a small pat of butter in a skillet over a medium heat, until foaming. Add the egg mixture with the ham, tomato, and bell pepper. Cook gently, stirring all the time, over a low heat for about 3 minutes. Remove from the heat. Adult supervision is required.

4 Lightly toast the bread, then spread with the remaining butter. Cut the toast into shapes with small novelty-shaped (see Cook's Tips) cookie cutters, if desired. Arrange the toast on serving plates, spoon over the ham and tomato scramble, and serve immediately.

COOK'S TIPS
► This is a good snack for themed days, such as Halloween or Valentine's Day, using appropriate cutters for the toast. If you don't have special cutters, cut the toast into shapes with a knife. Adult supervision is required.
► Add any of your favorite vegetables, such as corn or peas, to the scramble.

Dunkin' dippers

This dish is great for a party and all your friends will love dunking their favorite chips and vegetables into the rich and creamy dips. Watch out for dunkin' grown-ups— who are bound to want to join in all the fun!

bell peppers in a variety of colors

serves *8–10*

ingredients
for the cheese dip
- **soft cheese**, 8 ounces
- **milk**, 4 tablespoons
- **fresh chives**, small bunch
- **small carrot**, 1, peeled

for the saucy tomato dip
- **shallot**, 1
- **garlic**, 2 cloves
- **fresh basil leaves**, a handful, plus a few extra, torn, to garnish
- **ripe tomatoes**, 1¼ pounds, cut in half
- **olive oil**, 30ml/2 tbsp
- **salt** and **ground black pepper**
- **green chiles**, 2 (optional)

for the guacamole
- **red chiles**, 2 (optional)
- **ripe avocados**, 2
- **garlic**, 1 clove, peeled and chopped
- **shallot**, 1, peeled and chopped
- **olive oil**, 2 tablespoons, plus extra to serve
- **lemon**, juice of 1
- **salt**
- **fresh Italian parsley leaves**, a handful, to garnish

for dunking
- **cucumber**, 1
- **baby corn**, 4
- **red, orange** and **yellow bell peppers**, ½ of each, seeded
- **cherry tomatoes**, 8–10
- **tortilla chips** or **potato chips**

tools
- ✴ Mixing bowl
- ✴ Wooden spoon
- ✴ Cutting board
- ✴ Small sharp knife
- ✴ 3 serving bowls
- ✴ Grater
- ✴ Blender or food processor
- ✴ Teaspoon
- ✴ Fork

tortilla chips   *baby corn*

1 To make the cheese dip, spoon the soft cheese into a mixing bowl and beat it with a wooden spoon until soft and creamy.

2 Add the milk to the cheese, a little at a time. Beat the mixture well each time you pour more milk in.

3 Beat the mixture for 2 minutes. If necessary, add more milk to make it runnier. Chop the chives on a board. Adult supervision is required. Reserve some, then add the rest to the dip.

(!)

4 Finely grate the carrot. Reserve some and stir the rest into the dip.

5 Spoon into a small serving bowl and sprinkle over the remaining chives and carrot. Cover and set aside.

6 To make the saucy tomato dip, peel and halve the shallot and garlic cloves. Place in a blender with the basil leaves. Adult supervision is required.

7 Blend until finely chopped. Add the tomatoes and blend in short bursts until the tomatoes are finely chopped but not pureed.

(!)

8 With the motor running, pour in the olive oil. Adult supervision is required. Season. Spoon into a bowl.

(!) = Watch out! Sharp or electrical tool in use.   (🔥) = Watch out! Heat is involved.

10 **To make the guacamole**, prepare the chiles as in Step 9, if using, then chop them.

9 With adult supervision, cut the chiles in half lengthwise, if using, and cut out their seeds and membranes, or scrape out with a teaspoon. Slice the chile halves across their width into tiny strips and stir them into the tomato mixture. Wash your hands. Garnish with the basil.

11 Cut the avocados in half around their length. Adult supervision is required. Remove the pits and scoop out the flesh into a bowl. Mash with a fork.

12 Stir the garlic and shallot into the avocado with the oil and lemon juice. Add salt to taste. Spoon into a serving bowl. Drizzle with oil and scatter over the parsley.

13 **To make the dunks**, cut the cucumber, baby corn, and bell peppers into 3-inch lengths. Adult supervision is required.

14 Serve the dips with the dunks, tomatoes, and tortilla or potato chips.

snacks and light bites   **77**

Skinny dips

Baked potatoes in disguise, these delectable bites are served with a spicy dip. Although they aren't quick to make, they are very easy and extremely delicious.

serves 4

ingredients
- **baking potatoes**, 8, scrubbed
- **oil**, 2–3 tablespoons
- **salt**, a generous pinch
- **mayonnaise**, 6 tablespoons
- **plain yogurt**, 2 tablespoons
- **curry paste**, 5ml/1 tsp
- **fresh cilantro**, 2 tablespoons, roughly chopped

cilantro

tools
- ✳ Fork
- ✳ Large, shallow roasting pan
- ✳ Oven mitts
- ✳ Medium knife
- ✳ Cutting board
- ✳ Spoon
- ✳ Pastry brush
- ✳ Small bowl
- ✳ Wooden spoon

1 Preheat the oven to 375°F.

2 Prick the potatoes with a fork, then arrange in the roasting pan. Ask an adult to put in the oven and bake for 45 minutes, or until tender. Ask an adult to remove from the oven. Let stand until cool enough to handle.

3 With adult supervision, carefully cut each potato into quarters lengthwise, holding it with a clean dish towel if it's still hot.

(!)

4 Scoop out some of the center with a knife or spoon and put the skins back in the pan. Adult supervision is required. Save the cooked potato for use in another dish.

5 Brush the potato skins with oil and sprinkle with salt before asking an adult to put them back in the oven. Cook for 30–40 minutes more, until they are crisp and brown.

6 Put the mayonnaise, yogurt, curry paste, and 1 tablespoon of the cilantro in a small bowl.

7 Mix everything together well with a wooden spoon. Cover with plastic wrap and let the flavors develop while the skins are cooking.

8 Put the dip in a serving bowl and arrange the skins around the edge. Serve hot, sprinkled with the remaining cilantro.

(!) = Watch out! Sharp or electrical tool in use.   (🍳) = Watch out! Heat is involved.

Chile cheese nachos

Crispy tortilla chips smothered in melted cheese served with an avocado dip make the most delicious snack. You can omit the chiles if you prefer.

serves **4**

ingredients
- **Cheddar cheese**, 2 ounces
- **red Leicester cheese**, 2 ounces
- **pickled green jalapeño chiles**, 2 ounces (optional)
- **chili tortilla chips**, 4-ounce bag

for the dip
- **ripe avocado**, 1
- **beefsteak tomato**, 1
- **lemon juice**, 2 tablespoons
- **salt** and **ground black pepper**

tools
- ✳ **Grater**
- ✳ **2 mixing bowls**
- ✳ **Strainer**
- ✳ **Cutting board**
- ✳ **Medium sharp knife**
- ✳ **Teaspoon**
- ✳ **Heatproof plate or shallow casserole**
- ✳ **Oven mitts**

3 Peel away the skin, then roughly chop the avocado flesh. Roughly chop the beefsteak tomato. Adult supervision is required.

5 Ask an adult to preheat a broiler to medium-hot. Arrange the tortilla chips in a layer on a heatproof plate or shallow casserole, overlapping some slightly.

COOK'S TIP
▶ If the chips are burning before the cheese has melted, cover with foil and continue grilling. Adult supervision is required.

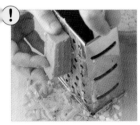

1 Grate both cheeses and put in a mixing bowl. Drain the chiles, if using, and slice on a cutting board. Wash your hands. Adult supervision is required.

4 Mix together the avocado and tomato in a mixing bowl. Add the lemon juice and season to taste. Mix well to combine everything, then set aside.

2 **To make the dip**, cut the avocado in half down its length. Remove the pit with a teaspoon. Adult supervision is required.

6 Sprinkle over both types of grated cheese and then add jalapeño chiles, or not, depending on your preference.

7 Ask an adult to put under the broiler and toast until the cheese has melted and browned. Ask an adult to remove and serve with the dip.

Cheese and basil tortillas

These tortilla wedges are a great easy-cook invention. You'll want to experiment with different fillings and leftovers will never go to waste again.

serves 2

ingredients
- **olive oil**, 1 tablespoon
- **soft flour tortillas**, 2
- **Gruyère cheese**, 4 ounces, thinly sliced
- **fresh basil leaves**, a handful
- **salt** and **ground black pepper**

basil leaves

tools
* **Medium skillet**
* **Metal spatula**
* **Cutting board**
* **Large sharp knife**

1 With adult supervision, heat the oil in a skillet over a low heat. Add one of the tortillas, and heat for 1 minute. Be careful to avoid overcooking them.

2 Arrange the Gruyère cheese slices and basil leaves on top of the tortilla and season. Adult supervision is required.

3 Place the remaining tortilla on top of the cheese and basil layer to make a sandwich.

4 Press down lightly on the tortilla to secure, then cook for 1 minute, so the cheese can melt slightly. Carefully flip over with the metal spatula. Adult supervision is required.

5 Cook for a few minutes, until the underneath is golden and crisp.

6 Slide the tortilla onto a cutting board or plate and cut into small wedges with a knife. Adult supervision is required. Serve immediately—the tortilla will become tough as it cools.

VARIATION
- The crispy tortillas make excellent snacks to share with friends. If you have a few slices of ham or salami in the refrigerator, add these to the tortillas as well. They are also tasty with a handful of sliced, pitted olives.

ham

(!) = Watch out! Sharp or electrical tool in use.   = Watch out! Heat is involved.

Chicken pita pockets

These scrummy pitas are packed with succulent chicken and a zesty, crunchy salad, and make a perfect substantial snack or weekend lunch.

makes 6

ingredients
- **small cucumber**, 1
- **scallions**, 2, chopped
- **tomatoes**, 3
- **olive oil**, 2 tablespoons
- **parsley**, a small bunch, finely chopped
- **mint**, a small bunch, finely chopped
- **preserved lemon**, ½, rinsed well and finely chopped
- **tahini**, 3–4 tablespoons
- **lemon**, juice of 1
- **garlic**, 2 cloves, crushed
- **salt** and **ground black pepper**
- **pitas**, 6
- **roast chicken breasts**, 2, flesh removed from the bone and cut into strips

pitas

tools
- ✳ **Vegetable peeler**
- ✳ **Cutting board**
- ✳ **Strainer**
- ✳ **Medium sharp knife**
- ✳ **Large mixing bowl**
- ✳ **Small bowl**
- ✳ **Spoon and fork**

1 Peel the cucumber, then chop into small chunks. Chop the scallions. Adult supervision is required.

2 Place the tomatoes in a heatproof bowl and ask an adult to pour over boiling water. Let stand for about 5 minutes, until the skins split. With adult supervision, rinse under cold water.

3 Peel away the skin, cut the tomatoes into quarters, and scoop out the seeds with a teaspoon. Chop the flesh into chunks and put in a large mixing bowl. Adult supervision is required.

4 Add the cucumber and the scallions. Stir in the oil, parsley, mint, and preserved lemon. Season.

5 In a second small bowl, mix the tahini with the lemon juice, then thin down the mixture by stirring in a little water, until it has the consistency of thick heavy cream.

6 Beat in the garlic with a fork and season to taste. Ask an adult to preheat the broiler to hot.

7 Lightly toast the pitas well away from the heat until they puff up. Adult supervision is required.

8 Open the pitas and stuff them liberally with the chicken and salad. Drizzle a generous amount of tahini sauce into each one and serve with any extra salad.

Chunky veggie salad

This crunchy snack is packed with vitamins and will give you loads of energy—ideal for after school to get you through your homework! Serve on slices of crusty bread.

serves **4**

ingredients
- **small white cabbage**, ¼
- **small red cabbage**, ¼
- **baby carrots**, 8
- **small mushrooms**, 2 ounces
- **cauliflower**, 4 ounces
- **small zucchini**, 1
- **cucumber**, 4-inch piece
- **tomatoes**, 2
- **cheese**, 2 ounces
- **sprouted seeds**, 2 ounces (see Fact File)
- **peanuts**, ½ cup (optional)
- **sunflower oil**, 2 tablespoons, plus extra for serving
- **lemon juice**, 1 tablespoon, plus extra for serving
- **salt** and **ground black pepper**

tools
- ✳ **Cutting board**
- ✳ **Medium sharp knife**
- ✳ **Vegetable peeler**
- ✳ **Grater**
- ✳ **Mixing bowl**
- ✳ **Wooden spoon**

1 On a cutting board, finely chop the white and red cabbages. Peel the carrots with a vegetable peeler, then slice into thin circles or sticks. Adult supervision is required.

2 Gently wipe the mushrooms clean, then cut into quarters.

3 With adult supervision, cut the cauliflower into small, even stalks ("florets").

4 Grate the zucchini with a coarse grater. Cut the cucumber into cubes and chop the tomatoes into similar-size pieces. Grate the cheese coarsely. Adult supervision is required.

5 Put all the prepared vegetables and sprouted seeds in a bowl and mix together well.

6 Stir in the peanuts, if using. Drizzle over the oil and lemon juice. Season well with salt and pepper, then let stand for 30 minutes to let the flavors develop.

7 Sprinkle grated cheese over just before serving with slices of crusty bread.

FACT FILE
SPROUTED SEEDS
These are the sprouts that start to grow when seeds are given the right conditions. They taste great and are full of goodness.

(!) = Watch out! Sharp or electrical tool in use.   = Watch out! Heat is involved.

Chicken and tomato salad

Warm salads are wonderful for eating all year round but especially in winter when you want a salad but need warm food. This one is delicious and nutritious.

serve 2

ingredients
- **baby spinach leaves**, 8 ounces, rinsed
- **cherry tomatoes**, 9 ounces
- **scallions**, 1 bunch
- **skinless chicken breast fillets**, 2
- **salt** and **ground black pepper**

for the dressing
- **olive oil**, 3 tablespoons
- **hazelnut oil**, 2 tablespoons (see Variation)
- **white wine vinegar**, 1 tablespoon
- **garlic**, 1 clove, peeled and crushed
- **chopped fresh mixed herbs**, 1 tablespoon

tools
- ✳ Small bowl or pitcher
- ✳ Whisk or fork
- ✳ Cutting board
- ✳ Medium sharp knife
- ✳ Large nonstick skillet
- ✳ Wooden spatula

VARIATION
- You can replace the hazelnut oil with more olive oil. Alternatively, you can experiment with other flavored oils, such as delicious avocado oil.

1 **To make the dressing,** place 2 tablespoons of the olive oil and the hazelnut oil in a small bowl or pitcher. Whisk together, then slowly add the vinegar, whisking well between each addition. Add the crushed garlic and mixed herbs and whisk well to combine everything thoroughly.

2 Trim any long stalks from the spinach leaves, then place in a large serving bowl.

3 Cut the tomatoes in half. Trim the scallions, then slice. Add to the bowl with the spinach leaves and toss together. Adult supervision is required.

4 Cut the chicken into strips. Heat the remaining olive oil in a skillet and stir-fry the chicken over a high heat for 7–10 minutes, until it is cooked and brown. Adult supervision is required.

5 Arrange the cooked chicken over the salad.

6 Whisk the dressing to blend, then drizzle it over the salad. Season to taste, toss lightly, and serve immediately.

Country pasta salad

Salads are a wonderful way of using up leftovers, including pasta. You can throw this together quickly and easily for a tasty, filling light lunch or snack.

serves 6

ingredients
- **dried fusilli**, 2¾ cups
- **green beans**, 5 ounces
- **potato**, 1 medium (about 5 ounces)
- **baby tomatoes**, 7 ounces
- **scallions**, 2
- **black olives**, 6–8, pitted
- **Parmesan cheese**, 3½ ounces
- **capers in vinegar**, 1–2 tablespoons

for the dressing
- **extra virgin olive oil**, 6 tablespoons
- **balsamic vinegar**, 1 tablespoon
- **chopped**, **fresh Italian parsley**, 1 tablespoon
- **salt** and **ground black pepper**

tools
- ✳ Large pan
- ✳ Colander
- ✳ Cutting board
- ✳ Vegetable peeler
- ✳ Large mixing bowl
- ✳ Small mixing bowl
- ✳ Whisk
- ✳ Wooden spoon

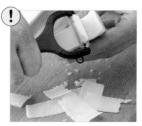

1 Fill two-thirds of a large pan with water and a pinch of salt. Bring to a boil. Add the pasta and bring back to a boil. Cook for 8–10 minutes, or according to package instructions, until the pasta is just tender (al dente). Drain in a colander, rinse under cold water. Drain again. Adult supervision is required.

2 Meanwhile, trim the ends from the beans with a knife, then cut into 2-inch lengths. Peel the potato and cut into cubes. Adult supervision is required.

3 Place the beans and potato in the pan. Cover with water. Bring to a boil, reduce the heat, and simmer for 5–6 minutes, or until tender. Drain and cool. Adult supervision is required.

4 Meanwhile, cut the tomatoes in half. Trim the scallions and slice. Slice the olives. Adult supervision is required.

5 With adult supervision, make shavings from the Parmesan with a vegetable peeler.

6 Put the tomatoes, scallions, Parmesan shavings, olive rings, and drained capers in a large bowl, then add the cold pasta, beans, and potato.

7 **To make the dressing,** put all the ingredients in a small bowl and season to taste. Whisk well to mix.

8 Pour the dressing over the pasta salad and toss well to mix. Cover with plastic wrap and let stand for 30 minutes. Serve or chill until required.

Tuna pasta salad

This is ideal for making when you are in a rush and need a sustaining snack or lunch, because most of the ingredients are pantry items.

serves 6–8

ingredients
- **short pasta**, such as **ruote**, **macaroni**, or **farfalle**, 1 pound
- **olive oil**, 4 tablespoons
- **canned tuna**, 14 ounces, drained
- **canned cannellini** or **borlotti beans**, 28 ounces, rinsed and drained
- **small red onion**, 1
- **celery**, 2 stalks
- **lemon**, juice of 1
- **chopped fresh parsley**, 2 tablespoons
- **salt** and **ground black pepper**

tools
- ✳ Large pan
- ✳ Colander
- ✳ Large mixing bowl
- ✳ 2 small mixing bowls
- ✳ Fork
- ✳ Cutting board
- ✳ Medium sharp knife
- ✳ Wooden spoon

2 Let drain, shaking the colander from time to time. Toss with the olive oil in the large mixing bowl, and set aside until cold.

1 Fill two-thirds of a large pan with water and a pinch of salt. Bring to a boil. Add the pasta and bring back to a boil. Cook for 8–10 minutes, or according to package instructions, until the pasta is just tender (al dente). Drain in a colander and rinse under cold water. Adult supervision is required.

3 Put the tuna in a small mixing bowl and separate into flakes with the fork. Add to the pasta with the beans.

4 Peel the onion, then slice. Trim the celery and slice. Adult supervision is required. Add to the pasta.

5 In a small bowl, mix the lemon juice with the parsley. Mix into the other ingredients. Season. Let the salad stand for at least 1 hour before serving.

COOK'S TIP
▶ It is important to run the pasta under cold water as soon as you have drained it because this will stop it from cooking any further. For most dishes this is not a problem, but for pasta salads you want the pasta to stay soft with some bite (al dente).

Quick and easy suppers

Being able to create a healthy, tasty meal in a short amount of time is a really useful skill to have and will really impress your parents. This collection of easy recipes ranges from warming soups and quick egg dishes to pasta, rice, pizza, and a mouthwatering selection of fish, meat, and chicken dishes.

Chilled tomato soup

Although cold soup may sound a bit odd, it tastes fantastic. The fresh vegetable flavors of this tomato soup are brought out by the tasty arugula pesto, which is ideal for a special supper.

serves 4

ingredients
- **ripe tomatoes**, 1¾ pounds
- **shallots**, 2
- **sun-dried tomato paste**, 1½ tablespoons
- **vegetable stock**, 2½ cups
- **salt** and **ground black pepper**
- **ice cubes**, to serve

for the arugula pesto
- **arugula leaves**, ½ ounce
- **olive oil**, 5 tablespoons
- **pine nuts**, 2 tablespoons
- **garlic**, 1 clove
- **freshly grated Parmesan cheese**, ⅓ cup

tools
- ✳ Cutting board
- ✳ Medium sharp knife
- ✳ Food processor or blender
- ✳ Strainer
- ✳ Metal spoon
- ✳ Large pan
- ✳ Plastic or rubber spatula
- ✳ Large bowl
- ✳ Mortar and pestle
- ✳ Ladle

6 Ladle the soup into serving bowls and add a few ice cubes to each. Spoon some of the arugula pesto into the center of each portion and serve.

1 On a cutting board, chop the tomatoes. Peel and chop the shallots. Adult supervision is required.

2 Place the tomato and shallots in a food processor or blender. Add the sun-dried tomato paste and blend until smooth. Adult supervision is required.

3 Push the mixture through a strainer into a large pan, scraping all the mixture out with the plastic or rubber spatula.

4 Add the stock and heat gently for 4–5 minutes. Adult supervision is required. Season, pour into a bowl, and let cool. Chill for 4 hours.

5 To make the arugula pesto, put the arugula leaves, olive oil, pine nuts, and garlic in a clean food processor or blender and blend to form a paste. Adult supervision is required. Alternatively, use a mortar and pestle. Stir in the Parmesan cheese using the pestle or a spoon.

COOK'S TIP
▶ A mortar is a bowl in which you grind food with a pestle, a baseball bat-shape baton.

   (!) = Watch out! Sharp or electrical tool in use.   🍴 = Watch out! Heat is involved.

Chilled avocado soup

This unusual no-cook recipe comes from Spain, where avocados grow really well. It is mild and creamy and perfect for a quick supper on a summer's day with a hunk of French bread.

serves 4

ingredients
- **ripe avocados**, 3
- **ground cumin**, ¼ teaspoon
- **paprika**, ¼ teaspoon
- **scallions**, 1 bunch, white parts only, trimmed and roughly chopped
- **garlic**, 2 cloves, chopped
- **lemon**, juice of 1
- **chicken** or **vegetable stock**, scant 2 cups
- **iced water**, 1¼ cups
- **salt** and **ground black pepper**
- **fresh Italian parsley**, to serve

avocado

tools
* **Cutting board**
* **Medium sharp knife**
* **Teaspoon**
* **Food processor or blender**
* **Wooden spoon**

1 On a cutting board, using a sharp knife, cut the avocados in half lengthwise. Twist each half in opposite directions and pull apart so you get two halves. Adult supervision is required. Using a teaspoon, carefully dig out the pits from each avocado and discard.

2 Using the teaspoon, scoop out the flesh from each half. Place in a food processor or blender.

3 Repeat with the remaining avocados. Add the cumin, paprika, scallions, garlic, and lemon juice. Blend until smooth. Adult supervision is required.

4 With the motor of the food processor or blender running, gradually add the stock until it is combined with the avocado. Adult supervision is required. Stir in the iced water, season, and garnish with parsley.

5 Serve immediately so it doesn't get warm.

COOK'S TIP
► If you can't serve the soup at once, put it in the refrigerator before you add the iced water, seasoning, and garnish, and when you are ready, take it out of the refrigerator and stir these in.

Broccoli soup

They call broccoli a "super food" because it is packed with goodness. This soup is also full of flavor. Instead of serving it with the garlic toast, you may prefer it with plain bread.

serves **6**

ingredients
- **broccoli spears**, 1½ pounds
- **chicken stock**, 7½ cups
- **salt** and **ground black pepper**
- **fresh lemon juice**, 1 tablespoon

to serve
- **white bread**, 6 slices
- **garlic**, 1 large clove, cut in half
- **freshly grated Parmesan cheese**

tools
- ✳ **Vegetable peeler**
- ✳ **Cutting board**
- ✳ **Small sharp knife**
- ✳ **Large pan**
- ✳ **Blender or food processor**
- ✳ **Wooden spoon**
- ✳ **Ladle**

COOK'S TIP

▶ When you rub garlic over toast, the rough surface catches the garlic, giving the toast a strong garlicky flavor. If you prefer a milder garlic flavor, just rub lightly over the toast once or twice, or alternatively don't use the garlic.

garlic

3 Simmer for 20 minutes, or until soft. Remove from the heat and cool. Adult supervision is required.

1 Using a vegetable peeler, peel the broccoli stems, starting from the bottom of the stalks and pulling gently up toward the florets. Chop the broccoli into small chunks. Adult supervision is required.

2 Pour the stock into a large pan and bring to a boil. Add the broccoli.

4 Carefully pour half into a blender and blend until smooth. Stir into the mixture in the pan. Season and add lemon juice. Adult supervision is required.

5 Toast the bread on both sides until crispy and golden, then rub with the garlic (see Cook's Tip).

6 Break each into several pieces and place in the bottom of each bowl. Reheat the soup until hot and ladle over the toast. Serve at once, with Parmesan cheese.

Chinese soup

You may have had this delicious meal-in-a-bowl soup in a Chinese restaurant before, and this homemade version will taste even better.

serves 4–6

ingredients
- **chicken breast fillets**, 8 ounces
- **sesame oil**, 1 tablespoon
- **scallions**, 4, roughly chopped
- **chicken stock**, 5 cups
- **soy sauce**, 1 tablespoon
- **frozen corn kernels**, 1 cup
- **medium egg noodles**, 4 ounces
- **salt** and **ground black pepper**
- **carrot**, 1, thinly sliced
- **shrimp crackers**, to serve (optional)

tools
- ✳ **Cutting board**
- ✳ **Medium sharp knife**
- ✳ **Large pan**
- ✳ **Wooden spoon**

egg noodles

soy sauce

1 Remove the skin from the chicken, then trim any fat off the chicken. Cut into small cubes. Adult supervision is required.

2 With adult supervision, heat the oil in a pan. Add the chicken and scallions. Cook, stirring often, until the meat has browned.

3 Add the stock and the soy sauce and bring the soup to a boil.

4 Stir in the corn, then add the egg noodles, breaking them up roughly with your fingers. Taste the soup and season, if needed. Adult supervision is required when using heat.

5 Simmer, uncovered, for 1–2 minutes, until the noodles and corn are beginning to soften.

6 Add the carrots and simmer for 5 minutes.

7 Serve immediately in bowls with shrimp crackers, if desired.

COOK'S TIP
▶ For a special fun touch that is often used in Chinese restaurants, you can make carrot decorations. After peeling the carrots, cut into thin slices along the length, with adult supervision. Using a small novelty cutter, such as a flower, stamp out carrot shapes to add to the soup.

Potato and pepper frittata

Packed with flavor, this tasty omelet contains potatoes and cannellini beans, making it a really satisfying supper dish that is best served with a salad.

serves **6**

ingredients
- **potatoes**, 2 medium, peeled and diced
- **olive oil**, 2 tablespoons
- **onion**, 1, chopped
- **red bell pepper**, 1, chopped
- **celery**, 2 stalks, chopped
- **canned cannellini beans**, 14 ounces, drained
- **eggs**, 8
- **salt** and **ground black pepper**
- **oregano sprigs**, to garnish
- **green salad** and **olives**, to serve

tools
- ✳ **Large pan**
- ✳ **Colander**
- ✳ **Large nonstick skillet**
- ✳ **Wooden spoon**
- ✳ **Small mixing bowl**
- ✳ **Fork**
- ✳ **Wooden spatula**
- ✳ **Oven mitts**

1 Cook the potatoes in boiling water for 8–10 minutes, until tender. Drain. Adult supervision is required.

2 With adult supervision, heat the oil in a skillet. Add the onion, red bell pepper, and celery. Cook for 3–5 minutes, stirring often, until soft but not colored.

3 Add the potatoes and beans and cook, stirring with a wooden spoon, for several minutes to heat through. Adult supervision is required when using heat.

4 In a small bowl, beat the eggs with a fork, then season well with salt and ground black pepper.

5 Pour the egg mixture over the vegetables in the skillet and stir gently.

6 Push the mixture toward the center of the pan using a spatula, letting the liquid egg to run onto the bottom and cook. Preheat the broiler. Adult supervision is required.

VARIATION
• Try using other vegetables, such as corn, peas, asparagus, drained artichokes, or peppers in oil.

7 When it is set, ask an adult to place under the broiler for 2–3 minutes, until the top is brown. Ask an adult to remove from under the broiler and cut into wedges. Garnish with oregano and serve with salad and olives.

(!) = Watch out! Sharp or electrical tool in use. = Watch out! Heat is involved.

Tomato omelet envelopes

Nothing beats an omelet when you're in a hurry and want something tasty. This one is filled with a colorful tomato-and-melted cheese mixture.

serves **2**

ingredients
- **small onion**, 1
- **tomatoes**, 4
- **vegetable oil**, 2 tablespoons
- **eggs**, 4
- **chopped fresh chives**, 2 tablespoons
- **salt** and **ground black pepper**
- **Camembert cheese**, 4 ounces, rind removed and cut into cubes
- **lettuce leaves** and **Granary bread**, to serve (optional)

lettuce

tools
- ✳ **Cutting board**
- ✳ **Medium sharp knife**
- ✳ **Large skillet**
- ✳ **Wooden spoon**
- ✳ **Whisk or fork**
- ✳ **Nonstick omelet pan or small skillet**
- ✳ **Nonstick baking sheet**

1 Preheat the oven to 340°F.

2 Cut the onion into thin wedges. Cut the tomatoes into wedges the same size. Heat 1 tablespoon of the oil in a skillet or omelet pan. Add the onion and cook, stirring, for 2 minutes. Adult supervision is required.

3 Increase the heat, add the tomatoes and cook for a further 2 minutes, then remove from the heat. Adult supervision is required.

4 Using a whisk or fork, beat the eggs with the chives in a bowl and season to taste. Heat the remaining oil in the skillet.

5 Add half the egg mixture and tilt the pan to spread thinly. Cook for 1 minute. Flip the omelet over and cook for 1 minute more. Remove to a baking sheet and keep hot in the oven. Make a second omelet with the remaining egg mixture as before. Adult supervision is required.

6 Return the tomato mixture to a high heat. Add the cheese and toss over the heat for 1 minute.

7 Divide the mixture between the omelets and fold them over. Serve immediately with crisp lettuce leaves and chunks of Granary bread, if desired.

Fiorentina pizza

If you like eggs, then you'll love this pizza. The egg is gently cooked as the pizza bakes to create a soft set that combines wonderfully with the spinach and cheese.

serves **2–3**

ingredients
- **fresh spinach**, 6 ounces
- **olive oil**, 3 tablespoons
- **small red onion**, 1, thinly sliced
- **pizza crust**, 1, about 10–12 inches in diameter
- **pizza sauce**, 1 small jar
- **nutmeg**, freshly grated
- **mozzarella cheese**, 5 ounces
- **egg**, 1
- **Gruyère cheese**, grated, ¼ cup

egg

tools
✳ Skillet
✳ Wooden spoon
✳ Nonstick baking sheet
✳ Pastry brush
✳ Small metal spoon
✳ Small sharp knife
✳ Cutting board
✳ Oven mitts
✳ Grater

1 Remove the stalks from the spinach.

2 Heat 1 tablespoon of the oil in a skillet. Add the onion and fry for 5 minutes, until soft. Add the spinach and fry until wilted. Drain off any excess liquid. Adult supervision is required.

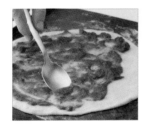

3 Preheat the oven to 425°F. Place the pizza crust on a baking sheet. Brush with half the remaining olive oil. Spread the pizza sauce evenly over the crust using the back of a metal spoon, leaving a small border all around the edge.

4 Top with the spinach mixture. Sprinkle over a little freshly grated nutmeg.

5 With adult supervision, slice the mozzarella and arrange over the spinach. Drizzle over the remaining oil. Bake for 10 minutes, then remove from the oven.

6 Make a small hole in the center of the topping and break the egg into the hole. Sprinkle the grated Gruyère on top. Return to the oven for an additional 5–10 minutes, until crisp and golden. Ask an adult to remove from the oven and serve immediately.

(!) = Watch out! Sharp or electrical tool in use. = Watch out! Heat is involved.

Ham and pineapple pizza

Easy to assemble and loved by all—you can really go to town experimenting with different toppings for this French bread pizza.

serves 4

ingredients
- **small baguettes**, 2
- **sliced cooked ham**, 3 ounces
- **canned pineapple**, 4 rings, drained well
- **small green bell pepper**, ½,
- **sharp Cheddar cheese**, 3 ounces

for the tomato sauce
- **olive oil**, 1 teaspoon
- **onion**, 1, finely chopped
- **garlic**, 2 cloves, finely chopped
- **canned chopped tomatoes**, 14 ounces
- **tomato paste**, 1 tablespoon
- **fresh chopped mixed herbs** (such as oregano, parsley, thyme, and basil), 1 tablespoon
- **sugar**, pinch of
- **salt** and **ground black pepper**

tools
- ✳ **Large pan**
- ✳ **Wooden spoon**
- ✳ **Large serrated knife**
- ✳ **Cutting board**
- ✳ **Nonstick baking sheet**
- ✳ **Oven mitts**
- ✳ **Medium sharp knife**
- ✳ **Grater**

1 **To make the tomato sauce**, heat the oil in a pan with adult supervision. Add the onion and garlic. Fry for 5 minutes, until softened.

2 Add the tomatoes, tomato paste, herbs, sugar, and seasoning. Stir. Adult supervision is required.

3 Bring the mixture to a boil. Reduce the heat slightly and simmer, uncovered, stirring often, for 10 minutes, or until the tomatoes have reduced to a thick pulp. Remove from the heat and set aside. Adult supervision is required.

4 Preheat the oven to 350°F. Cut the baguettes in half lengthwise with a large serrated knife on a cutting board. Place on a baking sheet. Bake for 5 minutes, until they begin to become crispy. Adult supervision is required.

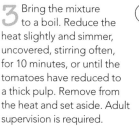

5 Ask an adult to remove the baking sheet from the oven. Spread the tomato sauce over the baguettes.

6 With adult supervision, cut the ham into strips, the pineapple into chunks, and the bell pepper into thin strips.

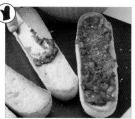

7 Arrange the ham, pineapple, and bell pepper on the baguettes.

8 Grate the Cheddar and sprinkle on top. Bake for 10 minutes, until crisp and golden. Ask an adult to remove from the oven and serve immediately.

Mexican tomato rice

This dish is a delicious mixture of rice, tomatoes, peas, and spices. If you don't like too much heat, reduce the number of chiles you use.

serves **4**

ingredients
- **canned chopped tomatoes**, 14 ounces
- **olive oil**, 2 tablespoons
- **onion**, ½, roughly chopped
- **garlic**, 2 cloves, roughly chopped
- **long-grain rice**, 2½ cups
- **vegetable stock**, 3 cups
- **salt**, ½ teaspoon
- **fresh mild chiles**, 1–2 (see Cook's Tip)
- **frozen peas**, 1 cup
- **ground black pepper**

tools
- ✳ **Blender or food processor**
- ✳ **Large heavy pan with a tight-fitting lid**
- ✳ **Wooden spoon**
- ✳ **Fork**

3 Stir in the rice and fry for 1–2 minutes. Add the tomatoes and cook, stirring, for 3–4 minutes, until the liquid has evaporated.

5 Remove the pan from the heat, cover it with the lid and let stand for about 5 minutes, so the flavors are absorbed.

1 Pour the tomatoes and their juice into a blender or food processor and blend until smooth. Adult supervision is required.

2 With adult supervision, heat the oil in a pan. Add the onion and garlic and cook over a medium heat, stirring, for 2 minutes, until softened.

4 Stir in the stock, salt, chiles, and peas. Bring to a boil. Cover and simmer for 6 minutes, until the rice is tender. Adult supervision is required when using heat.

6 Remove the chiles, fluff up the rice with a fork, and serve sprinkled with black pepper. The chiles can be used as a garnish, if you like.

COOK'S TIP
▶ Remember that the general rule is the smaller the chile the hotter it will be. This is because the smaller chiles tend to have more membranes and seeds (the part where most of the heat is). So, if you like a lot of spice, use small, hot chiles. For a milder flavor, use the larger variety and remove the seeds.

Quick and easy risotto

A traditional Italian risotto is made by very gradually stirring stock into rice as it cooks. This recipe is a cheat's dish because it all goes in the pan at the same time.

serves **3–4**

ingredients
- **mozzarella cheese**, 4 ounces
- **cooked ham**, 3-ounce slice
- **fresh parsley**, 2 tablespoons
- **chicken stock**, 4 cups
- **risotto rice**, 1½ cups
- **freshly grated Parmesan cheese**, 2 tablespoons, plus extra to serve
- **salt** and **ground black pepper**

tools
* Cutting board
* Medium sharp knife
* Large heavy pan with a tight-fitting lid
* Wooden spoon

3 Add the rice. Bring back to a boil. Cover and simmer, stirring often, for about 18–20 minutes, until the rice is tender. Adult supervision is required.

VARIATIONS
- This is a really easy recipe and the ingredients can be altered to suit your taste. For example, you can replace the ham with leftover, cooked chicken and add a handful of frozen corn or peas, or you can add sliced, cooked sausages and fresh broccoli florets.
- You can use Cheddar cheese instead of Parmesan cheese, if desired.

1 On a cutting board, cut the mozzarella into cubes. Cut the ham into similar-size squares and coarsely chop the parsley. Adult supervision is required.

5 Cover the pan with a lid and let stand for 2–3 minutes to let the cheese melt, then stir again to combine all the ingredients thoroughly.

2 With adult supervision, put the stock in a large pan and bring to a boil. Reduce the heat and bring to a simmering point.

4 Ask an adult to remove from the heat. Stir in the mozzarella, Parmesan, ham, and parsley. Season to taste.

6 Spoon into warmed serving bowls and serve immediately, with extra Parmesan cheese sprinkled over the top.

Presto pasta sauces

From fresh and tangy to rich and creamy, here are four classic pasta sauces to use for any occasion. Simply serve with your favorite cooked pasta.

spaghetti

all serve **4**

ingredients

for the basic tomato sauce
- **olive oil**, 1 tablespoon
- **butter**, 1 tablespoon
- **garlic**, 1 clove, peeled and finely chopped
- **onion**, 1 small, peeled and finely chopped
- **celery**, 1 stalk, finely chopped
- **canned chopped tomatoes**, 14 ounces
- **fresh basil leaves**, a handful, torn
- **salt** and **ground black pepper**

for the roasted vegetable sauce
- **red** or **orange bell peppers**, 2
- **onion,** 1 small
- **eggplant**, 1 small

- **tomatoes**, 2
- **garlic**, 2 cloves, unpeeled
- **olive oil**, 2–3 tablespoons
- **lemon juice**, 1 tablespoon

for the pesto sauce
- **basil leaves**, 1 cup
- **garlic**, 2 cloves, peeled and finely chopped
- **pine nuts**, 2 tablespoons

- **salt** and **ground black pepper**
- **olive oil**, ½ cup
- **freshly grated Parmesan cheese**, ½ cup

for the cream and Parmesan sauce
- **butter**, 4 tablespoons
- **heavy cream**, ½ cup
- **freshly grated Parmesan cheese**, ⅔ cup

tools
- ✳ Cutting board
- ✳ Medium sharp knife
- ✳ Large heavy pan
- ✳ Wooden spoon
- ✳ Nonstick baking sheet
- ✳ Oven mitts
- ✳ Metal spoon
- ✳ Blender or food processor
- ✳ Strainer (optional)
- ✳ Small pan
- ✳ Medium heavy pan

1 To make the basic tomato sauce, heat the oil and butter in a heavy pan. Add the garlic, onion, and celery. Cook over a low heat, stirring occasionally, for 15–20 minutes, or until the onion softens and begins to color. Adult supervision is required.

2 Stir in the tomatoes and bring to a boil. Reduce the heat, cover, and simmer for 10–15 minutes, stirring occasionally, until the mixture is thick. Adult supervision is required.

3 Add the basil leaves, season, and stir. Serve hot with cooked pasta.

4 To make the roasted vegetable sauce, cut the bell peppers, onion, eggplant and tomatoes in half. Remove any seeds and membranes. Adult supervision is required.

5 Ask an adult to preheat a broiler. Place the vegetables on a baking sheet with the garlic.

6 Ask an adult to place under the broiler and cook until the skins are blackened and the flesh is tender.

7 Ask an adult to remove from the heat and let stand until cool.

8 Peel the skins from the bell peppers, onions, and tomatoes. Scoop the flesh from the eggplant and squeeze the flesh from the garlic.

(!) = Watch out! Sharp or electrical tool in use.   = Watch out! Heat is involved.

12 Heat the sauce gently in a small pan. Serve hot with cooked pasta.

9 Place in a blender or food processor and blend to a smooth puree. Adult supervision is required.

10 Taste and add oil and lemon juice if necessary. If you prefer a smooth sauce, rub the puree through a strainer.

11 **To make the pesto sauce,** place the basil, garlic, pine nuts, and seasoning in a blender or food processor. Blend until smooth. With the motor running, add the oil in a thin stream. Add the cheese and blend. Adult supervision is required.

13 **To make the cream and Parmesan sauce,** gently heat the butter, cream, and Parmesan in a pan until melted. Adult supervision is required.

14 Increase the heat and simmer gently for 1 minute, until the sauce is reduced. Season to taste and serve hot with pasta. Adult supervision is required.

quick and easy suppers   99

Baked macaroni cheese

It is definitely worth knowing how to make this all-time favorite dish. Once you've made the sauce for this, you'll be able to make white sauces for all kinds of recipes.

serves 6

ingredients
- **milk**, 2 cups
- **bay leaf**, 1
- **butter**, 4 tablespoons
- **all-purpose flour**, ⅓ cup
- **salt** and **ground black pepper**
- **grated nutmeg**, a pinch
- **freshly grated Parmesan** or **Cheddar cheese**, or a **combination of both**, 1½ cups
- **fresh white bread crumbs**, ⅓ cup
- **macaroni**, 1 pound

tools
- ✳ **Small heavy pan**
- ✳ **Strainer**
- ✳ **Pitcher**
- ✳ **Medium pan**
- ✳ **Whisk**
- ✳ **Wooden spoon**
- ✳ **Heatproof bowl**
- ✳ **Large pan**
- ✳ **Casserole**
- ✳ **Colander**
- ✳ **Oven mitts**

macaroni

1 Put the milk in a small pan with the bay leaf. Heat gently, remove from the heat, and strain into a pitcher. Adult supervision is required.

2 Melt the butter in a medium pan. Add the flour and whisk. Cook, whisking, for 2–3 minutes, then remove from the heat.

3 Gradually mix the milk into the butter and flour mixture. Return to the heat and bring to a boil, beating, until the sauce thickens. Adult supervision is required.

4 Remove the pan from the heat and season with salt and pepper, adding the nutmeg, if using.

5 Add all of the cheese except 2 tablespoons and stir until melted. Transfer to a heatproof bowl. Cover with a layer of plastic wrap. Set aside.

6 Fill a large pan with water and bring to a boil. Preheat the oven to 400°F.

7 Grease a casserole and sprinkle with some bread crumbs.

8 Add the macaroni to the pan of boiling water, and cook according to the package instructions until it is just tender (al dente). Adult supervision is required.

9 Ask an adult to drain the macaroni in a colander. Combine it with the sauce. Pour it into the casserole. Sprinkle the top with the remaining bread-crumbs and cheese and bake for 20 minutes, until melted and golden.

(!) = Watch out! Sharp or electrical tool in use.   (🖑) = Watch out! Heat is involved.

Farfalle with tuna

This is a fantastic recipe that needs only six ingredients that you will find in most kitchen pantries. It's tasty and filling and good for you—perfect!

serves 4

ingredients
- **salt**, a pinch
- **dried farfalle pasta**, 14 ounces
- **olive oil**, 1 teaspoon
- **passata**, 2½ cups (*see* Cook's Tips)
- **pitted black olives**, 8–10, cut into rings (*see* Cook's Tips)
- **canned tuna in olive oil**, 6 ounces

black olives   canned tuna

tools
- ✳ **Large pan**
- ✳ **Small pan**
- ✳ **Wooden spoon**
- ✳ **Colander**
- ✳ **Fork**
- ✳ **Large heatproof bowl**

1 Fill two-thirds of a large pan with water and add the oil and a pinch of salt. Bring to a boil. Add the dried pasta and bring back to a boil. Cook for 8–10 minutes, or according to package instructions, until just tender (al dente). Adult supervision is required.

2 With adult supervision, place the passata in a small pan with the black olives and heat through gently over a medium heat. Stir occasionally with a spoon to prevent it from sticking and burning, until the sauce is simmering.

3 Drain the canned tuna in the colander and flake it with a fork.

4 Add the tuna to the tomato sauce with about 4 tablespoons of the hot water used for cooking the pasta. Taste the sauce and adjust the seasoning as necessary.

5 Ask an adult to drain the cooked pasta in a colander and tip it into a large heatproof bowl.

6 Pour the tuna and tomato sauce over the top of the pasta and toss lightly to mix. Serve immediately in warmed serving bowls.

COOK'S TIPS
▶ Prepared, sliced, pitted black olives are available in cans and jars from most large supermarkets.
▶ Passata is Italian strained tomatoes, available in some delis. You can use tomato sauce instead.

Tortellini with ham

There's a huge variety of fresh pasta available and it works well served with simple ingredients, such as this ham and creamy tomato sauce.

serves **4**

ingredients

- **large onion**, ¼
- **pancetta**, 4-ounce piece, cut into cubes
- **tortellini alla carne** (meat-filled tortellini), 9-ounce package
- **olive oil**, 2 tablespoons
- **strained crushed Italian plum tomatoes**, ⅔ cup
- **heavy cream**, scant ½ cup
- **freshly grated Parmesan cheese**, generous 1 cup
- **salt** and **ground black pepper**

tools

- ✳ **Cutting board**
- ✳ **Medium sharp knife**
- ✳ **2 large pans**
- ✳ **Wooden spoon**
- ✳ **Measuring cup**
- ✳ **Colander**

1 With adult supervision, peel and finely chop the onion. Set aside.

2 Fill two-thirds of a large pan with water and add a pinch of salt. Bring to a boil. Add the pasta and bring back to a boil. Cook for 8–10 minutes, according to package instructions, until just tender (al dente). Adult supervision is required.

3 Meanwhile, with adult supervision, heat the oil in another large pan. Add the onion. Cook over a low heat, stirring often, for 5 minutes, until softened.

4 Add the cubed pancetta and cook for 5 minutes, until it is golden. Add the tomatoes with ⅔ cup of water. Adult supervision is required.

5 Stir well, then season to taste.

6 Bring to a boil, then lower the heat and simmer for 3–4 minutes, stirring occasionally, until the sauce has reduced slightly. Adult supervision is required.

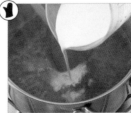

7 Stir in the cream. Ask an adult to drain the pasta and add it to the pan.

8 Add a handful of grated Parmesan to the pan and stir gently with a wooden spoon to combine, being careful not to break up the fragile cooked pasta.

9 Transfer the pasta to warmed serving bowls, top with the remaining Parmesan, and serve immediately.

(!) = Watch out! Sharp or electrical tool in use.   = Watch out! Heat is involved.

Spaghetti carbonara

This rich and creamy dish is really tasty and easy to make. The bacon adds a wonderful flavor, but you can leave it out if you prefer.

serves **4**

ingredients
- **small onion**, 1
- **garlic**, 1 large clove
- **rindless smoked bacon** or **pancetta**, 6 ounces
- **olive oil**, 2 tablespoons
- **fresh** or **dried spaghetti**, 12 ounces
- **eggs**, 4
- **crème fraîche**, 6–8 tablespoons
- **freshly grated Parmesan cheese**, 4 tablespoons, plus extra to serve
- **salt** and **ground black pepper**

tools
- ✳ Cutting board
- ✳ Medium sharp knife
- ✳ 2 large pans
- ✳ Wooden spoon
- ✳ Mixing bowl
- ✳ Whisk or fork
- ✳ Colander
- ✳ Tongs

1 Peel and chop the onion and garlic. Cut the bacon or pancetta into pieces. Adult supervision is required.

2 Heat the oil in a large pan. Add the onion and garlic and fry, stirring, for about 5 minutes, until softened. Add the bacon or pancetta and cook for 10 minutes, stirring frequently. Adult supervision is required.

3 Fill two-thirds of a large pan with water and add a pinch of salt. Bring to a boil. Add the pasta and cook for 8–10 minutes, or according to package instructions, until just tender. Adult supervision is required.

4 Put the eggs, crème fraîche, Parmesan, and black pepper in a bowl. Beat with a whisk or fork.

5 Ask an adult to drain the pasta thoroughly in a colander. Pour the pasta into the pan with the onion and pancetta or bacon and toss well to mix.

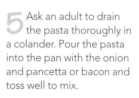

6 Turn off the heat, then immediately add the egg mixture to the pan and toss thoroughly so that it cooks and coats the pasta. Adult supervision is required.

7 Season to taste, then divide the pasta among four warm bowls and sprinkle with ground black pepper. Top with extra grated Parmesan and serve immediately.

VARIATION
• You can replace the crème fraîche with heavy cream, light cream, or sour cream, if you prefer.

Cabbage and potatoes

Whether you use leftovers or cook this classic recipe from fresh, be sure to fry it really well in the pan so it turns a rich honey brown.

serves 4

ingredients
- **potatoes**, 4 medium (about 1 pound 2 ounces), peeled and roughly chopped
- **vegetable oil**, 4 tablespoons
- **onion**, 1, finely chopped
- **cooked cabbage** or **Brussels sprouts**, finely chopped, 1½ cups
- **salt** and **ground black pepper**
- **pork chops**, broiled, to serve (optional)

potatoes

tools
❋ **Vegetable peeler**
❋ **Sharp knife**
❋ **Cutting board**
❋ **Large pan**
❋ **Colander**
❋ **Large heavy skillet**
❋ **Large mixing bowl**
❋ **Wooden spoon**
❋ **Spatula or palette knife**
❋ **Large flat plate**

1 Place the potatoes in a pan and cover with water. Bring to a boil and cook for 10 minutes, or until tender. Ask an adult to drain in a colander and return to the pan. Mash. Set aside.

3 Squeeze the cabbage or sprouts to remove excess water. Place in a bowl with the potatoes and season to taste. Mix well.

2 With an adult, heat 2 tablespoons of the oil in a skillet. Add the onion. Cook for 5 minutes, stirring, until soft.

4 Add the vegetables to the skillet with the cooked onions, stir, then press the vegetable mixture into a large, even shape. Adult supervision is required.

5 Cook over a medium heat for 5 minutes, until browned underneath. Check this by lifting up with the spatula or palette knife. Adult supervision is required.

6 Ask an adult to place a plate over the skillet, and, holding it tightly against the skillet, turn them both over together.

7 Return the empty skillet to the heat, and add the remaining oil. When hot, slide the cake back into the skillet, browned-side uppermost.

8 Cook over a medium heat for 10 minutes, or until the underside is brown. Serve hot, in wedges with pork chops, if you like.

   (!) = Watch out! Sharp or electrical tool in use.   (👋) = Watch out! Heat is involved.

Bean and tomato chili

Packed with flavor, this makes a great alternative to a meat chili. The cilantro adds a flavorsome touch, but you can use parsley instead, if desired.

serves **4**

ingredients
- **fresh red chile**, 1
- **tomato and herb sauce**, 14 ounces
- **canned mixed beans**, 28 ounces
- **salt** and **ground black pepper**
- **fresh cilantro**, a large handful
- **sour cream**, ½ cup

tools
- ✳ **Cutting board**
- ✳ **Medium sharp knife**
- ✳ **Medium pan with a lid**
- ✳ **Colander**
- ✳ **Wooden spoon**
- ✳ **Ladle**

3 Drain the canned beans in a colander and rinse well under cold running water.

4 Add the beans to the tomato sauce and beans and season well with salt and black pepper.

6 Set some cilantro aside for the garnish and add the remainder to the pan. Stir to mix.

COOK'S TIP
▶ Be careful when chopping chiles and always wash your hands in soapy water after touching them. They contain a chemical called capsaicin, which is a powerful irritant and will cause eyes to sting if it comes into contact with them.

1 On a cutting board, cut the chile in half and carefully cut out and discard the seeds and membranes. Thinly slice the chile into slivers. Adult supervision is required. Wash your hands.

2 Put the sliced chile in a medium pan with the tomato sauce.

5 With adult supervision, chop the cilantro.

7 Bring the mixture to a boil, then reduce the heat, cover, and simmer gently for 10 minutes, stirring occasionally. Add a little water if it starts to dry out. Adult supervision is required.

8 Ask an adult to remove from the heat and carefully ladle the chili into warmed individual bowls and top with sour cream. Sprinkle with the reserved cilantro and serve.

Tuna and corn fish cakes

This simple recipe is a wonderful way to use up leftover mashed potatoes. If you like, try making fish- or star-shape cakes using cookie cutters.

serves **4**

ingredients
- **potatoes**, 3 medium (about 12 ounces)
- **canned tuna fish**, 7 ounces, drained
- **canned** or **frozen corn**, ¾ cup
- **chopped fresh parsley**, 2 tablespoons
- **salt** and **ground black pepper**
- **fresh bread crumbs**, 1 cup
- **vegetable oil**, 2 tablespoons
- **baby plum tomatoes**, broiled, **salad**, and **lemon wedges**, to serve

tools
- ✳ Vegetable peeler
- ✳ Cutting board
- ✳ Medium sharp knife
- ✳ Large pan
- ✳ Potato masher
- ✳ Large mixing bowl
- ✳ Wooden spoon
- ✳ Large flat plate
- ✳ Skillet

1 Peel the potatoes and roughly chop them with a knife. Put in a large pan and cover with cold water. Bring to a boil and cook for 10 minutes or until tender. Adult supervision is required.

2 Ask an adult to drain, then return to the pan. Mash with a masher until smooth. Set aside to cool.

3 Place the mashed potatoes in a large mixing bowl and stir in the tuna fish, corn, and chopped fresh parsley. Season to taste with salt and black pepper and combine thoroughly.

4 Mix together, then divide the mixture into eight. Form into patty shapes with your hands.

5 Spread out the bread crumbs on a plate. Press the fish cakes into the bread crumbs and coat evenly on both sides.

6 Heat the oil in a skillet, add the cakes, and cook for 2 minutes on each side, until golden brown. Adult supervision is required. Serve with broiled tomatoes, salad, and lemon wedges.

COOK'S TIP
▶ When you shape fish cakes, patties, or meatballs of any kind, it really helps if you dip your hands in water before you start and whenever the mixture starts to stick to your hands. It is better to make smaller rather than larger ones because they cook better.

(!) = Watch out! Sharp or electrical tool in use.   = Watch out! Heat is involved.

Fast fishes

What a catch you'll make with these tasty homemade fish sticks. They are called "fast" because as well as being good swimmers, they cook in just 10 minutes!

serves **2**

ingredients
- **hoki** or **cod fillets**, 2, each 4 ounces
- **salt**
- **carrot**, 1, peeled
- **egg**, 1, beaten
- **fresh bread crumbs**, 2 cups
- **sesame seeds**, 4 teaspoons
- **vegetable oil**, 4 teaspoons
- **frozen peas**, 2 tablespoons
- **frozen corn kernels**, 4
- **new potatoes**, boiled, to serve

tools
- ✳ **2 cutting boards**
- ✳ **Long thin sharp knife**
- ✳ **Small shallow dish**
- ✳ **Whisk or fork**
- ✳ **Large flat plate**
- ✳ **Large skillet**
- ✳ **Spatula or palette knife**
- ✳ **Small pan**

1 Place the fish fillet on a cutting board, skin-side down. Dip the fingers of one hand in salt. Hold onto the fish with this hand.

2 Using a knife, carefully cut under the fish flesh along the skin. Adult supervision is required. Discard the skin. Rinse the fish and pat dry on paper towels. Cut into four pieces.

3 Cut the carrot into long thin slices, then cut out fin and tail shapes and tiny triangles for fish mouths. Adult supervision is required.

4 Put the egg in a small dish and whisk. Mix the bread crumbs and sesame seeds on a plate. Dip pieces of fish in egg first, then in the bread crumbs to coat on both sides.

5 Heat the oil in a skillet. Add the fish and fry over a medium-high heat for 4–5 minutes, turning with the spatula or palette knife, until golden brown. Adult supervision is required.

6 Meanwhile, bring a pan of water to the boil. Add the peas and corn and cook for 3–4 minutes, until tender. Ask an adult to drain.

7 Arrange the fish on two plates. Position the carrot pieces and use the corn as eyes and peas as bubbles. Serve with boiled new potatoes.

COOK'S TIP
▶ You can freeze the uncooked, breaded fish portions on a tray, then transfer to sealed containers. Thaw at room temperature and cook as Step 5.

Colorful chicken kebabs

You'll have a great time making your own kebabs. They're wonderful cooked under the broiler or on the barbecue in the summer.

serves **2–4**

ingredients
- **converted long-grain rice**, 4 ounces
- **ground turmeric**, 1 teaspoon
- **green bell pepper**, ½
- **orange bell pepper**, ½
- **chicken breast fillet**, 4 ounces, cut into thin strips
- **white mushrooms**, 4
- **baby corn**, 4
- **cherry tomatoes**, 4
- **salad dressing**, 4 tablespoons (see Cook's Tip)

tools
- ✳ **4 wooden skewers**
- ✳ **Shallow dish**
- ✳ **Large pan**
- ✳ **Strainer**
- ✳ **Cutting board**
- ✳ **Medium sharp knife**
- ✳ **Teaspoon**
- ✳ **Oven mitts**

5 Thread a tomato onto each of the skewers, then a piece of chicken, then a bell pepper, mushroom, and corn. Continue until the skewers are full.

COOK'S TIP

▶ For the dressing, put 4 tablespoons of sunflower oil, 2 tablespoons of vinegar, 1 tablespoon of honey, and a dash of pepper in a screw-top jar, then shake it well to combine all the ingredients.

1 Put the wooden skewers in a dish of cold water. Let them soak for about 30 minutes. This will stop them from burning.

2 Put the rice and turmeric in a large pan. Cover with boiling water, and bring to a boil. Reduce the heat slightly and simmer for 15 minutes, until tender. Adult supervision is required.

3 Ask an adult to drain the rice in a strainer. Return to the pan and cover. Ask an adult to preheat the broiler to high.

4 Cut the bell peppers on in half. Cut out the seeds and membranes and cut into chunks. Cut the mushrooms and baby corn into similar-size pieces. Adult supervision is required.

6 Spoon over some of the dressing. Broil for 5 minutes, then turn over and broil for another 5 minutes, until the chicken is cooked. Adult supervision is required.

7 Divide the rice between the serving plates and arrange the kebabs on top.

(!) = Watch out! Sharp or electrical tool in use.   = Watch out! Heat is involved.

Sticky chicken

These delicious bites are perfect for a tasty supper. The sticky, sweet marinade makes a fabulous coating—just don't forget to serve it with napkins!

serves **2–4**

ingredients
- **chicken drumsticks**, 4
- **vegetable oil**, 2 teaspoons
- **soy sauce**, 1 teaspoon
- **smooth peanut butter**, 1 tablespoon
- **ketchup**, 1 tablespoon
- **small baked potatoes**, **corn**, and **tomato wedges**, to serve

tools
- ✳ Small sharp knife
- ✳ Cutting board
- ✳ Heatproof bowl
- ✳ Medium bowl
- ✳ Pastry brush
- ✳ Wooden spoon
- ✳ Skewer
- ✳ Oven mitts

1 Preheat the oven to 400°F.

2 Rinse the drumsticks under cold water, pat dry on paper towels, and peel off the skin with your fingers. As you get to the thin end you will need to cut the skin off with a knife. Make three or four slashes and place in a heatproof bowl. Adult supervision is required.

3 Put the oil, soy sauce, peanut butter, and ketchup in a medium bowl and mix with a wooden spoon. Spread thickly over the top.

4 Cook in the oven for 15 minutes. Turn the drumsticks over and baste with the peanut butter mixture and meat juices. Adult supervision is required.

5 Cook for an additional 20 minutes, or until the juices run clear when the chicken is pierced with a skewer. Ask an adult to remove from the oven.

6 Cool slightly, then wrap aluminum foil around the end of each drumstick. Serve with baked potatoes, corn, and tomato wedges.

VARIATIONS
- Use chicken thighs or breasts instead of drumsticks, if desired.
- This recipe also works with sausages or pork ribs (cook these in the oven partway before spreading over the marinade and cooking for another 20 minutes).

sausages

Honey mustard chicken

This is a tasty variation of Sticky Chicken, using a sweet mustard dressing and succulent chicken thighs. It is perfect for a quick and easy meal.

serves **4**

ingredients
- **chicken thighs**, 8
- **whole-grain mustard**, 4 tablespoons
- **honey**, 4 tablespoons
- **salt** and **ground black pepper**
- **tomatoes**, 8
- **red onion**, ½
- **olive oil**, 1 tablespoon

tools
- ✳ **Roasting pan**
- ✳ **2 small glass bowls**
- ✳ **2 spoons**
- ✳ **Pastry brush**
- ✳ **Small knife**
- ✳ **Cutting board**

red onion

COOK'S TIP
▶ To check the chicken is cooked through, skewer it with a sharp knife or a metal skewer; the juices should run clear.
▶ For a really speedy supper, brush the chicken thighs with the marinade and refrigerate overnight or until needed.

1 Preheat the oven to 375°F.

2 Put the chicken thighs in a single layer in a roasting pan.

3 Mix together the mustard and honey in a small glass bowl with a spoon.

4 Season with salt and ground black pepper to taste.

5 Brush all over the chicken. Cook for 25–30 minutes, brushing the chicken with the pan juices occasionally, until cooked through (see Cook's Tip). Adult supervision is required.

(!)

6 Meanwhile, cut the tomatoes into quarters, chunks, or thick slices and place in a small bowl. Adult supervision is required.

7 Finely chop the red onion and add to the tomatoes in the bowl. Add the olive oil and stir to mix.

8 Ask an adult to remove the chicken from the oven. Serve immediately with the tomato salad.

   (!) = Watch out! Sharp or electrical tool in use.   = Watch out! Heat is involved.

Yellow bean chicken

Chinese food is really quick to make and uses some different ingredients that you may not have tried before. These can be found in Chinese stores or supermarkets.

serves **4**

ingredients
- **peanut oil**, 2 tablespoons
- **salted cashew nuts**, ¾ cup
- **scallions**, 4
- **skinless chicken breast fillets**, 1 pound
- **yellow bean sauce**, 5½ ounces
- **cooked rice**, to serve

tools
- ✳ Wok or large, deep skillet
- ✳ Wooden spatula
- ✳ Draining spoon
- ✳ 2 cutting boards
- ✳ 2 medium sharp knives

cashew nuts

VARIATION
- If you like fish, you can make this dish with diced monkfish fillet or shrimp instead of chicken. Cook the monkfish in the same way as the chicken. If you use shrimp, cook them in Step 3 until they change color. Alternatively, you can use strips of pork tenderloin or round steak.

shrimp

2 Chop the scallions with a knife. On a separate board, cut the chicken into strips, using a clean knife. Adult supervision is required.

1 Heat 1 tablespoon of the oil in a wok or skillet, add the nuts, and cook over a low heat, stirring frequently, for 2 minutes, until browned. You need to keep an eye on the nuts to prevent them from burning. Remove with a draining spoon and set aside. Adult supervision is required.

3 Heat the remaining oil in the wok or skillet and cook the scallions and chicken for 5–8 minutes, until the meat is cooked.

4 Return the nuts to the wok or skillet and add the sauce. Stir to combine and cook for 1–2 minutes, until heated through. Adult supervision is required when using heat.

5 Serve immediately with a bowl of cooked rice.

Turkey burgers

These delicious fresh-tasting burgers are a great midweek supper served in buns with potato wedges and salad. Choose a tasty relish to serve with them.

serves 4

ingredients
- **small red onion**, 1
- **ground turkey**, 1½ pounds
- **fresh thyme leaves**, small handful
- **lime-flavored olive oil**, 2 tablespoons
- **salt** and **ground black pepper**
- **burger buns**, 4, lightly toasted, to serve
- **relish** or **ketchup**, to serve

tools
- ❋ **Cutting board**
- ❋ **Medium sharp knife**
- ❋ **Mixing bowl**
- ❋ **Grill pan**
- ❋ **Pastry brush**
- ❋ **Spatula or palette knife**

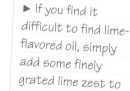

burger buns

COOK'S TIP

▶ If you find it difficult to find lime-flavored oil, simply add some finely grated lime zest to the ground turkey and cook the patties in ordinary olive oil.

lime

1 Peel and finely chop the onion. Put it in a mixing bowl with the turkey. Adult supervision is required.

2 Add the thyme and 1 tablespoon of the oil and season well with salt and ground black pepper. Cover and chill for up to 4 hours.

3 Divide the mixture into six equal portions and shape into round patties using damp hands. If the mixture starts to stick, dampen your hands again.

4 With adult supervision, preheat a grill pan. Brush the patties with half of the remaining oil.

5 Place the patties on the grill pan and cook for 10–12 minutes. Adult supervision is required.

6 Turn the patties over, brush with more oil, and cook for 10–12 minutes on the second side, or until cooked right through. Adult supervision is required.

7 Ask an adult to lift the patties from the grill pan. Serve in warmed buns, with relish or ketchup.

 ! = Watch out! Sharp or electrical tool in use.   🔥 = Watch out! Heat is involved.

Pitas with lamb koftas

These slightly spicy koftas can be made in advance and stored in an airtight container for three days, ready for you to broil or barbecue at a moment's notice.

serves 4

ingredients
- **ground lamb**, 1 pound
- **salt** and **ground black pepper**
- **small onion**, 1
- **harissa paste**, 2 teaspoons (see Cook's Tip)
- **fresh mint**, a small handful
- **plain yogurt**, ½ cup
- **pita breads**, 8
- **cucumber** and **tomato slices**, to serve

pita breads

tools
- ❋ 8 wooden bamboo skewers
- ❋ Large mixing bowl
- ❋ Cutting board
- ❋ Medium sharp knife
- ❋ Small mixing bowl
- ❋ Spoon
- ❋ Oven mitts

1 Ask an adult to prepare a barbecue or preheat the broiler. Soak eight wooden skewers in cold water for 1 hour to prevent them from burning.

2 Place the lamb in a large bowl and season generously with salt and black pepper.

3 Peel and finely chop the onion and add to the bowl of lamb with the harissa paste. Mix to combine. Adult supervision is required.

4 Divide the mixture into eight equal pieces and, using wet hands, press the meat onto the skewers in a sausage shape.

5 Cook for 10 minutes over the hot coals or under the broiler, turning occasionally, until cooked. Adult supervision is required.

6 Chop the mint and mix it with the yogurt. Season to taste and set aside. Warm the pita breads on the barbecue or under the broiler for a few seconds, then split in half. Adult supervision is required.

7 Place a kofta in each pita and remove the skewer. Add some cucumber and tomato slices. Drizzle with the yogurt sauce.

COOK'S TIP
▶ Harissa is a North African paste made from chiles and garlic. If you can't find it, try chopping one small chile and adding it to the lamb with a clove of crushed garlic and 1 teaspoon of ground cumin and 1 teaspoon of ground coriander instead.

Mexican tacos

Piling salad, cheese, and beef into taco shells is a fun way to eat. This recipe is ideal for easy party food that everyone will enjoy eating.

serves **4**

ingredients
- **iceberg lettuce**, ½ small head
- **onion**, 1 small, peeled
- **tomatoes**, 2
- **avocado**, 1
- **olive oil**, 1 tablespoon
- **lean ground beef** or **turkey**, 9 ounces
- **salt** and **ground black pepper**
- **garlic**, 2 cloves, crushed
- **ground cumin**, 1 teaspoon
- **mild chili powder**, 1–2 teaspoons
- **taco shells**, 8
- **sour cream**, 4 tablespoons
- **Cheddar cheese**, 4 ounces

taco shells

ground beef

tools
* **Cutting board**
* **Medium sharp knife**
* **Teaspoon**
* **Large, deep skillet**
* **Wooden spoon**
* **Oven mitts**

1 With adult supervision, shred the lettuce. Chop the onion and the tomatoes.

2 Cut the avocado in half lengthwise. Using a teaspoon, remove and discard the pit. Cut the halves in half, pull off the skin, and slice the flesh. Adult supervision is required.

3 Heat the oil in a skillet. Add the meat and brown over a medium heat, stirring frequently to break up any large lumps. Adult supervision is required.

4 Season to taste, add the garlic and spices, and cook for 10 minutes more, until cooked.

5 Meanwhile, warm the taco shells according to the package instructions. Don't let them get too crispy.

6 Spoon the lettuce, onion, tomatoes, and avocado into the taco shells. Top with the sour cream, followed by the ground beef or turkey mixture.

COOK'S TIP
▶ Tacos are eaten with the fingers and there's usually a certain amount of "fall out," so make sure you have plenty of napkins handy.

7 With adult supervision, grate the cheese, then sprinkle into the tacos. Serve immediately, as the cheese melts from the heat of the cooked meat.

Meatballs in tomato sauce

Here are tasty and easy meatballs that are simple to make. Use beef or pork, whichever you prefer. The sausages will add some subtle spice to their flavor.

serves 4

ingredients
- **ground beef**, 225g/8oz
- **salt** and **ground black pepper**
- **Sicilian-style sausages**, 4
- **canned pomodorino tomatoes**, 28 ounces
- **cooked pasta or rice**, to serve
- **Parmesan cheese shavings**, to serve

tools
* Mixing bowl
* Medium sharp knife
* Fork
* Large, shallow casserole
* Food processor or blender

COOK'S TIP

► Pomodorino tomatoes are another name for cherry tomatoes that are vine ripened. You can use cans of cherry tomatoes instead if desired, and these are widely available.

tomatoes

1 Put the ground beef in a bowl and season with salt and pepper. Slit the sausages and squeeze out the meat. Add to the bowl. Mash everything with a fork.

2 Shape into balls about the size of walnuts and arrange in a single layer in a casserole.

3 Cover the casserole and chill in the refrigerator for 30 minutes. Preheat the oven to 350°F.

4 Place the tomatoes in a food processor or blender and blend until just smooth. Adult supervision is required. Season with salt and pepper to taste.

5 Pour the tomato sauce over the meatballs in the casserole, making sure they are all well covered.

6 Cover with aluminum foil and bake for 30 minutes, until cooked. Ask an adult to remove the foil after 15 minutes and stir occasionally, .

7 Serve the meatballs hot with cooked pasta or rice, sprinkled with Parmesan shavings.

Pork satay

These tasty kebabs are perfect for cooking under the broiler or on the barbecue. Serve with plain yogurt for dipping for a super-duper supper.

makes *8–12*

ingredients
- **pork tenderloin**, 1 pound
- **light Barbados sugar** or **brown sugar**, 1 tablespoon
- **shrimp paste**, ½-inch cube
- **lemon grass stalks**, 1–2
- **coriander seeds**, 2 tablespoons
- **macadamia nuts** or **blanched almonds**, 6
- **onions**, 2, peeled and chopped
- **fresh red chile**, 1, seeded and chopped (wash your hands after touching chile)
- **ground turmeric**, ½ teaspoon
- **canned coconut milk**, 1¼ cups
- **sunflower oil**, 2 tablespoons

macadamia nuts

tools
- ✳ **2 cutting boards**
- ✳ **2 medium sharp knives**
- ✳ **Nonmetallic dish**
- ✳ **Aluminum foil**
- ✳ **Nonstick skillet**
- ✳ **Blender or food processor**
- ✳ **8–12 wooden skewers, soaked in water for 1 hour**
- ✳ **Oven mitts**

1 Cut the pork into chunks. Adult supervision is required. Spread out in a layer in a dish. Sprinkle with sugar, cover, and set aside.

2 Wrap the shrimp paste in aluminum foil. Heat a skillet, then add the parcel. Heat for a few minutes, then remove from heat.

3 Using a clean board and knife, cut off the lower 2 inches of the lemon grass and chop finely.

4 Dry-fry the coriander seeds in the nonstick pan for 2 minutes. Put in a blender or food processor and blend to a powder. Adult supervision is required.

5 Remove the foil from the shrimp paste. Add the nuts and lemon grass to the blender and blend briefly, then add the onions, chile, shrimp paste, and turmeric. Blend to a paste. Adult supervision is required.

6 Pour in the coconut milk and oil and blend briefly to combine.

7 Pour the mixture over the pork and let marinate for at least 1–2 hours at room temperature or overnight in the refrigerator. This will enhance the flavors. Ask an adult to preheat the broiler.

8 Thread 3–4 pieces of pork onto each skewer (reserving any leftover marinade) and place on a foil-lined broiler pan.

9 Cook for 8–10 minutes, until tender, basting frequently with the remaining marinade. Adult supervision is required. Serve immediately.

(!) = Watch out! Sharp or electrical tool in use.   (🖑) = Watch out! Heat is involved.

Honey chops

These tasty, sticky chops are very easy to prepare and broil, but they would be just as good cooked on a barbecue. Serve with herbed mash potatoes or fries.

serves **4**

ingredients
- **carrots**, 8 medium (about 1 pound)
- **butter**, 1 tablespoon
- **brown sugar**, 1 tablespoon
- **sesame seeds**, 1 tablespoon
- **herb mashed potatoes**, to serve

for the chops
- **pork loin chops**, 4
- **butter**, 4 tablespoons
- **honey**, 2 tablespoons
- **tomato paste**, 1 tablespoon

tools
- ✳ Cutting board
- ✳ Medium sharp knife
- ✳ Small heavy pan
- ✳ Aluminum foil
- ✳ Small mixing bowl
- ✳ Wooden spoon
- ✳ Oven mitts

1 With adult supervision, cut the carrots into matchsticks. Put in a small pan and just cover with water.

2 Add the butter and sugar and bring to a boil. Reduce the heat and simmer for 15 minutes, until most of the liquid has boiled away. Adult supervision is required.

3 Meanwhile, line a broiler pan with foil and arrange the pork chops on the broiler rack.

4 In a bowl, beat together the butter and honey with a wooden spoon. Beat in the tomato paste. Ask an adult to preheat the broiler to high.

5 Spread half the honey paste over the chops and broil them for about 5 minutes, until browned. Ask an adult to remove the pan from under the broiler.

6 Turn the chops over, spread them with the remaining paste, and ask an adult to return to the broiler.

COOK'S TIP
▶ This paste can also be used to coat sausages before broiling them, or drizzled over vegetables for roasting, such as peppers, zucchini, and tomatoes.

7 Broil the chops for 5 minutes more, until cooked. Transfer to plates. Sprinkle the sesame seeds over the carrots and serve with the chops and mash.

Main meals

The main meal of the day is very important, and needs to be yummy, healthy, and satisfying. This chapter contains a great range of family favorites, from colorful vegetable treats to meaty mouthfuls, all of which are bound to be popular. All you have to do is choose a dish, put on your apron, and get cooking!

Corn and potato chowder

This creamy, chunky soup is rich with the sweet taste of corn. It's yummy served with crusty bread and topped with some melted cheese for a warming dinner.

serves **4**

ingredients
- **onion**, 1, peeled
- **medium baking potato**, 1, peeled
- **celery**, 2 stalks
- **garlic**, 1 clove
- **small green bell pepper**, 1
- **sunflower oil**, 2 tablespoons
- **butter**, 2 tablespoons
- **stock** or **water**, 2½ cups
- **salt** and **ground black pepper**
- **milk**, 1¼ cups
- **canned cannellini beans**, 7 ounces
- **canned corn kernels**, 11 ounces
- **dried sage**, good pinch
- **Cheddar cheese**, grated, ½ cup, to serve

celery

tools
- ✳ Cutting board
- ✳ Large sharp knife
- ✳ Garlic press
- ✳ Large pan
- ✳ Wooden spoon
- ✳ Grater

1 On a cutting board, chop the onion, potato, and celery into small pieces. Crush the garlic clove using a garlic press. Adult supervision is required.

2 Cut the bell pepper in half, then remove and discard the membrane and seeds. Chop the rest into small pieces.

3 Put the onion, garlic, potato, celery and bell pepper into a large heavy pan with the oil and butter.

4 Heat until sizzling, then reduce the heat to low. Cover and cook for about 10 minutes, stirring occasionally. Adult supervision is required when using heat.

5 Pour in the stock or water, season to taste, and bring to a boil. Reduce the heat, cover, and simmer for 15 minutes, until the vegetables are tender.

6 Add the milk, beans, and corn—with their liquids—and the sage. Simmer, uncovered, for 5 minutes. Sprinkle with cheese and serve.

COOK'S TIP
▶ If you prefer soup without chunks, leave the soup to cool slightly, then put the soup in a blender or food processor (adult supervision is required) and blend. Return to the pan and reheat. Adult supervision is required.

(!) = Watch out! Sharp or electrical tool in use. (✋) = Watch out! Heat is involved.

Carrot soup

Carrots are said to improve your eyesight, so this delicious soup might help you see in the dark. Serve with toast or chunks of bread for a light meal.

serves **4**

ingredients
- **carrots**, 8 medium (about 1 pound)
- **onion**, 1
- **sunflower oil**, 1 tablespoon
- **split red lentils**, scant ½ cup
- **vegetable** or **chicken stock**, 5 cups
- **ground coriander**, 1 teaspoon
- **chopped fresh parsley**, 3 tablespoons
- **salt** and **ground black pepper**
- **fresh cilantro leaves** and **plain yogurt**, to serve

carrots

tools
- ✳ **Peeler**
- ✳ **Cutting board**
- ✳ **Medium sharp knife**
- ✳ **Large pan**
- ✳ **Wooden spoon**
- ✳ **Small bowl**
- ✳ **Strainer**
- ✳ **Blender or food processor**

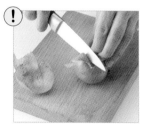

3 Add the carrots and cook gently, stirring, for about 4–5 minutes, until they start to soften.

1 Peel the carrots, then trim off the ends and slice into circles. Peel the onions and cut in half. Lay the halves flat and slice into half moon crescents. Adult supervision is required.

2 Heat the oil in a pan, add the onion, and cook, stirring, for 5 minutes. Adult supervision is required.

4 Meanwhile, put the lentils in a small bowl and cover with cold water. Pour off any parts that float on the surface. Pour into a strainer and rinse under cold running water.

5 With adult supervision, add the lentils, stock, and coriander to the pan. Bring to a boil. Lower the heat, cover, and simmer gently for 30 minutes, or until the lentils are tender.

6 Add the parsley, season, and cook for 5 minutes. Set the pan aside to cool slightly.

7 Pour the soup into a blender or food processor and blend until smooth. (You may have to do this in two batches.) Adult supervision is required.

8 Return the soup to the pan and reheat until piping hot. Ladle into bowls and garnish with cilantro and a spoonful of yogurt.

Super-duper soup

This fantastic vegetable soup is healthy, tasty, and extremely easy to make. You can vary the vegetables, using whichever ones you like best.

serves 4–6

ingredients
- **onion**, 1
- **carrots**, 2
- **potatoes**, 6 medium (about 1½ pounds)
- **broccoli**, 1 small head (about 4 ounces)
- **zucchini**, 1
- **mushrooms**, 4 ounces
- **vegetable oil**, 1 tablespoon
- **vegetable stock**, 5 cups
- **canned chopped tomatoes**, 1 pound
- **medium-hot curry powder**, 1½ teaspoon (optional)
- **dried mixed herbs**, 1 teaspoon
- **salt** and **ground black pepper**

tools
- ✳ Vegetable peeler
- ✳ Cutting board
- ✳ Medium sharp knife
- ✳ Large pan
- ✳ Metal spoon

1 Peel the onion, carrots, and potatoes. On a cutting board, slice the onion and carrots. Adult supervision is required.

2 Cut the potatoes into large chunks. Cut the broccoli into "florets". Slice the zucchini and the mushrooms. Set aside.

3 Heat the vegetable oil in a pan. Add the onion and carrots and fry gently for about 5 minutes, stirring occasionally, until they start to soften. Adult supervision is required.

4 Add the potatoes and fry gently for 2 minutes more, stirring frequently.

5 Add the stock, tomatoes, broccoli, zucchini, and mushrooms.

6 Add the curry powder (if using) and herbs. Season and bring to a boil. Cover and simmer for 30–40 minutes, or until the vegetables are tender. Serve immediately.

COOK'S TIP
▶ You can also add dried pasta to the soup 8–10 minutes before the end of cooking. Look out for special small pasta shapes in large supermarkets and delicatessens. Allow about 1 ounce per person and add a little extra water to the soup.

(!) = Watch out! Sharp or electrical tool in use.   = Watch out! Heat is involved.

Tomato and bread soup

This simple tomato and basil soup is thickened with stale bread, and makes a delicious, filling meal.

serves 4

ingredients

- **stale bread**, 6 slices (about 6 ounces)
- **onion**, 1 medium
- **garlic**, 2 cloves
- **olive oil**, 6 tablespoons
- **dried chile**, small piece, crumbled (optional)
- **ripe tomatoes**, 6 small (about 1½ pounds), peeled and chopped, or **canned peeled plum tomatoes**, 28 ounces, chopped
- **chopped fresh basil**, 3 tablespoons
- **salt** and **ground black pepper**
- **meat** or **vegetable stock** or **water**, or **a combination**, 6¼ cups
- **extra virgin olive oil**, to serve (optional)

tools

- ✳ **Cutting board**
- ✳ **Large serrated knife**
- ✳ **Medium sharp knife**
- ✳ **Large pan**
- ✳ **Slotted spoon**
- ✳ **Wooden spoon**
- ✳ **Medium pan**
- ✳ **Fork**

1 On a cutting board, cut away the crusts from the bread using a large serrated knife. Cut into cubes. Adult supervision is required.

2 Peel the onion. Cut in half lengthwise, then lay flat on the board and chop into small pieces. Peel and finely chop the garlic cloves.

3 Heat 4 tablespoons of the oil in a pan. Add the chile, if using, and stir over high heat for 1–2 minutes. Add the bread cubes and cook until golden, stirring. Adult supervision is required.

4 Remove with a slotted spoon and transfer to a plate lined with paper towels. Set aside.

5 With adult supervision, add the remaining oil, the onion, and garlic and cook, stirring occasionally until the onion softens.

6 Stir in the tomatoes, bread cubes and basil. Season to taste. Cook over moderate heat, stirring occasionally, for 15 minutes. Adult supervision is required.

7 Meanwhile, place the stock or water in a pan and bring to a boil. Add to the pan containing the tomato mixture and mix well. Bring to a boil, lower the heat slightly, and simmer for 20 minutes. Adult supervision is required.

8 Remove the soup from the heat. Use a fork to mash the tomatoes and the bread together. Season to taste.

9 Let the soup stand for 10 minutes. Just before serving, swirl in a little extra virgin olive oil, if desired.

Boston baked beans

This tasty speciality from Boston may take a long time to cook, but it is easy to prepare, is ideal for a cold day, and fills the kitchen with its wonderful aroma.

serves 8

ingredients
- **dried navy beans**, 2½ cups
- **bay leaf**, 1
- **cloves**, 4
- **onions**, 2, peeled
- **molasses**, ½ cup
- **dark brown sugar**, ¾ cup
- **Dijon-style mustard**, 1 tablespoon
- **salt**, 1 teaspoon
- **pepper**, 1 teaspoon
- **boiling water**, 1 cup
- **salt pork**, 8-ounce piece

tools
- ✳ Colander
- ✳ Large mixing bowl
- ✳ 2 large pans
- ✳ Large casserole or heavy pan with a lid
- ✳ Small mixing bowl
- ✳ Cutting board
- ✳ Small sharp knife
- ✳ Oven mitts

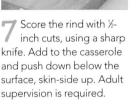

1 Rinse the beans in a colander under running water. Drain and place in a bowl. Cover with water and let soak overnight. Drain and rinse again.

2 Put in a pan with the bay leaf and cover with fresh cold water. Bring to a boil, cover, and simmer until tender, 1½–2 hours.

3 Preheat the oven to 275°F. Ask an adult to drain the beans, then put in a casserole or heavy pan. Stick two cloves in each of the onions and add them to the casserole or pan.

4 In a bowl, combine the molasses, sugar, and mustard. Season. Ask an adult to add the boiling water.

5 Pour this mixture over the beans. Add more water if necessary, so the beans are almost covered with liquid.

6 Fill the unused pan with water. Add the salt pork and bring to a boil. Boil for 3 minutes. Ask an adult to drain the pork in a colander. Let cool.

7 Score the rind with ½-inch cuts, using a sharp knife. Add to the casserole and push down below the surface, skin-side up. Adult supervision is required.

8 Cover and bake for 4½–5 hours. Uncover for the last 30 minutes. Ask an adult to remove from the oven and serve.

ⓘ = Watch out! Sharp or electrical tool in use.   🔥 = Watch out! Heat is involved.

Zucchini and potato bake

This delicious dish is great served with warm crusty bread and a crispy green salad. It is easy to make, satisfying, and looks good when brought to the table.

serves 6

ingredients
- **zucchini**, 4–5 medium (about 1½ pounds)
- **potatoes**, 4 medium (about 1 pound)
- **onion**, 1
- **garlic**, 3 cloves
- **large red bell pepper**, 1
- **canned chopped tomatoes**, 14 ounces
- **extra virgin olive oil**, ⅔ cup
- **hot water**, ⅔ cup
- **dried oregano**, 1 teaspoon
- **salt** and **ground black pepper**
- **fresh Italian parsley**, 3 tablespoons, chopped, plus a few extra sprigs, to garnish (optional)

tools
✳ **Cutting board**
✳ **Medium sharp knife**
✳ **Large casserole**
✳ **Vegetable peeler**
✳ **Wooden spoon**
✳ **Oven mitts**

1 Preheat the oven to 375°F. Slice the zucchini into even-size rounds and put in a casserole. Peel the potatoes and cut them into chunks. Adult supervision is required.

2 With adult supervision, peel and chop the onion and garlic and deseed and chop the bell pepper.

3 Add the onion, garlic, red bell pepper, and tomatoes to the casserole and mix well, then stir in the olive oil, hot water, and dried oregano.

4 Spread the mixture evenly in the casserole, then season to taste with salt and pepper. Bake for 30 minutes.

5 Ask an adult to remove from the oven. Stir in the parsley and a little more water.

6 Ask an adult to return the casserole to the oven and cook for 1 hour more, increasing the temperature to 400°F for the final 10–15 minutes, so that the potatoes brown.

7 Ask an adult to remove the casserole from the oven. Let cool for 5 minutes before serving garnished with sprigs of Italian parsley, if you like.

COOK'S TIP
▶ You can prepare this dish a day in advance. Simply make up to the end of Step 3, cover, and chill. The next day, continue from Step 4.

Creamy coconut noodles

When everyday vegetables, such as carrots and cabbage, are given the Thai treatment, the result is a delectable creamy dish that everyone will enjoy. If you like your food spicy, add a little more red curry paste.

serves **4**

ingredients
- **vegetable oil**, 2 tablespoons
- **lemon grass stalk**, 1, finely chopped
- **Thai red curry paste**, 1 tablespoon
- **onion**, 1, halved and sliced
- **zucchini**, 3, sliced into circles
- **Savoy cabbage**, shredded, 4 ounces
- **carrots**, 2, sliced into circles
- **broccoli**, 1 small (about 5 ounces), cut into florets
- **canned coconut milk**, 28 ounces
- **vegetable stock**, 2 cups
- **dried egg noodles**, 5 ounces
- **cilantro**, 4 tablespoons
- **Thai fish sauce**, 1 tablespoon
- **soy sauce**, 2 tablespoons

lemon grass

tools
- ✳ **Large pan or wok**
- ✳ **2 wooden spoons**
- ✳ **Cutting board**
- ✳ **Large sharp knife**

1 Heat the oil in a large pan or wok until just smoking. Add the lemon grass and red curry paste and stir-fry for 2–3 seconds, keeping it moving all the time. Adult supervision is required when using heat.

2 Add the onion and reduce the heat to medium. Cook, stirring occasionally with a wooden spoon, for about 5–10 minutes, until the onion has softened but not browned.

3 Add the zucchini, cabbage, carrots, and broccoli florets to the pan. Using two spoons, toss the vegetables to combine everything well. Reduce the heat to low.

4 Cook the mixture, stirring often, for an additional 5 minutes. Increase the heat to medium, then stir in the coconut milk, stock, and noodles and bring to a boil.

5 With adult supervision, chop the cilantro. Add to the pan with the fish sauce and soy sauce. Stir to combine and cook for 1 minute. Transfer to bowls and serve immediately.

⚠ = Watch out! Sharp or electrical tool in use. = Watch out! Heat is involved.

Crunchy summer rolls

These rolls are crunchy, pretty, and tasty to eat—perfect for a quick light meal in the summer. There are loads of dipping sauces available in Asian stores, but you can just use soy sauce, if you like.

serves 4

ingredients
- **round rice papers**, 12
- **small cucumber**, 1
- **carrots**, 2–3
- **scallions**, 3
- **lettuce**, 1 head, leaves separated and ribs removed
- **mung bean sprouts**, 1 cup (8 ounces)
- **fresh mint leaves**, 1 bunch
- **cilantro leaves**, 1 bunch
- **Asian dipping sauce**, such as **nuoc cham**, **tuk tre**, or **soy sauce**, to serve

tools
- ✳ **Shallow dish**
- ✳ **Vegetable peeler**
- ✳ **Spoon**
- ✳ **Cutting board**
- ✳ **Medium sharp knife**

1 Pour some lukewarm water into a shallow dish. Soak the rice papers, 2–3 at a time, for 5 minutes, until they are soft. Place on a clean dish towel and cover to keep them moist.

2 Peel the cucumber, carefully cut it in half lengthwise, then remove the seeds with a spoon. Cut the remaining flesh into short matchsticks. Adult supervision is required.

3 Peel the carrots and cut them in half widthwise, then lengthwise. Slice into short matchsticks. Trim the scallions, cut into short pieces, then cut into matchsticks. Adult supervision is required.

4 Work with one paper at a time. Place a lettuce leaf toward the edge nearest to you, leaving around 1 inch to fold over. Place a mixture of the vegetables on top, followed by some mint and cilantro.

5 Fold the edge nearest to you over the filling, tuck in the sides, and roll tightly to the edge on the far side. Repeat with the other papers and vegetables. Serve with dipping sauce.

Chinese omelet parcels

A filled omelet makes a nourishing dinner. If you are not fond of stir-fries, then use any other ingredients instead. Wash your hands after touching the chiles.

FACT FILE
CORIANDER AND CILANTRO
The coriander plant provides two ingredients: the fresh leafy herb called cilantro, which is used in this recipe, and coriander seeds, which are usually dry-fried in a skillet before being ground up and used to add a distinctive taste to a range of spiced dishes. The fragrant, bright green leaves of the fresh type add a wonderful flavor, color, and aroma to many dishes, especially Asian ones, and can be bought from supermarkets or in speciality Asian stores.

fresh cilantro

serves 4

ingredients
- **broccoli**, 1 small head (about 4½ ounces), cut into florets
- **peanut oil**, 2 tablespoons
- **fresh ginger**, ½-inch piece, peeled and finely grated
- **garlic**, 1 large clove, finely chopped
- **red chile**, 1, seeded and sliced
- **scallions**, 4, sliced diagonally
- **bok choy**, trimmed and chopped, 3 cups
- **fresh cilantro leaves**, 2 cups, plus extra to garnish
- **bean sprouts**, ½ cup
- **zucchini**, 1, cut into strips
- **black bean sauce**, 3 tablespoons
- **eggs**, 4
- **salt** and **ground black pepper**
- **soy sauce**, to serve

tools
- ✴ **Medium pan**
- ✴ **Slotted spoon**
- ✴ **Wok or large, deep skillet**
- ✴ **Wooden spoon**
- ✴ **Cutting board**
- ✴ **Medium sharp knife**
- ✴ **Small bowl**
- ✴ **Fork**
- ✴ **Omelet pan**
- ✴ **Spatula or palette knife**

1 Bring a pan of water to a boil, add the broccoli, and cook for 2 minutes. Lift out with a slotted spoon and rinse under cold water. Adult supervision is required.

2 Meanwhile, heat 1 tablespoon of the oil in a wok or skillet. Add the ginger, garlic, and half the chile and stir-fry for 1 minute. Adult supervision is required when using heat.

3 Add the scallions, broccoli, and bok choy and stir-fry for 2 minutes.

4 With adult supervision, chop three-quarters of the cilantro.

5 Add the cilantro, bean sprouts and zucchini strips to the wok or skillet and stir-fry for 1 minute. Add the black bean sauce, stir to combine and heat through for 1 minute more.

⚠ = Watch out! Sharp or electrical tool in use.   🧤 = Watch out! Heat is involved.

8 Turn out onto a plate and keep warm while you make three more omelets, adding a little oil each time.

9 Spoon the cooked vegetables onto one side of each omelet and roll up. Cut in half and serve garnished with cilantro and chile, if desired, and soy sauce.

6 Beat the eggs in a small bowl with a fork and season with salt and pepper. Heat a little of the remaining oil in an omelet pan and add one-quarter of the egg.

7 Swirl the egg until it covers the bottom of the pan in a thin layer, then scatter over one-quarter of the cilantro leaves. Cook until set, turning over with a spatula or palette knife.

Raving ravioli

Making your own pasta is loads of fun and impressive. If you have a pasta machine, follow the manufacturer's instructions, otherwise just use a rolling pin.

serves **4**

Ingredients
- **fresh spinach**, 3 ounces
- **white bread flour**, 2½ cups
- **eggs**, 3, beaten
- **vegetable oil**, 1 tablespoon
- **salt** and **ground black pepper**
- **heavy cream**, 1¼ cups
- **fresh cilantro**, 1 tablespoon, chopped

- **freshly grated Parmesan cheese**, 2 tablespoons, plus extra to serve

for the filling
- **trout fillet**, 4 ounces
- **ricotta cheese**, ⅓ cup
- **lemon**, 1, grated rind
- **chopped fresh cilantro**, 1 tablespoon
- **salt** and **ground black pepper**

FACT FILE
PARMESAN CHEESE
Used in many different dishes, Parmesan cheese is a strongly flavored hard cheese from Italy. Because it has a powerful flavor, you only need to use a small amount.

Parmesan cheese

tools
- ✳ Medium pan
- ✳ Blender or food processor
- ✳ Large deep skillet
- ✳ Colander
- ✳ Small mixing bowl
- ✳ Large rolling pin
- ✳ Medium sharp knife or pastry wheel
- ✳ Teaspoon
- ✳ Small pan

1 Remove the stalks from the spinach and tear up the leaves. Place in a medium pan with 1 tablespoon water and heat gently, covered, until the spinach has wilted. Adult supervision is required.

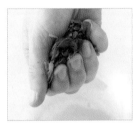

2 Cool, then squeeze out as much water as you can. Put the leaves into a blender or food processor, with the flour, eggs, and oil.

3 Season to taste and blend until it forms a smooth dough. Adult supervision is required.

4 Transfer the dough to a lightly floured surface and knead it for about 5 minutes, until it is smooth. Wrap it well with plastic wrap and chill in the refrigerator for at least 30 minutes.

5 **To make the filling,** place the trout fillet in a skillet. Cover with water and bring to a boil. Reduce the heat slightly and simmer gently for 3–4 minutes, until tender and flaking easily. Adult supervision is required.

6 Ask an adult to drain in a colander. Let cool. Remove the skin and flake the flesh into a bowl.

7 Sprinkle a counter lightly with flour. Roll out the dough to make a 20 x 18-inch rectangle the thickness of a thin piece of cardboard. Let it dry for about 15 minutes.

8 Use a sharp knife or pastry wheel to trim the edges, then cut the dough in half. Adult supervision is required.

⚠ = Watch out! Sharp or electrical tool in use.   🖐 = Watch out! Heat is involved.

9 Meanwhile, add the ricotta, lemon rind, and cilantro to the trout. Season and beat together.

10 Put four small spoonfuls of the trout filling across the top of the dough, leaving a small border around the edge of each. Carry on putting the filling mixture in lines to make eight rows.

11 Lift up the second sheet of pasta on the rolling pin and lay it over the first sheet. Run your finger between the bumps to remove any air and to press the dough together.

(!)

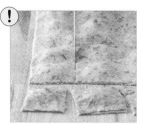

12 Using the knife or pastry wheel, cut the ravioli into small parcels and trim around the edge as well to seal each one.

13 Cook in lightly salted boiling water for 2–3 minutes. Ask an adult to drain. Return to the pan.

14 Put the cream, remaining cilantro, and the Parmesan in a small pan and heat gently, without boiling, until the cheese has melted. Adult supervision is required. Pour over the ravioli and stir.

15 Transfer to serving dishes and serve immediately, garnished with a sprig of cilantro and grated Parmesan.

Fantastic potatoes!

Baked potatoes are really easy to cook and, served with one of these scrumptious toppings, are a real treat. Each topping makes enough to fill four potatoes.

COOK'S TIP

▶ Choose potatoes that are even-sized and have undamaged skins, and scrub them thoroughly. If they are cooked before you want to serve them, ask an adult to take them out of the oven and wrap them up in a warm cloth until they are needed.

serves **4**

ingredients
- **medium baking potatoes**, 4
- **olive oil**
- **sea salt**
- **a filling of your choice** (see below)

for the stir-fried vegetables
- **sunflower oil**, 3 tablespoons
- **leeks**, 2, thinly sliced
- **carrots**, 2, cut into sticks
- **zucchini**, 1, thinly sliced
- **baby corn**, 4 ounces, halved
- **white mushrooms**, sliced, 1½ cups
- **soy sauce**, 3 tablespoons
- **dry sherry** or **vermouth**, 2 tablespoons
- **sesame oil**, 1 tablespoon
- **sesame seeds**, to garnish

for the red bean chile
- **canned red kidney beans**, 15 ounces, drained
- **cream cheese**, scant 1 cup
- **mild chili sauce**, 2 tablespoons
- **ground cumin**, 1 teaspoon

for the cheese and creamy corn
- **canned creamed corn**, 15 ounces
- **grated Cheddar cheese**, 1 cup
- **mixed dried herbs**, 1 teaspoon
- **fresh parsley sprigs**, to garnish

tools
- ✳ **Small sharp knife**
- ✳ **Nonstick baking sheet**
- ✳ **Oven mitts**
- ✳ **Cutting board**
- ✳ **Wok or skillet**
- ✳ **Wooden spoon**
- ✳ **Metal spoon**
- ✳ **Small mixing bowl**
- ✳ **2 small pans**

1 Preheat the oven to 400°F.

2 With adult supervision, score the potatoes with a cross. Rub the skins all over with olive oil. Place on a baking sheet and cook for 45–60 minutes, until a knife inserted into the center of the potatoes comes out clean.

3 Ask an adult to remove the potatoes from the oven and let cool slightly for a few minutes.

4 Place the potatoes on a cutting board and cut them open along the scored lines with a knife. Push up the flesh. Season to taste and fill with your chosen filling.

5 **To make the stir-fried vegetables**, heat the oil in a wok or large skillet until really hot. Adult supervision is required.

6 Add the leeks, carrots, zucchini, and baby corn and stir-fry together for about 2 minutes, then add the mushrooms and stir-fry for another minute.

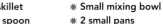

7 Mix together the soy sauce, sherry or vermouth, and sesame oil in a small bowl.

8 Pour the mixture over the vegetables in the wok or skillet. Heat through until just bubbling, then scatter over the sesame seeds. Serve immediately with the potatoes.

   (!) = Watch out! Sharp or electrical tool in use.   (🖐) = Watch out! Heat is involved.

9 To make the red bean chile, heat the beans in a small pan for 5 minutes or in a microwave for about 3 minutes, until hot. Adult supervision is required.

10 Stir in the cream cheese, chili sauce, and cumin. Heat for 1 minute. Spoon onto the potatoes and top with more chili sauce.

11 To make the cheese and creamy corn filling, heat the corn in a small pan with the cheese and herbs for about 5 minutes, until hot. Mix well. Adult supervision is required.

12 Spoon the mixture onto the potatoes and garnish with fresh parsley sprigs.

Vegetable paella

This extremely easy all-in-one-pan meal includes loads of colorful, tasty vegetables and is a sure hit with vegetarians and meat eaters alike.

serves 6

Ingredients
- **leeks**, 2
- **celery**, 3 stalks
- **red bell pepper**, 1
- **zucchini**, 2
- **cremini mushrooms**, 6 ounces
- **onion**, 1, peeled and chopped
- **garlic**, 2 cloves, peeled and chopped
- **frozen peas**, 1½ cups
- **long-grain brown rice**, 2 cups
- **vegetable stock**, 3¾ cups
- **saffron**, a few threads
- **canned cannellini beans**, 14 ounces, drained
- **cherry tomatoes**, 2 cups (about 8 ounces)
- **chopped fresh mixed herbs**, 3–4 tablespoons

tools
- ✳ **Cutting board**
- ✳ **Medium sharp knife**
- ✳ **Paella pan or large, deep skillet**
- ✳ **Wooden spoon**

1 Slice the leeks and chop the celery, reserving any leaves. Adult supervision is required when cutting.

2 Cut the bell pepper in half and remove the seeds and membranes. Slice. Slice the zucchini and the mushrooms.

3 Put the onion, garlic, leeks, celery, pepper, zucchini, and mushrooms in a paella pan.

4 Add the peas, brown rice, vegetable stock, and saffron threads to the pan and mix well with a wooden spoon to combine.

5 Bring the mixture to a boil, stirring often. Lower the heat and simmer, uncovered, stirring often, for 30 minutes, until almost all the liquid has been absorbed and the rice is tender. Add the beans and cook for 5 minutes more. Adult supervision is required.

6 Meanwhile, cut the cherry tomatoes in half and add to the pan with the chopped herbs. Serve immediately, garnished with the reserved celery leaves.

VARIATION
- If preferred, use long-grain white rice instead of brown.

(!) = Watch out! Sharp or electrical tool in use.   (✋) = Watch out! Heat is involved.

Fish and rice paella

If you have had paella on vacation in Spain then you'll be eager to try this recipe. Using a mixture of frozen fish saves doing too much fussy preparation.

serves 4

ingredients
- **red bell pepper**, 1
- **oil**, 2 tablespoons
- **onion**, 1, peeled and sliced
- **mushrooms**, chopped, 2 cups
- **ground turmeric**, 2 teaspoons
- **rice** and **grain mix** (or just rice), scant 1½ cups
- **fish, chicken**, or **vegetable stock**, 3 cups
- **salt** and **ground black pepper**
- **frozen premium seafood selection**, 14 ounces, thawed
- **frozen large jumbo shrimp**, 4 ounces, thawed

tools
* Cutting board
* Medium sharp knife
* Paella pan or large, deep skillet
* Wooden spoon

1 With adult supervision, cut the bell pepper in half, remove the seeds, and chop.

2 Heat the oil in a paella pan. Add the onion and fry for 5 minutes, stirring. Add the mushrooms and bell pepper and fry for 1 minute. Adult supervision is required.

3 Stir in the turmeric and then the grains. Stir until well mixed, then carefully pour on the stock.

4 Season, cover, and let simmer gently for 15 minutes. Uncover and stir once or twice during the cooking time.

5 Uncover and add the seafood selection and shrimp. Stir and bring the liquid back to a boil.

6 Cover and simmer for another 3–5 minutes, stirring once or twice, until the fish and shellfish are opaque. Serve immediately.

VARIATION
• You can use whatever mixture of fish you like in this dish, or simply use either shrimp or some canned tuna if you prefer to keep it simple.

canned tuna

Flounder with tomato sauce

These crispy fishy morsels beat store-bought fish sticks hands down. Instead of reaching for the ketchup, try serving with this tasty tomato sauce.

serves **4**

ingredients
- **all-purpose flour**, ¼ cup
- **eggs**, 2, beaten
- **dried bread crumbs**, ¾ cup
- **flounder**, 4 small, skinned
- **salt** and **ground black pepper**
- **butter**, 2 tablespoons
- **sunflower oil**, 2 tablespoons
- **lemon**, 1, quartered, to serve

for the tomato sauce
- **red onion**, 1
- **garlic**, 1 clove
- **olive oil**, 2 tablespoons
- **canned chopped tomatoes**, 14 ounces
- **tomato paste**, 1 tablespoon
- **fresh basil leaves**, torn, 1 tablespoon

tools
- ✱ **Cutting board**
- ✱ **Medium sharp knife**
- ✱ **Large pan**
- ✱ **Wooden spoon**
- ✱ **3 large shallow dishes**
- ✱ **2 large skillets**
- ✱ **Spatula or palette knife**

1 **To make the tomato sauce**, finely chop the red onion and garlic. Adult supervision is required.

2 Heat the oil in a large pan, add the onion and garlic, and cook for 2–3 minutes, stirring occasionally until softened but not brown. Adult supervision is required.

3 Stir in the chopped tomatoes and tomato paste. Bring to a boil and simmer for 10 minutes.

4 Meanwhile, spread out the flour in one shallow dish, pour the beaten eggs into another, and spread out the bread crumbs in a third.

5 Lightly season the fish pieces on both sides. Dip each in turn first in the flour on both sides, then in egg on both sides, and finally in the bread crumbs. Aim for an even coating of bread crumbs that is not too thick. Gently shake off any excess bread crumbs and set the fish aside.

6 Heat the butter and oil in a skillet until foaming. Add the fish and fry for about 5 minutes on each side, until the outside is brown and the fish is cooked. Adult supervision is required.

7 Ask an adult to remove with a spatula or palette knife and transfer to paper towels to drain.

8 Season the tomato sauce to taste, then stir in the basil. Transfer the fish to plates and serve with the sauce. Offer lemon wedges separately for squeezing over the top.

⚠ = Watch out! Sharp or electrical tool in use.　　✊ = Watch out! Heat is involved.

Fish and cheese pies

This creamy mixture of fish, corn, and cabbage topped with potato and cheese is easy to make, warming, and filling—perfect for a winter's dinner.

serves 2

ingredients

- **potato**, 1 medium, peeled and chopped
- **green cabbage**, shredded, ⅓ cup
- **cod** or **hoki fillets**, 4 ounces, skinned
- **milk**, ⅔ cup
- **butter**, 1 tablespoon
- **all-purpose flour**, 1 tablespoon
- **frozen corn**, 2 tablespoons
- **red Leicester** or **mild Cheddar cheese**, grated, ¼ cup
- **sesame seeds**, 1 teaspoon
- **cooked carrot sticks** and **snow peas**, to serve

tools

- ✳ 2 large pans with lids
- ✳ Colander
- ✳ Table knife
- ✳ Strainer
- ✳ Wooden spoon
- ✳ 2 small casseroles
- ✳ Potato masher
- ✳ Oven mitts

1 Bring a large pan filled three-quarters with water to a boil. Add the potato and cook for 10 minutes. Add the cabbage and cook for 5 minutes more, until tender. Adult supervision is required.

2 Ask an adult to drain in a colander. Return to the pan and cover with a lid.

3 Meanwhile, place the skinned fish fillets and all but 2 teaspoons of the milk in another large pan. Bring to a boil, then cover, reduce the heat, and simmer gently for 8–10 minutes, until the fish flakes easily when pressed gently with the tip of a table knife. Adult supervision is required.

4 Ask an adult to strain, reserving the liquid.

5 Wash the pan, then melt the butter in it. Stir in the flour and cook, stirring, for 1–2 minutes. Adult supervision is required.

6 Remove from the heat and stir in the reserved cooking liquid. Return to the heat and bring to a boil, stirring until thickened.

7 Ask an adult to preheat the broiler to medium-hot. Add the fish and corn to the sauce with half the cheese. Spoon into the casseroles.

8 Mash the potato and cabbage with the remaining milk. Stir in half the remaining cheese. Spoon over the fish. Sprinkle with the sesame seeds and the remaining cheese.

9 Broil until browned. Adult supervision is required. Serve.

Tandoori-style chicken

Create an Indian classic at home with this easy recipe, then use the same marinade to tandoori your favorite meats and fish.

serves 6

Ingredients

- **chicken thighs**, 6 (see Cook's Tips)
- **plain yogurt**, ½ cup
- **paprika**, 1¼ teaspoons
- **hot curry paste**, 1 teaspoon
- **coriander seeds**, 1 teaspoon, roughly crushed (see Cook's Tips)
- **cumin seeds**, ½ teaspoon, roughly crushed
- **ground turmeric**, ½ teaspoon
- **vegetable oil**, 2 teaspoons

to serve
- **scallions**, 2
- **fresh mint leaves**, a small handful
- **plain yogurt**, ⅔ cup
- **cucumber**, ½
- **cooked basmati rice**, **mixed salad**, and **lemon wedges**, to serve (optional)

turmeric

tools

- ✳ **2 cutting boards**
- ✳ **2 medium sharp knives**
- ✳ **Nonmetallic shallow bowl**
- ✳ **1 small bowl**
- ✳ **Spoon**
- ✳ **Tongs**
- ✳ **Wire rack** (to fit over roasting pan)
- ✳ **Medium roasting pan**
- ✳ **Kettle or pan**
- ✳ **Oven mitts**
- ✳ **Skewer**
- ✳ **Grater**
- ✳ **Spatula or palette knife**

1 On a cutting board, carefully cut away the skin from the chicken thighs with a sharp knife—you will need to pull it off to free it completely. Use the knife to make two or three deep slashes in the meaty parts. Adult supervision is required.

2 Rinse the chicken, then pat dry on paper towels. Place in a shallow bowl.

3 Place the yogurt, paprika, curry paste, coriander and cumin seeds, and turmeric in a small bowl and mix together.

4 Spoon over the chicken thighs and turn over to coat in the paste.

5 Cover the chicken in its marinade with plastic wrap and let marinate in the refrigerator for at least 2 hours.

6 Preheat the oven to 400°F. Arrange the marinated chicken thighs on a wire rack set over a roasting pan, leaving a little room between them. Spread with any leftover marinade and drizzle with a little oil.

ⓘ = Watch out! Sharp or electrical tool in use.   🔥 = Watch out! Heat is involved.

10 Ask an adult to remove the roasting pan from the oven and lift off the chicken with a spatula or palette knife.

11 Transfer the chicken to serving dishes and serve with the yogurt mixture, rice, salad, and lemon wedges, if using. The cooked chicken is delicious eaten warm, or cold the next day, if desired.

7 Ask an adult to pour a little boiling water into the bottom of the roasting pan (to create steam). Cook in the preheated oven for 40 minutes, or until the juices run clear when the chicken is pierced deeply with a skewer.

8 With adult supervision, chop the scallions and mint on a cutting board.

9 Put the yogurt in a serving bowl. Grate the cucumber and stir in. Add the scallions and mint and mix. Season to taste.

Chicken fajitas

These fabulous fajitas are perfect for the weekend, and it's a lot of fun preparing all the different fillings and bringing them to the table so people can help themselves.

COOK'S TIP
► Soak the wooden skewers for at least 1 hour before using to stop them from burning as you cook the onions under the broiler.

serves **6**

ingredients
- **lime**, 2, finely grated rind of 1 and the juice of 2
- **olive oil**, ½ cup
- **garlic**, 1 clove, peeled and finely chopped
- **dried oregano**, ½ teaspoon
- **dried red chili flakes**, a good pinch
- **roasted coriander seeds**, 1 teaspoon, crushed
- **salt** and **ground black pepper**
- **boneless chicken breast fillets**, 6
- **Bermuda onions**, 3, peeled and thickly sliced
- **large red, yellow, or orange bell peppers**, 2, seeded and cut into strips
- **chopped fresh cilantro**, 2 tablespoons

for the salsa
- **tomatoes**, 3 medium, (about 1 pound), peeled, seeded, and chopped
- **garlic**, 2 cloves, peeled and finely chopped
- **red onion**, 1 small, peeled and finely chopped
- **green chile**, 1, seeded and finely chopped (optional)
- **lime**, ½, finely grated rind
- **fresh cilantro**, 2 tablespoons, chopped
- **superfine sugar**, a pinch
- **roasted cumin seeds**, ½–1 teaspoon, ground

to serve
- **soft flour tortillas**, 12–18
- **guacamole**
- **sour cream**, ½ cup
- **crisp lettuce leaves**
- **fresh cilantro sprigs**
- **lime wedges**

tools
✳ **Casserole**
✳ **Grater**
✳ **Juicer**
✳ **2 small sharp knives**
✳ **2 cutting boards**
✳ **Medium sharp knife**
✳ **Wooden skewer** (see Cook's Tip)
✳ **Broiler rack**
✳ **Oven mitts**
✳ **Grill pan**
✳ **Large skillet**
✳ **Wooden spoon**

1 In a casserole, mix the lime rind and juice, 5 tablespoons of the oil, the garlic, oregano, chili flakes, and coriander seeds, and season. With adult supervision, slash the skin on the chicken several times. Turn them in the mixture.

2 Cover and set aside to marinate for 2 hours.

3 To make the salsa, combine the tomatoes, garlic, onion, chile (if using), lime rind, and cilantro. Season with salt, pepper, superfine sugar, and cumin.

4 Set the salsa aside for 30 minutes, then taste and adjust the seasoning, adding more cumin and sugar, if necessary.

(!)

5 Ask an adult to heat the broiler. Thread the onions onto a skewer.

6 Brush the onions with 1 tablespoon of the remaining oil and season. Broil for about 10 minutes, until the onions are softened and charred in places. Adult supervision is required. Preheat the oven to 400°F.

7 Cover the casserole containing the marinated chicken with foil, then cook in the oven for 20 minutes. Remove from the oven, then cook in a grill pan for 8–10 minutes, until browned and fully cooked. Adult supervision is required.

(!) = Watch out! Sharp or electrical tool in use.   ( ) = Watch out! Heat is involved.

9 Add the chicken cooking juices and fry over a high heat, stirring frequently, until the liquid evaporates. Stir in the chopped cilantro. Adult supervision is required.

10 Reheat the tortillas following the instructions on the package.

11 Using a sharp knife, cut the chicken into strips and transfer to a serving dish. Place the pepper mixture and the salsa in separate dishes.

8 Meanwhile, with adult supervision, heat the remaining oil in a large skillet, add the bell peppers, and cook for 10 minutes, until softened and browned in places. Add the broiled onions and fry briskly for 2–3 minutes.

12 Serve the dishes of chicken, onions and bell peppers, and salsa with the tortillas, guacamole, sour cream, lettuce, and cilantro for people to help themselves. Serve lime wedges on the side so that people can choose whether to squeeze over the lime juice, depending on their personal preference.

main meals   **141**

Turkey croquettes

These crunchy potato and turkey bites served with a really tomatoey sauce are so tasty you may want to make double the amount!

serves 4

ingredients
- **potatoes**, 4 medium, peeled and diced
- **eggs**, 3
- **milk**, 2 tablespoons
- **salt** and **ground black pepper**
- **turkey strips**, 6 ounces, chopped
- **scallions**, 2, finely sliced
- **fresh bread crumbs**, 2 cups
- **vegetable oil**, for deep-frying

for the sauce
- **olive oil**, 1 tablespoon
- **onion**, 1, finely chopped
- **canned chopped tomatoes**, 14 ounces
- **tomato paste**, 2 tablespoons
- **chopped fresh parsley**, 1 tablespoon

tools
- ✳ **2 medium pans**
- ✳ **Colander**
- ✳ **Potato masher**
- ✳ **Mixing bowl**
- ✳ **Wooden spoon**
- ✳ **2 small shallow dishes**
- ✳ **Heavy pan or deep-fat fryer**
- ✳ **Draining spoon**

1 Put the potatoes in a pan and cover with water. Bring to a boil and boil for 10–15 minutes, until tender. Adult supervision is required.

2 Ask an adult to drain in a colander. Return to the pan. Heat gently for 1–2 minutes to make sure all the excess water evaporates. Remove from the heat.

3 Mash the potatoes with two eggs and the milk, until smooth. Season well. Stir in the turkey and scallions. Transfer to a mixing bowl, cover, and chill for 1 hour.

4 Meanwhile, **to make the sauce**, heat the oil in a medium pan and fry the onion for 5 minutes, stirring occasionally, until softened. Drain and add the tomatoes and tomato paste, stir, and bring to a boil. Simmer for 10 minutes. Stir in the parsley and season to taste. Adult supervision is required.

5 Remove the potato mixture from the refrigerator and divide into eight pieces. Wet your hands and shape each into a sausage shape. Place the remaining egg in a dish and spread the bread crumbs on another dish. Dip the croquettes into the egg and then bread crumbs to coat.

6 Ask an adult to heat the oil in a heavy pan or deep-fat fryer to 330°F and add the croquettes. Cook for 5 minutes, or until golden and crisp. Ask an adult to remove with a draining spoon and drain on paper towels. Reheat the sauce gently and serve with the croquettes.

ⓘ = Watch out! Sharp or electrical tool in use.   = Watch out! Heat is involved.

Turkey surprise packages

You'll have cooking all wrapped up with this easy supper recipe. Cooking in paper packages is really healthy because it doesn't require any added oil.

serves **4**

ingredients
- **scallions**, 2
- **fennel**, 2 ounces
- **carrot**, 1
- **celery**, 1 small stalk
- **turkey breast steaks**, 4, weighing 5–6 ounces each
- **chopped parsley**, 2 tablespoons
- **fatty bacon**, 8 strips
- **lemon**, 1, grated rind and juice
- **salt** and **ground black pepper**
- **lemon** or **lime wedges**, to serve

fennel

tools
✳ **2 cutting boards**
✳ **Medium sharp knife**
✳ **Pastry brush**
✳ **Large, shallow roasting pan**
✳ **Oven mitts**
✳ **Spatula or palette knife**

1 On a cutting board, cut the scallions, fennel, carrot, and celery into thin sticks of about the same thickness. Set aside. Adult supervision is required.

2 Lay the turkey breast steaks flat on a separate board and pat chopped parsley over each.

3 Wrap two strips of bacon around each turkey breast in a cross shape. Preheat the oven to 375°F.

4 Cut four 12-inch circles out of parchment paper, brush lightly with oil, and put a turkey breast just off center on each one.

5 Arrange the vegetable strips on top of the turkey breasts, sprinkle the lemon rind and juice over, and season well.

6 Fold each paper circle over the meat and vegetables and, starting at one side, twist and fold the paper edges together.

7 Work your way around the semicircles of parchment paper, sealing the edges of the packages together neatly.

8 Put the packages in the roasting pan and cook for 35–45 minutes, or until the meat is cooked and tender when tested with the tip of a knife. Ask an adult to remove from the oven and lift out the packages with a spatula.

9 Serve the packages with the lemon wedges on the side to squeeze over them.

Pork and pineapple curry

This easy curry is packed with juicy chunks of meat and pineapple in a fragrant, creamy sauce. Serve with plenty of long-grain rice to soak up all those delicious juices.

serves **4**

ingredients
- **pineapple**, ½ medium
- **canned coconut milk**, 14 ounces
- **Thai red curry paste**, 2 teaspoons
- **pork tenderloin**, 14 ounces, cut into bite-size pieces
- **Thai fish sauce**, 1 tablespoon
- **Barbados** or **brown sugar**, 1 teaspoon
- **tamarind paste**, 1 teaspoon
- **kaffir lime leaves**, 2
- **fresh red chile**, 1, cut into thin slices (optional)
- **cooked rice**, to serve (optional)

pineapple

tools
- ❋ **Cutting board**
- ❋ **Large sharp knife**
- ❋ **Small sharp knife**
- ❋ **Medium mixing bowl**
- ❋ **Measuring cup**
- ❋ **Large pan**
- ❋ **Wooden spoon**

1 Ask an adult to help you slice the bottom and top off the pineapple. Stand upright. Cut away the skin by "sawing" down. Using the tip of a small, sharp knife, cut out the "eyes" (dark round pieces). Cut the pineapple in half lengthwise, then cut out the core. Chop one half into bite-size pieces.

2 Pour the coconut milk into a bowl and let the cream rises to the surface. Scoop the cream into a measuring cup—you should have about 1 cup. If required, add a little of the liquid.

3 Pour the coconut cream into the pan and bring it to a boil. Adult supervision is required.

4 Cook over a medium heat for 8 minutes, until the cream separates, stirring frequently.

5 Stir in the red curry paste. Cook, stirring occasionally, for about 3 minutes, until the sauce thickens slightly.

6 Add the pork, fish sauce, and sugar. Mix the tamarind paste with 1 tablespoon of warm water in the cup, then add to the sauce and stir well. Cook, stirring, for 2–3 minutes, until the sugar has dissolved and the pork is cooked. Adult supervision is required.

7 Add the remaining coconut milk and the lime leaves and pineapple chunks to the pan and bring to a boil. Reduce the heat and simmer gently for 3 minutes, or until the pork is fully cooked.

8 Transfer to serving dishes, add the chile, if using, and serve with rice.

Thai pork burgers

These zesty burgers make a tasty change from the usual burger. Serve with slices of tomato and crunchy lettuce in a warm bread roll for a flavorsome snack.

serves 4

ingredients
- **ground pork**, 1 pound
- **salt** and **ground black pepper**
- **fresh ginger**, 1-inch piece, peeled
- **lemongrass**, 1 stalk
- **sunflower oil**, 2 tablespoons
- **4 bread rolls**, to serve
- **2 tomatoes**, to serve
- **lettuce**, ½ head, to serve

tools
- ✳ **Large mixing bowl**
- ✳ **Grater**
- ✳ **Cutting board**
- ✳ **Medium sharp knife**
- ✳ **Wooden spoon**
- ✳ **Plate**
- ✳ **Nonstick grill pan**

1 Place the pork in a large mixing bowl and season well with salt and ground black pepper.

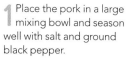
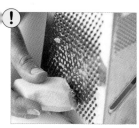

2 Grate the ginger using a fine grater. Remove the tough outer layers from the lemongrass stalk and discard, then chop the center finely. Adult supervision is required.

3 Add the ginger and lemongrass to the bowl and mix well. Wet your hands slightly and shape the meat into four patties, place on a plate, cover with plastic wrap, and chill for 20 minutes.

4 Heat the oil in a large, nonstick grill pan and add the patties.

5 Cook for 3–4 minutes on each side, until golden and cooked through. Adult supervision is required.

6 With adult supervision, cut the bread rolls in half, slice the tomatoes, and shred the lettuce. Drain the patties on paper towels, then serve in the rolls with the tomatoes and lettuce.

FACT FILE
LEMONGRASS
Readily available from most Asian stores, lemongrass has a wonderful fresh, lemony flavor and aroma. If you have some left over, don't throw it away. Place it into a sealed food bag and freeze for up to 3 months.

lemongrass

Sausage casserole

This casserole is guaranteed to keep you warm on a chilly winter night, and it's great for serving to guests.

serves **4–6**

ingredients

- **large pork, beef, lamb or vegetarian sausages**, 1 pound
- **vegetable oil**, 1 tablespoon
- **onion**, 1, peeled and chopped
- **carrots**, 4 medium (about 8 ounces), peeled and chopped
- **all-purpose flour**, 1 tablespoon
- **beef stock**, scant 2 cups
- **tomato paste**, 3 teaspoons
- **light brown sugar**, 3 teaspoons
- **Worcestershire sauce**, 1 tablespoon
- **Dijon mustard**, 2 teaspoons
- **bay leaf**, 1
- **dried chile**, 1, chopped
- **salt** and **ground black pepper**
- **canned mixed beans in water**, 14 ounces, drained
- **mashed potatoes**, to serve

tools

- ✳ Small sharp knife
- ✳ Fork
- ✳ Large skillet
- ✳ Spatula or tongs
- ✳ Casserole with lid
- ✳ Draining spoon
- ✳ Wooden spoon
- ✳ Oven mitts

1 Preheat the oven to 350°F. Separate the sausages if necessary by cutting the links with the knife, then prick several times all over with the fork.

2 With adult supervision, heat the vegetable oil in a large skillet over a medium-high heat.

3 Add the sausages and cook, turning frequently with the spatula or tongs, for about 10 minutes, until evenly browned on all sides but not cooked through. Transfer the browned sausages to the casserole bowl with the draining spoon. Adult supervision is required.

4 Add the onion and carrots to the skillet and fry for about 5 minutes, until lightly browned. Add the flour, stir, then transfer to the casserole.

5 Stir in ⅔ cup of the beef stock and 1 teaspoon each of the tomato paste and sugar.

6 Add the Worcestershire sauce, remaining beef stock, tomato paste, sugar, mustard, bay leaf, and chile to the pan. Season, bring to a boil, then pour into the casserole. Cover and cook for 30 minutes. Add the beans and cook for another 5 minutes. Serve immediately with mashed potatoes.

(!) = Watch out! Sharp or electrical tool in use.   (🧤) = Watch out! Heat is involved.

Mini "toads-in-the-hole"

The toads in this dish are little sausages, while the holes are made in a batter.

serves 2

ingredients

- **all-purpose flour**, 4 tablespoons
- **salt**, a pinch
- **egg**, 1
- **milk**, 4 tablespoons
- **chipolata sausages**, 3
- **vegetable oil**, 1 teaspoon
- **baked beans** and **steamed green beans**, to serve

tools

- ✳ Strainer
- ✳ Large mixing bowl
- ✳ Whisk
- ✳ Pitcher
- ✳ 2 small sharp knives
- ✳ Two 4-inch muffin pans
- ✳ Pastry brush
- ✳ Oven mitts

1 Sift the flour into a large bowl. Add a pinch of salt. Make a well in the center. Whisk the egg and add to the well. Gradually whisk in the milk, beating until a smooth batter is formed. Pour into a pitcher.

2 Preheat the oven to 425°F.

3 Press the center of each sausage with your finger to separate the meat into two pieces. Twist in the middle, then cut in half. Brush two 4-inch muffin pans with oil. Add three pieces of sausage to each, put in the oven, and cook for 5 minutes, until the sausages are opaque.

4 Ask an adult to remove the pans from the oven and immediately pour in the batter. Return to the oven and bake for 15 minutes, until risen and golden.

5 Ask an adult to remove from the oven. Loosen with a knife. Serve with baked beans and green beans.

COOK'S TIP

▶ To make sure you get a light, well-risen batter it is important that the batter is added to a very hot pan and returned to the oven as quickly and carefully as possible. It is also necessary to avoid opening the oven during the cooking time.

Lamb and potato pies

These easy-to-make pies are made with chunks of lamb, potato, onion, and an unsweetened pastry. They taste truly great and look very impressive.

serves **4**

ingredients

for the pastry
- **all-purpose flour**, 5 cups
- **butter**, generous 1 cup, cubed
- **chilled water**, 120ml/4fl ½ cup

- **boneless lamb** or **mutton**, 1 pound
- **onion**, 1, finely chopped
- **carrots**, 2, finely chopped
- **potato**, 1, finely chopped
- **celery**, 2 stalks, finely chopped
- **salt** and **ground black pepper**
- **egg**, 1, beaten

tools
- ✴ **Large bowl**
- ✴ **Table knife**
- ✴ **Parchment paper**
- ✴ **Small sharp knife**
- ✴ **Cutting board**
- ✴ **Spoon**
- ✴ **Rolling pin**
- ✴ **Serving plate**
- ✴ **Pastry brush**
- ✴ **2 baking sheets**
- ✴ **Oven mitts**

1 **To make the pastry**, put the flour into a large bowl and add the butter. Rub the butter into the flour with your fingertips until the mixture resembles coarse bread crumbs.

2 Add the chilled water. Mix with a knife until the mixture clings together.

3 Turn onto a floured counter and knead once or twice until smooth. Wrap in parchment paper and chill for 20 minutes before using.

4 Trim any fat or gristle from the meat and cut it up into very small pieces. Place in a large bowl and add the chopped onion, carrots, potato, and celery. Mix well and season to taste.

5 Preheat the oven to 350°F. Cut off one-third off the pastry ball and reserve to make the lids. Roll out the rest.

6 Cut out six circles by placing a plate on the pastry and cutting around it.

7 Divide the meat mixture between the circles, piling it in the middle.

8 Roll out the reserved pastry. Cut out six circles, about 4 inches across.

9 Lay the lids on top of the meat. Dampen the edges of the bottoms, bring the pastry up, and pinch the edges together.

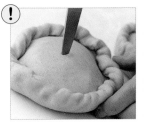

10 Make a hole in the top of each pie, brush with egg, and slide onto baking sheets. Bake for 1 hour. Serve hot or cold.

(!) = Watch out! Sharp or electrical tool in use.   = Watch out! Heat is involved.

Shepherd's pie

You can't go wrong with a shepherd's pie—especially in the cold winter months. Double or triple the quantities, depending on how many you want to serve.

serves **2**

ingredients
- **onion**, ½ small, peeled
- **lean ground beef**, 6 ounces
- **all-purpose flour**, 2 teaspoons
- **ketchup**, 2 tablespoons
- **beef stock**, ⅔ cup
- **dried mixed herbs**, a pinch
- **salt** and **ground black pepper**
- **rutabaga**, 2 ounces, peeled
- **parsnip**, ½ (about 2 ounces), peeled
- **potato**, 1 medium (4 ounces), peeled
- **milk**, 2 teaspoons
- **butter**, 1 tablespoon
- **cooked carrots** and **peas**, to serve

tools
- ✳ Cutting board
- ✳ Medium sharp knife
- ✳ Large nonstick skillet
- ✳ Wooden spoon
- ✳ Large pan
- ✳ Colander
- ✳ Potato masher
- ✳ 2 casseroles or ovenproof bowls
- ✳ Fork
- ✳ Oven mitts

1 Preheat the oven to 375°F. On a cutting board, finely chop the onion. Adult supervision is required. Place in a large skillet with the beef.

3 Add the flour, stirring, then add the ketchup, stock, and herbs. Season. Bring to a boil, reduce the heat, cover, and simmer for 30 minutes, stirring often. Adult supervision is required.

5 Place the vegetables in a pan with water and bring to a boil. Reduce the heat and simmer for about 20 minutes, until tender. Ask an adult to drain in a colander. Return to the pan.

2 Dry-fry (fry without oil) over a low heat, stirring constantly, until the beef is evenly browned.

4 With adult supervision, chop the rutabaga, parsnip, and potato.

6 Mash the vegetables with the milk and half of the butter.

7 Spoon the meat into two casseroles. Place the vegetables on top and fluff up with a fork. Dot with the remaining butter.

8 Place on a baking sheet and cook for 25–30 minutes, until browned on top. Serve with cooked carrots and peas.

Crown roast

This cut of meat is really just lamb chops that are still joined together. Here, two racks are interlocked, creating a cavity that is stuffed with fruity rice.

serves 4

ingredients

- **racks of lamb**, 2, with at least four chops in each piece
- **butter**, 2 tablespoons
- **scallions**, 4, roughly chopped
- **basmati rice**, ⅔ cup
- **stock**, 1¼ cups
- **ripe mango**, 1 large, peeled and roughly chopped
- **salt** and **ground black pepper**
- **boiled new potatoes** and **minted peas**, to serve

tools
- ✴ **Small sharp knife**
- ✴ **Cutting board**
- ✴ **Large nonstick pan**
- ✴ **Wooden spoon**
- ✴ **Roasting pan**
- ✴ **Spoon**
- ✴ **Kitchen string**
- ✴ **Oven mitts**

1 Use a sharp knife to cut the meat off the ends of the bones. Discard the skin. Scrape the bones clean. Chop the trimmings into pieces. (The butcher can do all this, if you prefer.) Adult supervision is required.

2 With adult supervision, melt the butter in a pan, add the scallions and scraps and fry until the meat has browned.

3 Add the rice, stir well, and pour in the stock. Bring to a boil, lower the heat, put a lid on the pan, and let the mixture simmer for 8–10 minutes, until the rice is tender. Adult supervision is required.

4 Remove the pan from the heat, stir in the mango, check the seasoning, and adjust as necessary. Preheat the oven to 375°F.

5 Place the two racks of lamb next to each other and spoon the stuffing in between them. Interlock the bones and tie together with a piece of string. Stand in a roasting pan.

6 Wrap the ends of the bones in aluminum foil. Cook for 1½–2 hours, until the lamb is cooked (see Cook's Tips). Serve with new potatoes and peas.

COOK'S TIP
▶ To test if the lamb is done, insert a skewer deep into the thickest part of the meat. For slightly pink lamb, the juices that run from the hole should be just tinged with pink. For well-done lamb, the meat juices should be clear.

⚠ = Watch out! Sharp or electrical tool in use.   ✊ = Watch out! Heat is involved.

Lamb stew

Tender cubes of lamb and vegetables smothered in a rich gravy are the perfect partner to hot, creamy mashed potato or crusty bread…mmmm!

serves 2

ingredients
- **lamb fillet**, 4 ounces
- **onion**, ¼ small
- **carrot**, 1 small (about 2 ounces)
- **parsnip**, ½ small (about 2 ounces)
- **potato**, 1 small
- **oil**, 1 teaspoon
- **lamb stock**, ⅔ cup
- **dried rosemary**, a pinch of
- **salt** and **ground black pepper**
- **crusty bread**, to serve

tools
- ✳ **2 medium sharp knives**
- ✳ **2 cutting boards**
- ✳ **Vegetable peeler**
- ✳ **Large nonstick pan with a lid**
- ✳ **Wooden spoon**

1 Rinse the lamb under cold running water, then pat dry on paper towels. Cut away any fat or gristle and cut into small cubes. Adult supervision is required.

2 Using a separate, clean knife and cutting board, peel and chop the onion, carrot, and parsnip. Peel the potato and cut into larger pieces. Adult supervision is required.

3 Heat the oil in a pan. Add the lamb and onion, and fry gently for about 10 minutes, stirring occasionally, until the meat is browned. Adult supervision is required when using heat.

4 Add the carrot, parsnip, and potato and fry for 3 minutes, stirring occasionally, until the vegetables have softened.

5 Add the lamb stock, dried rosemary, and a little salt and pepper to the pan and stir to mix. Bring to a boil, cover, reduce the heat slightly, and simmer for 35–40 minutes, or until the meat and vegetables are tender.

6 Spoon the stew into shallow bowls and serve immediately with crusty bread.

VARIATION
- This stew would work just as well with braising beef and beef stock, or pork tenderloin and stock. For vegetarians, omit the meat and add 4 ounces of extra root vegetables, such as carrots or parsnips.

carrots

Steak with tomato salsa

Nothing beats a nice juicy steak, and since they require very little cooking, they are quick and easy to rustle up. Serve with a wonderfully tangy tomato salsa.

serves 2

ingredients
- **large plum tomatoes**, 3
- **steaks**, 2, about ¾ inch thick (*see* Cook's Tip)
- **salt** and **ground black pepper**
- **scallions**, 2, thinly sliced
- **balsamic vinegar**, 2 tablespoons

tools
* Small sharp knife
* Large heatproof bowl
* Cutting board
* Teaspoon
* Large nonstick skillet
* Tongs
* Wooden spoon

COOK'S TIP
► Choose top round, sirloin, or porterhouse steak. If you prefer to broil the steak, the timing will be the same as in the recipe, but you must take into account the thickness of the meat—thick pieces take longer.

1 Preheat the oven to 330°F. Score a cross in the top of the tomatoes. Place in a heatproof bowl, then ask an adult to pour over boiling water. Let stand for 5 minutes. When the tomato skins start to split, drain and rinse under cold water. Peel away the skin.

2 With adult supervision, cut the tomatoes in half. Scoop out the seeds with a teaspoon and discard. Chop the flesh into small pieces. Set aside.

3 Trim any excess fat from the steaks, then season on both sides. Adult supervision is required.

4 Heat the skillet and cook the steaks for about 3 minutes on each side for medium rare. Cook for a little longer if you like your steak well cooked. Remove from the skillet with tongs and transfer to plates. Adult supervision is required. Keep warm while you prepare the salsa.

5 Add the scallions to the skillet with the tomatoes, balsamic vinegar, 2 tablespoons of water, and some seasoning. Stir briefly until warm, scraping up any meat residue. Spoon the salsa over the steaks and serve.

(!) = Watch out! Sharp or electrical tool in use.   = Watch out! Heat is involved.

Cheesy burgers

These look the same as ordinary burgers, but contain a hidden heart of soft, melted cheese. Serve with your favorite accompaniments, such as salad and salsa.

serves **4**

ingredients
- **lean ground beef**, 1 pound
- **bread**, 2 slices, crusts removed
- **egg**, 1
- **scallions**, 4, roughly chopped
- **garlic**, 1 clove, peeled and chopped
- **salt** and **ground black pepper**
- **mango chutney**, 1 tablespoons
- **dried mixed herbs**, 2 teaspoons
- **mozzarella cheese**, 2oz
  (see Variation)
- **burger buns**, 4, to serve
- **salad greens**, to serve (optional)

tools
- ✳ **Blender or food processor**
- ✳ **Cutting board**
- ✳ **Small sharp knife**
- ✳ **Spatula or palette knife**
- ✳ **Oven mitts**

1 Put the ground beef, bread, egg, chopped scallions, and garlic in a blender or food processor. Season, then blend in short bursts until everything is well combined. Adult supervision is required.

2 Add the chutney and herbs and blend again.

3 Divide the mixture into four equal portions. Wet your hands (to stop sticking) and shape each portion into a burger.

4 With adult supervision, cut the cheese into four pieces. Push one into the center of each burger and shape the meat around it.

5 Cover with plastic wrap and chill for about 30 minutes. Ask an adult to preheat the broiler to medium-hot.

6 Put the burgers on a foil-lined broiler pan and cook under the broiler for 10–18 minutes, turning once with a spatula or palette knife, until cooked through and brown. Adult supervision is required.

7 Split the buns in half, position some greens, if using, on the bottom, and place the burger on top. Sandwich with the other half.

VARIATION
- You can use any cheese instead of the mozzarella, if desired. Good ones that melt well and have a strong flavor include Cheddar cheese, American, Gruyère, Emmental, Monterey Jack, or Danish blue.

Danish blue

main meals   **153**

Desserts and drinks

Always the best part of a meal, desserts are well worth making yourself. This wonderful selection contains the works—from sticky chocolatey treats and fruity crumbles to creamy mousses, ice creams, and an impressive cheesecake. There is also a choice of super cool drinks, including fabulous fruit slushes and juices, as well as thick smoothies and milkshakes.

Magic chocolate pudding

Abracadabra…this gooey chocolate dessert, with a secret layer of sauce under a moist sponge topping, really is a magical dish to have up your sleeve.

serves **4**

ingredients

- **butter**, 4 tablespoons, plus extra for greasing
- **self-rising flour**, scant 1 cup
- **ground cinnamon**, 1 teaspoon
- **cocoa powder**, 5 tablespoons
- **light Barbados** or **brown sugar**, 1 cup
- **milk**, 2 cups
- **crème fraîche**, **strained plain yogurt**, **whipped cream**, or **vanilla ice cream**, to serve

tools

- ✳ 1½-quart ovenproof bowl
- ✳ Baking sheet
- ✳ Strainer or sifter
- ✳ 2 mixing bowls
- ✳ Medium pan
- ✳ Wooden spoon

1 Preheat the oven to 350°F. Lightly grease an ovenproof bowl, place it on a baking sheet, and set aside.

2 Sift the flour and ground cinnamon into a mixing bowl. Sift over 1 tablespoon of the cocoa and mix well.

3 Place the remaining butter in a medium pan. Add ½ cup of the Barbados sugar and ⅔ cup of the milk. Heat gently without boiling, stirring occasionally, until the butter has melted and all the sugar has dissolved. Remove from the heat. Adult supervision is required.

4 Stir the flour mixture into the pan. Pour the mixture into the prepared bowl and level the surface.

5 Mix the remaining sugar and cocoa in a bowl, then sprinkle over the pudding mixture. Pour the remaining milk evenly over the pudding.

FACT FILE

BARBADOS SUGAR

This type of sugar is unrefined, which means it has not been processed.

Barbados sugar

6 Bake for 45–50 minutes, or until the sponge has risen to the top and is firm to the touch. Serve hot, with the crème fraîche, yogurt, cream, or ice cream.

Rice pudding

A firm family favorite, rice pudding is delicious, easy to make, and perfect for a cold winter day. Stir in either honey or warm jelly for an extra-special treat.

serves 4

ingredients
- **raisins**, ½ cup
- **water**, 5 tablespoons
- **short-grain rice**, ½ cup
- **pared lemon peel**, 3 or 4 strips
- **water**, 1 cup
- **milk**, 2 cups
- **cinnamon stick**, 1, about 3 inches in length
- **sugar**, 1 cup
- **salt**, a pinch
- **butter**, 1 tablespoon, diced
- **toasted sliced almonds** (see Cook's Tip), to decorate (optional)
- **chilled orange segments**, to serve

tools
- ✳ Small pan
- ✳ Wooden spoon
- ✳ Large heavy pan
- ✳ Fork
- ✳ Strainer

short-grain rice

1 Put the raisins and water in a pan. Heat until warm, then remove from the heat. Adult supervision is required.

2 Mix the rice, lemon peel, and water in a pan and bring to a boil. Lower the heat, cover, and simmer, stirring occasionally, for 20 minutes. Remove the lemon peel.

3 Add the milk and the cinnamon to the pan, then stir. Continue to cook over a gentle heat until the rice has absorbed the milk.

4 Stir in the sugar and salt. Add the butter and stir constantly until the butter has melted. Adult supervision is required.

5 Drain the raisins in a strainer and stir into the rice mixture. Cook for 2–3 minutes, stirring to prevent it from sticking.

6 Transfer to serving bowls, top with the toasted sliced almonds, and serve with the orange segments.

COOK'S TIP
▶ To toast flaked almonds, either add to a heated small non-stickskillet (with no oil) and heat gently, stirring often, until golden. Or, spread on a baking sheet lined with foil and toast under a medium broiler for 1–2 minutes, until golden. Adult supervision is required.

Lazy fruit pastry

You don't need to be neat to make this dessert—it looks best when it's really craggy and rough. It is scrummy served hot or cold with whipped cream.

serves 6

ingredients
- **all-purpose flour**, 2 cups
- **superfine sugar**, 1 tablespoon
- **ground allspice**, 1 tablespoon
- **butter** or **margarine**, ⅔ cup
- **egg**, 1, separated
- **cooking apples**, 1 pound
- **lemon juice**, 2 tablespoons
- **raisins**, ⅔ cup
- **raw sugar**, ½ cup
- **hazelnuts**, ¼ cup, toasted and chopped (optional)

tools
* Mixing bowl
* Wooden spoon
* Rolling pin
* Nonstick baking sheet
* Vegetable peeler
* Small sharp knife
* Cutting board
* Pastry brush
* Oven mitts

1 Preheat the oven to 400°F. Put the flour, sugar, and spice in a bowl. Add the butter or margarine and rub it into the flour with your fingertips, until it resembles bread crumbs.

2 Add the egg yolk and use your hands to bring the mixture together. (You may need to add a little water).

3 Turn the dough onto a lightly floured counter and knead gently until smooth. Roll out the pastry with a rolling pin to make a rough circle about 12 inches across. Use the rolling pin to carefully lift the pastry onto a baking sheet. The pastry may hang over the edges slightly—this doesn't matter.

4 Peel the apples and cut them into quarters, then cut out the core. Discard the core and slice the apples on the cutting board. Adult supervision is required. Toss them in the lemon juice to stop them from turning brown.

5 Scatter some of the apples over the middle of the pastry, leaving a 4-inch border all around. Scatter some of the raisins over the top. Reserve 2 tablespoons of the sugar, then scatter some of the remaining sugar on top. Keep making layers of apple, raisins, and sugar until you have used them up.

6 Preheat the oven to 400°F. Fold up the pastry edges to cover the fruit, overlapping it where necessary. Brush the pastry with the egg white and sprinkle over the reserved sugar. Scatter over the nuts (if using). Cover the central hole with aluminum foil. Cook for 30–35 minutes, until the pastry is browned.

(!) = Watch out! Sharp or electrical tool in use.   = Watch out! Heat is involved.

Plum crumble

If you like to get your hands dirty when you cook, then you'll love rubbing a crumble mixture together. Whipped cream or ice cream are the perfect partners.

plums

serves **4–6**

ingredients
- **ripe red plums**, 2 pounds
- **superfine sugar**, ¼ cup

for the topping
- **all-purpose flour**, 1 cup
- **butter**, ½ cup, cut into pieces
- **superfine sugar**, ¼ cup
- **marzipan**, 6 ounces
- **rolled oats**, 4 tablespoons
- **sliced almonds**, 4 tablespoons
- **whipped cream**, to serve

tools
- ✳ Cutting board
- ✳ Knife
- ✳ Medium pan
- ✳ Large, shallow casserole
- ✳ Large mixing bowl
- ✳ Wooden spoon
- ✳ Grater
- ✳ Baking sheet
- ✳ Oven mitts

3 Spoon the plums into a shallow casserole.

1 Preheat the oven to 375°F. Cut the plums into quarters. Remove and discard the pits. Adult supervision is required.

2 Place the plums in a pan with the sugar and 2 tablespoons of water. Cover and simmer for 10 minutes, until the plums have softened. Adult supervision is required.

4 **To make the topping,** place the flour in a large mixing bowl. Add the pieces of butter and, using your fingertips, rub the butter into the flour until the mixture looks like bread crumbs. Stir in the superfine sugar.

5 Grate the marzipan on the largest holes of the grater. Adult supervision is required. Stir into the mixture with the oats and almonds. Spoon over the plums.

6 Place on a baking sheet and cook for 20–25 minutes, until golden brown. Let cool slightly and serve with whipped cream.

VARIATIONS
- You can vary the fruits, according to what is in season. Try cooking apples, peaches, or pears.
- If the plums are very tart, you may need to add extra sugar.
- You can also use hazelnuts, pecans, or pine nuts.

Lemon surprise pudding

The surprise comes when you come to serve this heavenly dessert and find that beneath the layer of fluffy sponge lies a smooth, tangy lemon sauce.

serves **4**

ingredients
- **butter**, 4 tablespoons, plus extra for greasing
- **lemons**, 2, grated rind and juice
- **superfine sugar**, ½ cup
- **eggs**, 2, separated
- **self-rising flour**, ½ cup
- **milk**, 1¼ cups
- **confectioners' sugar**, for dusting

tools
- ✳ 1¼-quart shallow casserole
- ✳ Wooden spoon or electric mixer
- ✳ 2 mixing bowls
- ✳ Whisk
- ✳ Large metal spoon
- ✳ Aluminum foil
- ✳ Roasting pan
- ✳ Oven mitts
- ✳ Strainer or sifter

1 Preheat the oven to 375°F. Lightly grease a 1¼-quart shallow casserole with butter.

2 Using a wooden spoon or an electric mixer, beat the remaining butter, lemon rind, and sugar in a bowl until creamy and pale in color. Add the egg yolks and flour and beat together. Adult supervision is required.

3 Gradually beat in the lemon juice and milk in several batches (the mixture may curdle, but don't worry). Be careful not to splash it everywhere.

4 In a large clean bowl, using a clean whisk, whisk the egg whites until they form stiff, dry peaks when the whisk is lifted out of the mixture.

5 Using a large metal spoon, fold the egg whites gently into the lemon mixture, then pour into the casserole.

6 Line a large roasting pan with a sheet of double-folded aluminum foil and position the casserole on top, so the sides of the foil come about 2 inches above the rim of the bowl.

7 Ask an adult to put the roasting pan in the oven and pour in hot water to come halfway up the sides of the casserole. Cook for 45 minutes, until golden brown.

8 Ask an adult to remove from the oven and take the casserole out of the roasting pan. Dust with sifted confectioners' sugar.

ⓘ = Watch out! Sharp or electrical tool in use.   ✊ = Watch out! Heat is involved.

Baked bananas

They may look slightly unappealing, but soft, cooked bananas served in their skins are simply delicious, especially with ice cream and a hot hazelnut sauce.

serves 4

ingredients
- **large bananas**, 4
- **lemon juice**, 1 tablespoon
- **vanilla ice cream**, 8 scoops

for the sauce
- **unsalted butter**, 2 tablespoons
- **hazelnuts**, ½ cup, toasted and coarsely chopped
- **light corn syrup**, 3 tablespoons
- **lemon juice**, 2 tablespoons

tools
- ✳ Nonstick baking sheet
- ✳ Pastry brush
- ✳ Small heavy pan
- ✳ Wooden spoon
- ✳ Oven mitts
- ✳ Small sharp knife

hazelnuts

1 Preheat the oven to 350°F. Place the unpeeled bananas on a baking sheet and generously brush the skins with lemon juice using a pastry brush.

2 Bake in the oven for about 20 minutes, until the skins are turning black and the bananas feel soft when gently squeezed.

3 Meanwhile, **make the sauce**. Melt the butter in a small heavy pan. Add the hazelnuts and cook over a low heat, stirring frequently, for 1 minute. Adult supervision is required.

4 Add the corn syrup and lemon juice and heat gently, stirring constantly with a wooden spoon, for 1 minute more.

5 To serve, ask an adult to remove the bananas from the oven. With adult supervision, slit each banana open along its length with a sharp knife and open out the skins.

6 Transfer to serving plates and serve with generous scoops of vanilla ice cream. Pour over the hazelnut sauce.

VARIATION
- To make a chocolate sauce, place ⅔ cup of heavy cream in a heavy pan with 3 ounces of milk chocolate, broken into squares, and 1 tablespoon of butter. With adult supervision, heat gently, stirring occasionally, until the chocolate has melted and the ingredients have combined to make a sauce. Pour over the bananas.

Banana and toffee ice cream

serves **4–6**

A combination of bananas, toffees, condensed milk, and cream are used to make this indulgent ice cream.

- **ingredients**
- **ripe bananas**, 3
- **lemon**, 1, juice of
- **canned sweetened condensed milk**, 12½ ounces
- **whipping cream**, ⅔ cup
- **toffees**, 5 ounces, plus extra to decorate

bananas

tools
* **Blender or food processor**
* **Plastic or rubber spatula**
* **Freezerproof container**
* **Metal spoon**
* **Kitchen scissors or hammer and cutting board (optional)**
* **Fork**

whipping cream

sweetened condensed milk

COOK'S TIP

▶ If you have an ice cream machine, mix the banana puree with the condensed milk and cream in a bowl, then transfer to the machine and churn, according to the manufacturer's instructions, until thick. Transfer to a freezerproof container, stir in the chunks of toffee, freeze the mixture for 3–5 hours, and serve as in the recipe.

3 Mix well to combine, cover, and freeze for about 4 hours, or until semi-frozen and mushy.

1 Peel the bananas and put them in a blender or food processor. Blend until smooth, then add the lemon juice and blend to mix. Adult supervision is required. Scrape into a freezerproof container.

2 Pour the condensed milk into the container, stirring with a metal spoon, then stir in the cream.

4 Meanwhile, cut the toffees into small pieces with scissors. Alternatively, put the toffees in the refrigerator until cold and hard, then transfer to a cutting board and smash with a small hammer.

5 Beat the semi-frozen ice cream with a fork to break up the ice crystals, then stir in the toffees.

6 Return to the freezer for 3–5 hours, or until firm. Remove from the freezer and let soften slightly, then scoop into bowls or glasses and decorate with chopped toffees. Serve immediately.

   (!) = Watch out! Sharp or electrical tool in use. = Watch out! Heat is involved.

Pineapple sorbet on sticks

Make sure you choose a ripe pineapple
so that you get maximum sweetness.

makes about 12

ingredients
- **pineapple**, 1 medium (about 2½ pounds)
- **superfine sugar**, ½ cup
- **lime juice**, 2 tablespoons

tools
- ✳ **Cutting board**
- ✳ **Medium and small sharp knives**
- ✳ **Blender or food processor**
- ✳ **Plastic strainer**
- ✳ **Mixing bowl**
- ✳ **Small heavy pan**
- ✳ **Wooden spoon**
- ✳ **Freezerproof container**
- ✳ **Electric mixer**
- ✳ **12 popsicle molds and sticks**

1 Ask an adult to help you slice off the bottom and top of the pineapple. Stand it upright on a board. Cut away the skin by cutting down with a sawing action. Use a small knife to cut out the "eyes" (small, dark, rough pieces).

2 Cut the pineapple in half lengthwise and cut away the core in the middle.

3 Pulp the pineapple in a blender or food processor. Adult supervision is required. Press through a strainer placed over a bowl to extract as much juice as you can.

4 Ask an adult to help you heat the sugar and 1¼ cups water in a pan, stirring frequently, until the sugar dissolves. Boil for 3 minutes, without stirring.

5 Remove from the heat and let cool. Stir the lime and pineapple juice into the syrup, then chill until cold. Pour into a nonmetallic freezerproof container and freeze for 3–4 hours.

6 Twice during the first 2 hours, beat with an electric mixer until smooth, then return to the freezer. Adult supervision is required.

COOK'S TIP
▶ If you don't have popsicle molds, you can use clean yogurt containers instead.

7 Spoon the mixture into 12 popsicle molds. Press a popsicle stick into the center of each. Freeze overnight until firm.

8 To serve, dip the molds in hot water for 1–2 seconds, then pull each popsicle from its mold.

Strawberry mousse

Creamy and fruity, this long-standing favorite is easy to make and tastes great.

serves **4**

ingredients
- **strawberries**, 9 ounces, hulled
- **superfine sugar**, ½ cup
- **cold water**, ⅔ cup
- **powdered gelatin**, 1 tablespoon, or **leaf gelatin**, 8 sheets
- **boiling water**, ¼ cup
- **heavy cream**, 1¼ cups
- **fresh mint leaves**, to decorate

strawberries

tools
- ❋ Small sharp knife
- ❋ Cutting board
- ❋ Food processor or blender
- ❋ Measuring cup
- ❋ Large heatproof bowl
- ❋ Metal spoon
- ❋ Large mixing bowl
- ❋ Whisk

1 With adult supervision, chop most of the strawberries, reserving a few whole ones for decoration.

2 Transfer to a food processor or blender, add the sugar and ⅓ cup of water, and blend to a smooth puree. Adult supervision is required.

3 Put the remaining cold water in a large bowl and sprinkle over the gelatin (or immerse the leaf gelatin, if using).

4 Let the gelatin soak for 5 minutes, then ask an adult to add the boiling water and let stand for 2–3 minutes, or until the gelatin has dissolved completely.

5 Add the strawberry-and-sugar mixture to the bowl of gelatin and mix to combine. Chill for about 30 minutes in the refrigerator, until the mixture has thickened.

6 Lightly whip the cream in a large bowl, until soft peaks form, then fold into the strawberry mixture.

7 Spoon the mousse into serving glasses and chill overnight. Just before serving, garnish with a whole strawberry and some mint leaves.

VARIATION
- You can use other types of berries, such as raspberries or red currants, or ripe peaches and nectarines to make this mousse instead of strawberries. Taste and add more sugar if necessary.

(!) = Watch out! Sharp or electrical tool in use.   = Watch out! Heat is involved.

Strawberries and meringue

Perfect for summer when strawberries are at their best, this dessert consists of a mixture of whipped cream, crushed meringue, and sliced strawberries.

serves **4**

ingredients
- **ripe strawberries**, 1 pound
- **elderflower syrup** or **fruit juice** (such as orange, apple, or pomegranate), 3 tablespoons
- **heavy cream**, 1¼ cups
- **meringues** or **meringue baskets**, 4

tools
- ✳ **Cutting board**
- ✳ **Small sharp knife**
- ✳ **3 mixing bowls**
- ✳ **Whisk**
- ✳ **Large metal spoon**

meringue basket

COOK'S TIPS
▶ This dessert is popular in the English school Eton College, where it is served at the annual summer picnic.
▶ Do not let the dessert chill for more than about 12 hours or it will turn mushy.
▶ This is a great way of using up leftover pieces of meringue.

1 Remove the green leaves from the top of the strawberries by twisting and pulling them out (known as hulling).

2 Slice the fruit. Set aside a few pretty slices for decoration, then put the rest into a bowl. Adult supervision is required.

3 Sprinkle the strawberry slices with the elderflower syrup or fruit juice. Cover the bowl and chill in the refrigerator for about 2 hours.

4 In a clean bowl, whisk the cream until it has thickened and is standing up in soft peaks.

5 Put the meringues in a bowl and use your hands to crush them into small pieces. Reserve a small handful for decoration.

6 Add the strawberries, syrup or juice, and most of the meringue to the cream and fold in gently using a large metal spoon.

7 Spoon into serving dishes and chill until required. Before serving, decorate with the reserved strawberries and meringue.

Chocolate banana fools

You won't be a fool if you make these scrummy desserts. If you don't know how to make fresh custard, you can use a custard mix and follow the package instructions.

serves 4

ingredients
- **semisweet chocolate**, 4 ounces, chopped
- **fresh custard**, 1¼ cups
- **bananas**, 2

tools
* Heatproof bowl
* Medium pan (optional)
* Mixing bowl
* Large metal spoon
* Cutting board
* Small sharp knife

COOK'S TIP

▶ To make chocolate decorations, line a baking sheet with parchment paper. Melt about 2 ounces of chopped chocolate in a heatproof bowl in the microwave, with adult supervision. Spoon into an icing bag and pipe shapes such as hearts on to the parchment. Chill until set, then peel away the shapes.

1 Put the chocolate in a heatproof bowl and melt in the microwave on high power for 1–2 minutes. Alternatively, place over a pan of barely simmering water, making sure the water doesn't touch the bottom of the bowl. Heat until the chocolate has melted. Adult supervision is required.

2 Remove the bowl from the pan (if using), stir, then set aside to cool.

3 Pour the custard into a mixing bowl and partially fold in the melted chocolate using a large metal spoon. Do not mix it in completely—aim to create a rippled effect.

4 Peel and slice the bananas and gently stir these into the chocolate-and-custard mixture, being careful not to overstir or you will lose the rippled effect.

5 Spoon the dessert into four glasses and chill for 30–60 minutes, until thick, before serving.

(!) = Watch out! Sharp or electrical tool in use.   🧤 = Watch out! Heat is involved.

Banana and apricot trifle

This trifle is perfect if you are having a party—if it's a sleepover, you will be sneaking down for leftovers!

serves **6–8**

ingredients
- **apricot**, **lemon**, or **tangerine gelatin**, ¼ package
- **apricot conserve**, 4 tablespoons
- **ginger cake**, 6–8 ounces
- **bananas**, 3
- **fresh custard** or **custard mix**, prepared following package instructions, 1¼ cups
- **sugar**, ½ cup, plus extra for sprinkling
- **heavy cream**, 1¼ cups

bananas

tools
✳ 2 heavy pans	✳ Cutting board	✳ Rolling pin
✳ Wooden spoon	✳ Baking sheet	✳ Mixing bowl
✳ Small sharp knife	✳ Aluminum foil	✳ Whisk

1 Put the flavored gelatin, apricot conserve, and 4 tablespoons of water in a heavy pan and heat, stirring once or twice, until dissolved. Adult supervision is required. Set aside until cool.

2 Cut the ginger cake into cubes and place in a deep serving bowl or dish.

3 Cut two of the bananas into thick slices. Adult supervision is required.

4 Pour the cooled gelatin mixture over the cake. Arrange the banana slices on top of the gelatin, then pour over the custard. Chill for 1–2 hours, until the custard is set.

5 **To make the caramel,** cover a baking sheet with foil. Ask an adult to help you heat the sugar with 4 tablespoons of water in a heavy pan until the sugar dissolves. Increase the heat and boil without stirring until just golden. Pour onto the foil and let stand until hard. Smash to break into pieces.

6 Place the cream in a bowl and whisk until it stands in soft peaks.

7 Spread the cream over the custard, then cut the reserved banana into slices and arrange on top of the cream with the caramel pieces. Serve the trifle immediately.

Very berry cheesecake

Making this creamy, sweet cheesecake involves several easy stages, but it tastes and looks so good it is well worth the effort and time it requires.

serves *8–10*

ingredients

for the base
- **butter**, ¾ cup
- **graham crackers**, 8 ounces

for the topping
- **lemons**, 2, rind and juice
- **gelatin**, scant ½-ounce envelope
- **cottage cheese**, 1 cup
- **cream cheese**, scant 1 cup
- **canned condensed milk**, 14 ounces
- **strawberries**, 4 cups, hulled
- **raspberries**, 1 cup

COOK'S TIPS

▶ If you don't have a blender or food processor, make cookie crumbs by placing the cookies in two plastic sandwich bags, one inside the other for extra strength. Gently smash with a rolling pin until you have crumbs. Use plain cookies if you don't have graham crackers.

cookies

▶ A lot of people think gelatin is tricky to use, but it is actually easy as long as you follow a few simple rules: always add gelatin to the liquid, never the other way around or it will turn lumpy and be unusable; make sure that the gelatin and the liquid are the same temperature or it will turn stringy; always add the gelatin gradually, stirring it into the liquid well each time so it is completely combined before you add a little more.

tools
- ✳ Pencil
- ✳ 8-inch round, loose-bottom, nonstick, spring-clip cake pan
- ✳ Parchment paper
- ✳ Scissors
- ✳ 2 medium pans
- ✳ Blender or food processor
- ✳ Spoon
- ✳ Heatproof bowl
- ✳ Strainer
- ✳ Cutting board
- ✳ Sharp knife
- ✳ Palette knife

1 With a pencil, draw around the bottom of an 8-inch round, loose-bottom, nonstick spring-clip cake pan onto parchment paper. Cut out the parchment circle and use to line the bottom of the pan.

2 To make the base, put the butter in a pan and melt over a low heat. Break the cookies in pieces, put them in a blender or food processor, and blend until they are crumbs (see Cook's Tips). Stir into the butter. Adult supervision is required.

3 Tip the buttery crumbs into the cake pan and use a spoon to spread the mixture in a thin, even layer over the bottom, pressing down well with the back of the spoon. Put the pan in the refrigerator while you make the topping.

4 To make the topping, put the lemon rind and juice in a small bowl. Sprinkle over the gelatin. Stand the bowl in a pan of water. With adult supervision, heat gently, until the gelatin has melted. Stir, remove the bowl, and let cool.

⚠ = Watch out! Sharp or electrical tool in use.   🔥 = Watch out! Heat is involved.

6 Pour in the dissolved gelatin mixture and blend once more.

7 On a cutting board, roughly chop half the strawberries. Adult supervision is required. Scatter over the base with half the raspberries, reserving the rest for decoration.

8 Pour the cheese mixture over the fruit. Level the top with the back of a spoon. Cover and chill in the refrigerator overnight, until set.

5 Drain the cottage cheese in a strainer, then transfer to a blender or food processor and blend for 20 seconds. Add the cream cheese and condensed milk and blend again until smooth. Adult supervision is required.

9 Loosen the edges of the cheesecake with a palette knife. Stand the pan on a can and open the clip at the side of the pan. Let the pan slide down. Put the cheesecake on a serving plate and decorate with the reserved fruit.

Fruit fondue

A scrumptiously healthy way to eat up loads of fruit, this dessert is perfect for sharing with family and friends because everyone will enjoy helping themselves.

serves 6

ingredients
- **custard mix**, 1 package, prepared following the package instructions
- **milk chocolate**, 3 ounces, , broken into squares
- **apples**, 3
- **bananas**, 3
- **satsumas** or **clementines**, 3
- **strawberries**, 175g/6oz
- **seedless grapes**, medium-size bunch

tools
* **Medium pan**
* **Wooden spoon**
* **Cutting board**
* **Small sharp knife**

COOK'S TIP
► For ease and safety for younger cooks, add the chocolate to a bowl of custard. With adult supervision, microwave on Full Power (100%) for 1½ minutes, or until the chocolate has melted. Stir well.

1 Pour the custard into a medium pan and add the chocolate. Heat gently, stirring constantly for about 5 minutes, until the chocolate has melted. Alternatively, melt the chocolate into the custard in the microwave (*see* Cook's Tips). Adult supervision is required. Cool slightly.

2 Meanwhile, cut the apple into quarters. Carefully cut away the core and then cut the apple into bitesize pieces. Adult supervision is required.

3 Slice the bananas thickly and break the satsumas or clementines into segments.

4 Remove the stalks and leaves from the strawberries by twisting and pulling them out (known as hulling). Break the grapes off their stalks.

5 Pour the warm chocolate custard into a medium serving bowl and stand on a large plate.

6 Arrange the fruit around the bowl on the plate and serve immediately with fondue forks, standard forks, or toothpicks for spearing and dipping the fruit.

(!) = Watch out! Sharp or electrical tool in use.   (🖐) = Watch out! Heat is involved.

Cantaloupe melon salad

This simple salad is a wonderful way to use fragrant summer melons and strawberries. It makes a refreshing dessert to serve after a meaty barbecue.

serves **4**

ingredients

- **cantaloupe melon**, ½
- **strawberries**, 1 cup
- **confectioners' sugar**, 1 tablespoon, plus extra for dusting

cantaloupe melon

tools

- ✳ **Small metal spoon**
- ✳ **Cutting board**
- ✳ **Large sharp knife**
- ✳ **Nonstick baking sheet or shallow casserole**
- ✳ **Strainer or tea strainer**
- ✳ **Oven mitts**

1 Ask an adult to preheat the broiler to high. Scoop out the seeds from the half melon using a small spoon.

2 With adult supervision, cut the melon in half lengthwise. Stand the melon pieces skin-side down on the board.

3 Carefully remove the skin by running the knife close to the skin. Cut the flesh into wedges. Arrange on a serving plate.

4 Remove the stalks and leaves from the strawberries by twisting and pulling them out (known as hulling). Cut in half.

5 Arrange the fruit in a single layer, cut-side up, on a baking sheet or in a shallow casserole and dust with the sugar (see Cook's Tip).

6 Broil the strawberries for 4–5 minutes, until the sugar starts to bubble. Adult supervision is required.

7 Place the caramelized strawberries on top of the melon. Dust everything with confectioners' sugar and serve immediately.

COOK'S TIP

▶ "Dusting" means to sift a fine layer of powder, such as confectioners' sugar, over food and is often used as a way of decorating desserts. For a light dusting of sugar it's easier to use a small strainer.

Chocolate puffs

Everybody loves chocolate puffs or éclairs, and choux pastry is easy to make—as long as you have good strong arm muscles!

serves **4–6**

ingredients
- **water**, ⅔ cup
- **butter**, ¼ cup
- **all-purpose flour**, generous ½ cup, sifted
- **eggs**, 2, lightly beaten

for the filling and icing
- **heavy cream**, ⅔ cup
- **confectioners' sugar**, 1½ cups
- **cocoa powder**, 1 tablespoon
- **water**, 2–4 tablespoons

cocoa powder

tools
❋ Medium pan
❋ Wooden spoon
❋ Electric mixer
❋ 2 baking sheets
❋ 2 metal spoons
❋ Oven mitts
❋ Palette knife
❋ Wire rack
❋ Large mixing bowl
❋ Piping bag fitted with a plain or star nozzle
❋ Small mixing bowl

COOK'S TIPS
- As the pastry cooks, the water in the dough turns to steam and puffs up the pastry, so when making, don't let the water boil before the butter completely melts or some of this essential water will evaporate and be lost.
- When adding the flour, only beat until the paste begins to leave the sides of the pan; overbeating makes it oily.
- Eggs lighten the pastry and should be added a little at a time. The mixture will be slightly lumpy at first, but beat vigorously after each addition until the egg and paste are thoroughly mixed together. This will ensure you have a smooth, glossy texture.
- If you are in a rush, you can use an electric mixer (with adult supervision) to beat the mixture. Be very careful to avoid overmixing the paste or you will ruin it.

1 **To make the puffs**, put the water in a medium pan, add the butter, and heat gently until the butter melts. Increase the heat to high. Adult supervision is required when using heat.

2 As soon as the water-and-butter mixture boils, pour in all the flour at once. The easiest way to do this is to tip the flour onto a piece of paper so you can pour it in quickly.

3 Beat the ingredients with a wooden spoon until the mixture leaves the sides of the pan and comes together in a ball. It should be very stiff. Let cool slightly in the pan.

4 Preheat the oven to 425°F.

5 Add the eggs, a little at a time. Beat well each time with a wooden spoon or electric mixer, until the mixture is thick and glossy (you may not need to use all of the egg to achieve this). Adult supervision is required.

6 Dampen two baking sheets with a light sprinkling of cold water.

⚠ = Watch out! Sharp or electrical tool in use.   🔥 = Watch out! Heat is involved.

7 Place walnut-size spoonfuls of the mixture on the baking sheets, leaving some space between them in case they spread. Bake for 25–30 minutes, until they are golden brown and well risen.

8 Ask an adult to remove from the oven and gently lift onto a rack using a palette knife. Make a small hole in each with the handle of a wooden spoon. Let stand until cold.

9 To make the filling, whisk the cream in a bowl until thick. Put it into a piping bag fitted with a plain or star nozzle. Push the nozzle into the hole in each puff and squirt a little cream inside.

10 To make the icing, mix the sugar and cocoa in a small bowl. Add enough water to make a thick icing. Spread a spoonful of icing on each puff and serve immediately.

Chocolate heaven

Get those cold hands wrapped around a steaming mug of creamy hot chocolate, and then dunk homemade chocolate-tipped cookies in it…perfect!

serves **2** (makes **10** cookies)

ingredients
for the hot chocolate
- **milk**, 2½ cups
- **drinking chocolate powder**, 6 tablespoons, plus extra for sprinkling
- **sugar**, 2 tablespoons, or to taste
- **aerosol whipped cream**, 2 large squirts (optional)

for the chocolate-tipped cookies
- **soft margarine**, ½ cup, plus extra for greasing
- **confectioners' sugar**, 3 tablespoons, sifted
- **all-purpose flour**, 1¼ cups
- **vanilla extract**, a few drops
- **semisweet chocolate**, 3 ounces

tools
- ✳ 2 small pans
- ✳ Whisk
- ✳ 2 nonstick baking sheets
- ✳ Large mixing bowl
- ✳ Wooden spoon
- ✳ Piping bag fitted with a star nozzle
- ✳ Oven mitts
- ✳ Palette knife
- ✳ Wire rack
- ✳ Small heatproof bowl

VARIATIONS
- Make the same quantity of round cookies if you prefer, and dip half of each cookie in melted chocolate.
- To melt the chocolate more quickly, put it in a heatproof bowl and cook in the microwave on high for 60–90 seconds, or until it has melted. Adult supervision is required.
- Try adding an Arabian twist to the hot chocolate by gently smashing a couple of cardamom pods with a rolling pin and putting them in the pan with the cold milk. With adult supervision, bring the milk to a boil, then fish out the cardamom pods with a slotted spoon and stir in the chocolate powder and sugar. Alternatively, add a spicy kick by smashing a whole green chile and using that instead of the cardamom pods, so its spicy flavor goes into the milk as it heats up.

cardamom pods

1 **To make the hot chocolate**, put the milk in a small pan and bring to a boil. Add the chocolate powder and sugar and bring it back to a boil, whisking. Adult supervision is required.

2 Divide between two mugs. Top with a squirt of whipped cream, if desired.

3 **To make the chocolate-tipped cookies**, preheat the oven to 350°F.

4 Lightly grease two baking sheets. Beat together the margarine and confectioners' sugar in a large mixing bowl until creamy. Mix in the flour and vanilla extract.

5 Put the cookie mixture in a large piping bag fitted with a large star nozzle and squeeze out 4–5-inch lines on the greased baking sheets, spaced apart a little.

ⓘ = Watch out! Sharp or electrical tool in use.   = Watch out! Heat is involved.

6 Bake in the oven for 15–20 minutes, until pale golden. Ask an adult to remove from the oven. Let cool slightly before lifting onto a wire rack with a palette knife. Let cool on the rack completely.

7 Put the chocolate in a small heatproof bowl. Stand the bowl over a pan of hot water and let melt. Do not let the bottom of the bowl touch the water. Adult supervision is required.

8 Dip both ends of each of the cooled cookies in turn in the melted chocolate, so that about 1 inch each is coated. Gently shake to remove any excess chocolate.

9 Place the cookies on the wire rack and let stand for about 15 minutes for the chocolate to set.

10 Serve the cookies with the hot chocolate. If you have any cookies left over, put them in an airtight container, where they will keep for 2–3 days.

Fresh orange fizz

This delicious drink is much healthier than store-bought ones. It will keep in the refrigerator for a few days.

makes about **4** glasses

ingredients
- **superfine sugar,**
  scant ½ cup
- **oranges,** 6 large
- **plain** or **carbonated mineral water,**
  to serve

tools
- ❋ **Small heavy pan**
- ❋ **Wooden spoon**
- ❋ **Cutting board**
- ❋ **Medium sharp knife**
- ❋ **Juice squeezer or juicing machine**
- ❋ **Large pitcher**

oranges

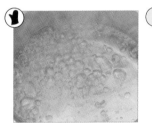

1 Put the sugar in a small, heavy pan with scant ½ cup of water. Heat gently, stirring carefully until the sugar has dissolved. Bring to a boil and boil rapidly for 3 minutes. Adult supervision is required.

2 Carefully remove the pan from the heat and let the syrup cool.

3 Meanwhile, cut the oranges in half and squeeze the juice from all the pieces. You can do this in a juicer or using a juicing machine, if you have one. Adult supervision is required.

4 Pour the orange juice into a large pitcher. You should have about 2½ cups of juice.

5 Pour the cooled sugar syrup into the pitcher of orange juice and mix, then chill in the refrigerator.

6 To serve, pour some of the drink into a pitcher or individual glasses and dilute to taste with plain or carbonated mineral water. Drop in some ice cubes and serve with straws.

VARIATION
- This recipe also works well with fresh lemon juice in place of the orange juice and will make a delicious bubbly lemonade if you add carbonated mineral water. You may need to add a little extra sugar to taste.

(!) = Watch out! Sharp or electrical tool in use.   = Watch out! Heat is involved.

Ruby red soda

A colorful and bubbly drink, this scrumptious syrup is made with vibrant blueberries or blackberries.

makes about **6** glasses

ingredients

- **blackberries** or **blueberries**, 3 cups
- **golden superfine sugar**, scant ¾ cup
- **ice cubes**
- **carbonated mineral water**, to serve

tools

- ✳ Juicing machine or a strainer and a large bowl
- ✳ Small heavy pan
- ✳ Wooden spoon
- ✳ Pitcher

blueberries

1 Examine the blackberries or blueberries carefully, removing any tough stalks or leaves from the fruit, and then wash them thoroughly. Let the fruit dry.

2 Push through a juicing machine, if you have one, or through a sieve set over a large bowl. Adult supervision is required.

3 Put the sugar in a small, heavy pan with scant ½ cup of water. Heat gently, stirring carefully until the sugar has dissolved. Bring to a boil and boil rapidly for 3 minutes. Adult supervision is required.

4 Remove the pan from the heat and let the syrup cool.

5 Mix the strained fruit juice with the syrup in a pitcher. The fruity syrup will keep well in the refrigerator for a few days.

6 For each serving, pour about ¼ cup of the fruity syrup into a glass and add ice. Fill up with carbonated mineral water and serve.

COOK'S TIP

▶ If you happen to have loads of berries, it makes sense to make a lot of this syrup and freeze it in single portions in ice-cube trays. Then you simply have to tip a couple of cubes into a glass and fill up with water for a really cool drink.

Totally tropical

This gorgeous juice makes use of the best naturally sweet tropical fruit. It is packed with vitamins and is a good way to help you on your way to eating five a day.

makes **2** glasses

ingredients
- **small pineapple**, ½
- **seedless white grapes**, small bunch
- **mango**, 1
- **mineral water** (optional)
- **fruit straws**, to decorate (see Cook's Tip)

tools
- ✳ **Cutting board**
- ✳ **Large sharp knife**
- ✳ **Small sharp knife**
- ✳ **Blender or food processor**
- ✳ **Metal spoon**
- ✳ **Spatula**

mineral water

mango

COOK'S TIP

▶ To make fruit straws to garnish your glasses, simply push bite-size pieces of fruit, such as grape, mango, and pineapple, onto a drinking straw.

grapes

1 Ask an adult to help you slice the bottom and top off the pineapple. Stand it upright on a cutting board. Carefully cut away the skin from the pineapple by "sawing" down. Using the tip of a small, sharp knife carefully cut out the "eyes" (rough dark round pieces).

2 Cut the pineapple in half and in half again down its length and cut away the tough core; discard. Roughly chop half the flesh. Remove the grapes from their stalks and put in a blender or food processor with the pineapple.

3 Place the mango flat on the cutting board, with the long, flat pit that runs across the middle of the mango standing upright. Carefully cut downward alongside the pit using a sharp knife, keeping as close to the pit as possible. Adult supervision is required.

4 Turn the mango over and repeat on the other side. Discard the pit. Scoop out the flesh with a spoon and add to the blender or food processor.

5 Blend, scraping the mixture down from the side with a spatula. Adult supervision is required.

6 Pour the fruit puree into glasses and fill up with mineral water, if using. Serve immediately, decorating each glass with a fruit straw (see Cook's Tip), if desired.

   (!) = Watch out! Sharp or electrical tool in use.   (🔥) = Watch out! Heat is involved.

Fruit punch

This wonderful recipe is great for any party, picnic, or just for when you are in need of a summer cooler. Serve in a punch bowl or a big pitcher.

serves 6

ingredients
- **orange juice**, 1¼ cups
- **pineapple juice**, 1¼ cups
- **pineapple**, ½ small
- **fresh cherries**, 6
- **tropical fruit juice**, 1¼ cups
- **lemon-flavored soda**, 2 cups

tools
✳ **2 ice-cube trays**
✳ **Cutting board**
✳ **Medium sharp knife**
✳ **Spoon**
✳ **Large pitcher**

3 Rinse the cherries and dry with paper towels. With adult supervision, make a slit in the bottom of each cherry, so they can sit on the rims of the glasses.

1 Pour the orange juice and pineapple juice into two separate ice-cube trays and freeze until solid.

2 Place the pineapple on its side and cut off the base. Cut two thick slices across the width, then cut into eight pieces and reserve. Adult supervision is required.

4 Mix together the tropical fruit juice and lemon-flavored soda in a large pitcher with a spoon.

5 Turn out some of the ice cubes by flexing the plastic and put a mixture of each flavor in each glass. Pour the fruit punch mixture over.

6 Decorate the glasses with the pineapple slices and cherries and serve immediately.

VARIATION
- Use a combination of your favorite fruit juices, such as grape and raspberry juice, to make ice cubes, with apple juice and lemon-flavored soda. Or try mango juice and coconut juice (available from Asian stores) to make ice cubes, with pineapple juice and lemon-flavored soda.

pineapple juice

What a smoothie

An exquisite blend of raspberries and orange mixed with yogurt makes a great after-school pick-you-up.

makes **2–3** glasses

Ingredients
- **raspberries**, 1⅓ cups
- **plain yogurt**,
  scant 1 cup
- **freshly squeezed orange juice**,
  1¼ cups

orange juice

raspberries

tools
- ✳ **Blender, food processor, or strainer**
- ✳ **Spatula**
- ✳ **Bowl (optional)**
- ✳ **Spoon (optional)**

1 Chill two or three tall glasses, the raspberries, yogurt, and orange juice in the refrigerator for about 1 hour.

2 Place the raspberries and yogurt in a blender or food processor. Blend thoroughly until smooth, scraping the mixture down with a spatula, if necessary. Adult supervision is required.

3 Alternatively, if you don't have a blender or food processor, or don't like the little raspberry seeds in your drink, press the raspberries through a strainer, collecting the puree in a bowl below it.

4 Add the yogurt to the raspberry puree in the bowl and stir to combine thoroughly.

5 Add the orange juice to the raspberry-and-yogurt mixture and process for another 30 seconds, or stir until combined if you have pressed the raspberries through a strainer. Adult supervision is required.

6 Pour the smoothie into the chilled glasses and serve immediately with straws, if desired.

COOK'S TIP
▶ This is delicious poured over crushed ice. If you have a processor or blender that is strong enough (check manufacturer's instructions), blend (with adult help) until crushed. Or, wrap some ice cubes in a clean dish towel and bash with a rolling pin until crushed.

(!) = Watch out! Sharp or electrical tool in use.   = Watch out! Heat is involved.

Strawberry and apple cooler

This fragrant, sweet drink was invented for enjoying on long, lazy summer days in the yard. It is best served well-chilled.

makes **2** tall glasses

ingredients
- **ripe strawberries**, 2½ cups
- **crisp apples**, 2 small
- **vanilla syrup**, 2 teaspoons
- **crushed ice** (see Cook's Tip on opposite page)

apples

tools
- ✳ **Cutting board**
- ✳ **Medium sharp knife**
- ✳ **Juicer, blender, or food processor**
- ✳ **Strainer (optional)**
- ✳ **Pitcher (optional)**
- ✳ **Spoon**

strawberries

1 Pick out a few pretty strawberries and reserve. Remove the stalks and leaves from the other strawberries by slicing them off (with adult supervision) or twisting and pulling them out.

2 On a cutting board, cut the apples into quarters, carefully cut out the core, and roughly chop. Adult supervision is required.

3 Push the fruits through a juicer, if you have one, or blend in a blender or food processor until smooth. Adult supervision is required. If you want it to be very smooth, push the mixture through a strainer into a pitcher positioned below.

4 Stir the vanilla syrup into the collected juice.

5 Fill two tall serving glasses halfway with crushed ice. Add straws or stirrers and position the reserved strawberries (slicing them, if desired) in with the ice, saving a few for the top, if desired.

6 Pour over the juice and top the drink with the reserved strawberries. Serve immediately.

COOK'S TIPS
▶ If you can't find vanilla syrup, you can add a few drops of vanilla extract to 2 teaspoons of honey.
▶ Try freezing the mixture in ice-cube trays. Then simply pile into chilled glasses and wait until they start to thaw a little.

Rainbow juice and fruit slush

makes **6** glasses

Fruity flavors are great for making drinks, such as rainbow juice, a stripy medley of tropical goodness, or fruit slush, a blend of semi-frozen blueberry and orange.

ingredients

for the rainbow juice
- **kiwis**, 8
- **pineapple**, 1 small
- **strawberries**, generous 1 cup, stalks and leaves removed

for the fruit slush
- **oranges**, 2
- **blueberries**, 2¼ cups
- **superfine sugar**, 4 tablespoons

kiwi

COOK'S TIPS

▶ To peel a pineapple, ask an adult to help you cut the top and bottom off the fruit. Stand the pineapple upright on the board and cut down with a "sawing" action to remove large strips of skin. Cut out any remaining "eyes" (small dark, rough pieces) with the tip of a sharp knife, and chop or slice. Alternatively, you can get wonderful gadgets that gouge out a continuous coil of pineapple flesh, leaving the shell and core intact.

▶ For an extra-cool drink, chill or semi-freeze the prepared fruit and the glasses before blending.

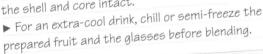

pineapple

tools
✳ Cutting board
✳ Small sharp knife
✳ Blender or food processor
✳ Spatula
✳ 2 small bowls
✳ Spoon
✳ Juicer or strainer
✳ Large bowl (optional)
✳ Nonmetallic freezer container
✳ Fork

1 To make the rainbow juice, cut away the peel from the kiwis using a sharp knife. Cut away the skin from the pineapple (see Cook's Tip), then halve and remove the core. Roughly chop the flesh. Adult supervision is required.

2 Put the pineapple in a blender or food processor along with 2 tablespoons of water. Process to a smooth puree, scraping the mixture down from the side, if necessary. Adult supervision is required. Pour into a small bowl.

3 Add the kiwis to the blender and blend until smooth. Pour into a separate bowl.

4 In a clean blender, blend the strawberries until smooth. Adult supervision is required.

5 Pour the strawberry puree into three glass tumblers. Carefully spoon the kiwi puree into the glasses to form a separate layer. Spoon the pineapple puree over the kiwi puree and serve with spoons or thick straws.

6 To make the fruit slush, using a small, sharp knife, carefully cut away the skin and pith from the oranges, then cut the oranges into 8–10 chunky wedges. Adult supervision is required.

(!) = Watch out! Sharp or electrical tool in use. = Watch out! Heat is involved.

8 Add the sugar and 1¼ cups of cold water to the juice and stir until the sugar has dissolved. Pour into a shallow, nonmetallic freezer container and freeze for 1–2 hours, or until the juice is beginning to freeze all over.

7 Reserve a few blueberries, then push the rest through a juicer, alternating them with the orange wedges. Adult supervision is required. If you don't have a juicer, push the fruit through a strainer placed over a large bowl.

9 Use a fork to break up any solid areas of the mixture and put into a blender or food processor. Blend until smooth and slushy. Spoon the drink into glasses and serve, topped with blueberries or other fruit.

desserts and drinks 183

Vanilla milkshake

You could open your very own diner with this recipe, serving the best vanilla shakes in town.

makes **2** glasses

ingredients
- **vanilla bean**, 1 (*see* Fact File)
- **whole milk**, 1⅔ cups
- **light cream**, scant 1 cup
- **vanilla ice cream**, 4 scoops

vanilla beans and extract

tools
* Small sharp knife
* Small pan
* Slotted spoon
* Cutting board
* Blender or food processor
* Ice cream scoop

whole milk

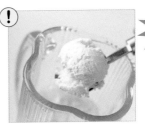

1 Using a sharp knife, score the vanilla bean down the center and open out along the cut. Place the milk in a pan, add the vanilla bean, and bring slowly to a boil. Adult supervision is required.

2 When the milk has reached boiling point, remove from the heat. Let stand until the milk is cold (known as steeping).

3 Remove the vanilla bean from the cooled milk with a slotted spoon and carefully scrape out the seeds with the tip of a small sharp knife.

4 Transfer the vanilla seeds to the blender or food processor with the milk and cream. Blend until well combined. Adult supervision is required.

5 Add the vanilla ice cream to the blender or food processor and blend well for 30 seconds, or until the mixture is deliciously thick and frothy.

6 Pour the milkshake into two large glasses. Add ice cubes, if desired, and serve immediately with stirrers and straws, if desired.

FACT FILE
VANILLA
You will usually find vanilla beans in the spice section of supermarkets. They have an intense flavor, so you need only a small amount. If you prefer, use 2 teaspoons of vanilla extract instead.

(!) = Watch out! Sharp or electrical tool in use.   = Watch out! Heat is involved.

Strawberry shake

If you like strawberries, then you will love this drink. If you have wild strawberries, it will be all the more delicious!

makes **2** glasses

ingredients
- **ripe strawberries**, 3½ cups
- **confectioners' sugar**, 2–3 tablespoons, sifted
- **drained plain yogurt**, scant 1 cup
- **light cream**, 4 tablespoons

plain yogurt

tools
- ✳ **Strainer**
- ✳ **Paper towels**
- ✳ **Small sharp knife (optional)**
- ✳ **Food processor or blender**
- ✳ **Spatula**

1 Pick out a couple of the prettiest strawberries and reserve. Remove the stalks and leaves from the other strawberries by slicing them off or pulling them out (known as hulling). Adult supervision is required.

2 Place the strawberries in a food processor or blender with 2 tablespoons of confectioners' sugar.

3 Blend the mixture to a smooth puree, scraping the mixture down from the side with a spatula, if necessary. Adult supervision is required.

4 Keep the pretty green leaves on the reserved strawberries. Carefully slice them in half using a small sharp knife. Adult supervision is required.

5 Add the yogurt and cream to the blender and blend again until smooth and frothy. Check the sweetness, adding a little sugar if necessary.

6 Pour the milkshake into two medium glasses. Top with the sliced strawberries and serve immediately with straws, if desired.

COOK'S TIP
▶ If strawberries are not in season, you can replace them with other fruits. Try using fresh bananas instead to make another very popular milkshake.

banana

Candy stripe

This wickedly indulgent drink combines blended strawberries with a marshmallow-flavor cream.

makes **4** large glasses

ingredients

- **white** and **pink marshmallows**, 5 ounces
- **whole milk**, generous 2 cups
- **red currant jelly**, 4 tablespoons
- **strawberries**, 4 cups
- **heavy cream**, 4 tablespoons
- **extra strawberries** and **marshmallows**, to decorate

tools

- ✳ **2 medium heavy pans**
- ✳ **Wooden spoon**
- ✳ **Blender or food processor**
- ✳ **Spatula**
- ✳ **Tablespoon**
- ✳ **Pitcher**
- ✳ **Teaspoon**

1 With adult supervision, put the marshmallows in a heavy pan with half the milk. Heat gently, stirring often, until the marshmallows have melted. Let stand until cool.

2 Heat the jelly in the other pan for 4 minutes, until melted. Set aside.

3 Remove the green stalks from the strawberries by twisting them off (known as hulling). Put them in a blender or food processor and process until smooth, scraping down the sides with a spatula if necessary. Adult supervision is required.

4 Stir 2 teaspoons of the strawberry puree into the jelly. Cover and set aside at room temperature.

5 Pour the remaining puree into a pitcher and stir in the marshmallow mixture, the cream, and the remaining milk.

6 Cover and chill the milkshake and four large glasses in the refrigerator for at least 1 hour.

7 To serve, use a teaspoon to drizzle lines of the strawberry syrup down the insides of the glasses—this creates a candystripe effect when filled. Fill the glasses with the milkshake.

8 Serve topped with the extra marshmallows and strawberries and drizzle with any leftover strawberry syrup.

(!) = Watch out! Sharp or electrical tool in use.   (✊) = Watch out! Heat is involved.

Banana high

Rich, creamy, and full of banana and toffee flavors, this drink is a real treat. Keep any leftover syrup for spooning over ice cream.

makes **4** tall glasses

ingredients
- **bananas**, 4 large
- **whole milk**, 2½ cups
- **vanilla sugar**, 1 tablespoon
- **ice cubes**, 8

for the toffee syrup
- **light Barbados** or **brown sugar**, scant ½ cup
- **heavy cream**, ⅔ cup

Barbados sugar

tools
- ✳ Small heavy pan
- ✳ Wooden spoon
- ✳ Blender or food processor
- ✳ Large mixing bowl
- ✳ Whisk
- ✳ Tablespoon

banana

1 **To make the toffee syrup**, put the sugar in a pan with 5 tablespoons of water. Heat gently, stirring until the sugar dissolves. Add 3 tablespoons of the cream and simmer for 4 minutes. Adult supervision is required. Remove from the heat and let cool for 30 minutes.

2 Peel the bananas, then break them into large pieces. Place the pieces in a blender or food processor with the milk, vanilla sugar, ice cube and another 3 tablespoons of the cream. Blend for about 1 minute, until smooth and frothy. Adult supervision is required.

3 Pour the remaining cream into a large, clean bowl and whisk gently until thickened and standing in soft peaks.

4 Add half the toffee syrup to the banana milkshake and blend, then pour into glasses.

5 Drizzle more syrup around the insides of the glasses. Spoon the cream over the top and drizzle with any remaining syrup. Serve immediately.

COOK'S TIP
► To make vanilla sugar, place a vanilla bean in a jar of sugar and let stand for at least 1 day.

Weekend treats

Yummy—it's time for a weekend treat! Lazy weekends are the best time to pamper yourself with your favorite sandwiches, cakes, and cookies. Making your own adds to the enjoyment and means you can make whatever combination of treats you want.

Griddle cakes

Also known as Scotch pancakes, these make a delectable breakfast, brunch, or snack served with butter and drizzled with honey.

makes 8–10

ingredients
- **butter**, 2 tablespoons, diced, plus extra for greasing
- **all-purpose flour**, 1 cup
- **baking soda**, 1 teaspoon
- **cream of tartar**, 1 teaspoon
- **egg**, 1, beaten
- **milk**, about ⅔ cup
- **butter**, a pat and **honey**, to serve

tools
- ✳ Grill pan or heavy skillet
- ✳ Strainer or sifter
- ✳ Large mixing bowl
- ✳ Wooden spoon
- ✳ Wooden spatula
- ✳ Clean dish towel

COOK'S TIP
▶ Placing the cooked griddle cakes in a clean, folded dish towel while you cook the remaining batter helps to keep them soft and moist until you are ready to serve them.

1 Lightly grease a grill pan or heavy skillet with a little butter. Sift the flour, baking soda, and cream of tartar together into a large mixing bowl.

2 Add the butter and rub it into the flour with your fingertips until the mixture resembles fine, evenly textured bread crumbs.

3 Make a well in the center of the flour mixture, then stir in the egg with a wooden spoon.

4 Add the milk a little at a time, stirring it in each time to check the consistency. Add just enough milk to give the batter the consistency of heavy cream.

5 Heat the grill pan or skillet to medium heat. Drop three or four spoonfuls of the mixture onto it. Cook for 3 minutes, until bubbles rise to the surface and burst. Adult supervision is required.

6 Turn the cakes over with a spatula and cook for another 2–3 minutes, until golden underneath.

7 Place the cooked griddle cakes between the folds of a clean dish towel while you cook the remaining batter in the same way. Serve warm, with butter and honey.

(!) = Watch out! Sharp or electrical tool in use. = Watch out! Heat is involved.

Buttermilk biscuits

These deliciously light biscuits are delicious for an afternoon snack, served fresh from the oven and spread with butter and raspberry or strawberry jam.

makes about **12** large or **18** small biscuits

ingredients
- **all-purpose flour**, 4 cups
- **salt**, ½ teaspoon
- **baking soda**, 1 teaspoon
- **butter**, ¼ cup, at room temperature
- **superfine sugar**, 1 tablespoon
- **egg**, 1 small, lightly beaten
- **buttermilk**, about 1¼ cups
- **butter** and **jam**, to serve

tools
- ✳ 2 baking sheets
- ✳ Strainer or sifter
- ✳ Large mixing bowl
- ✳ Metal spoon
- ✳ Rolling pin
- ✳ Fluted cutter
- ✳ Oven mitts
- ✳ Wire rack

1 Preheat the oven to 425°F. Grease two baking sheets.

2 Sift the flour, salt, and baking soda into a large mixing bowl, lifting the strainer or sifter up high. Add the butter and rub it in with your fingertips until the mixture resembles fine bread crumbs.

3 Add the sugar and mix in well. Make a well in the middle and add the egg and enough buttermilk to make a soft dough.

4 Turn the dough onto a lightly floured counter and knead lightly into shape. Roll out to about ½ inch thick with a floured rolling pin.

5 Stamp out 12 large or 18 small biscuits with a fluted cutter, gathering the trimmings and rerolling as necessary. Space well apart on baking sheets.

6 Bake for 15–20 minutes, until risen and golden brown, asking an adult to turn the sheets around halfway through.

VARIATION
- For biscuits with golden raisins, add ⅓–⅔ cup of golden raisins with the sugar in Step 3.

golden raisins

7 Ask an adult to remove from the oven, transfer to a wire rack, and let cool slightly. Serve warm.

Buttermilk pancakes

It is traditional to have these pancakes with crispy fried bacon and a generous drizzle of maple syrup, but try it with honey instead of the syrup.

makes about 6

ingredients
- **all-purpose flour**, 1¼ cups
- **baking powder**, ½ teaspoon
- **eggs**, 3
- **buttermilk**, ½ cup
- **oil**, for frying
- **honey**, to serve

tools
- ✳ **Strainer or sifter**
- ✳ **Large mixing bowl or food processor**
- ✳ **Wooden spoon (optional)**
- ✳ **Large, heavy skillet or grill pan**
- ✳ **Small bowl**
- ✳ **Tablespoon**
- ✳ **Spatula or palette knife**
- ✳ **Clean dish towel**

FACT FILE

BUTTERMILK

Originally a product left over after making butter, nowadays buttermilk is made from skim milk with a special bacterial "culture" to give it the same tangy flavor it had before.

1 Sift the flour and baking powder into a large bowl or food processor.

2 Add the eggs and beat with a wooden spoon or pulse to mix. Still beating or pulsing, pour in just enough buttermilk to make a thick, smooth batter. Adult supervision is required.

3 Heat a skillet or grill pan, then add enough oil to coat the bottom and swirl it around until coated. Pour off any excess oil. Adult supervision is required.

4 Drop three or four tablespoonfuls of the mixture, spaced slightly apart, onto the skillet or grill pan.

5 Cook the pancakes over a medium heat for about 1 minute, until the bottoms are golden brown. Carefully flip the pancakes over with a spatula or palette knife and cook for another 1 minute, until both sides are golden brown and cooked. Adult supervision is required.

6 Place the cooked pancakes between the folds of a clean dish towel while you cook the remaining batter in the same way. Serve warm, with honey.

French toast

This egg-coated fried bread makes a delicious breakfast, brunch, or even afternoon treat. This version is made with a special Italian bread called panettone.

serves **4**

ingredients
- **panettone**, 4 large slices
- **eggs**, 2 large
- **butter**, ¼ cup
- **fresh berries**, to serve
- **superfine sugar**, 2 tablespoons

tools
- ✷ **Cutting board**
- ✷ **Serrated bread knife**
- ✷ **Small bowl**
- ✷ **Fork or whisk**
- ✷ **Shallow dish**
- ✷ **Large nonstick skillet**
- ✷ **Spatula or palette knife**
- ✷ **Strainer or colander**

1 On a cutting board, cut the slices of bread in half (if you have small slices, leave as they are). Adult supervision is required.

2 Break the eggs into a small bowl. Use a fork or whisk to whisk lightly until well combined, then transfer to a shallow dish.

3 Heat the butter in a skillet. Adult supervision is required.

4 Dip the bread in the egg to coat on both sides. Add to the skillet. Fry for 2–3 minutes on each side, turning over with the spatula or palette knife, until brown. Adult supervision is required.

5 Wash the berries in a strainer or colander, drain, and pat dry with paper towels.

6 Drain the cooked toast on absorbent paper towels and dust with sugar. Scatter over the prepared berries and serve immediately.

VARIATION
- Make a simple fruit compote to serve with the toast by mixing berries, such as raspberries, blueberries, and strawberries, with sugar to taste. Add a little fruit juice or syrup mixed with a little water, cover, and let soak for at least 30 minutes.

blueberries

Banana muffins

Don't throw out nearly black bananas lurking in the fruit bowl. They will be perfect for these moist muffins.

makes **12**

ingredients

- **all-purpose flour**, 2 cups
- **baking powder**, 1 teaspoon
- **baking soda**, 1 teaspoon
- **salt**, a pinch
- **ground cinnamon**, ½ teaspoon
- **grated nutmeg**, ¼ teaspoon
- **ripe bananas**, 3 large
- **egg**, 1
- **dark brown sugar**, ¼ cup
- **vegetable oil**, ¼ cup, plus extra for greasing
- **raisins**, ⅓ cup

bananas

tools
- ✴ **12-hole muffin pan** (plus muffin liners, if liked)
- ✴ **Strainer or sifter**
- ✴ **2 large mixing bowls**
- ✴ **Fork**
- ✴ **Wooden spoon**
- ✴ **2 metal spoons**
- ✴ **Oven mitts**
- ✴ **Wire rack**

3 Put the bananas in a separate large mixing bowl.

1 Preheat the oven to 375°F. Lightly grease a 12-hole muffin pan, or position paper muffin liners in the holes, if using.

2 Sift together the flour, baking powder, baking soda, salt, cinnamon, and nutmeg into a large mixing bowl, lifting the strainer or sifter high. Set aside.

4 Mash the bananas to a fine pulp with a fork or with a wooden spoon.

5 Add the egg, sugar, and oil to the mashed bananas and beat with a wooden spoon to combine thoroughly.

6 Add the dry ingredients to the banana and egg and beat in gradually with a wooden spoon. It is important to avoid overmixing the mixture until it is smooth—it should look a little lumpy.

7 With the wooden spoon, gently stir in the raisins until just combined. Do not overmix.

8 Spoon the mixture into the muffin pan or liners with metal spoons, filling them about two-thirds full.

9 Bake for 20–25 minutes, until the tops spring back when touched lightly with your finger. Ask an adult to remove from the oven, cool slightly in the pan, then transfer to a wire rack to cool completely before serving.

Double choc chip muffins

What better way to enjoy the weekend than with this ultimate chocolate treat, which can be eaten warm fresh from the oven or cold.

makes 16

ingredients

- **all-purpose flour**, 3½ cups
- **baking powder**, 1 tablespoon
- **cocoa powder**, 2 tablespoons
- **dark Barbados** or **brown sugar**, ⅔ cup
- **eggs**, 2
- **sour cream**, ⅔ cup (*see Cook's Tip*)
- **milk**, ⅔ cup
- **sunflower oil**, 4 tablespoons
- **white chocolate**, 6 ounces, chopped into small pieces
- **semisweet chocolate**, 6 ounces, chopped into small pieces
- **cocoa powder**, for dusting (optional)

tools

- ✳ 16 muffin liners
- ✳ 16-hole muffin pan
- ✳ Strainer or sifter
- ✳ Large mixing bowl
- ✳ Wooden spoon
- ✳ Small bowl
- ✳ Fork
- ✳ 2 metal spoons
- ✳ Oven mitts
- ✳ Wire rack

1 Preheat the oven to 350°F. Place paper muffin liners in a 16-hole muffin pan.

2 Sift the flour, baking powder, and cocoa into a large mixing bowl, lifting the strainer or sifter high to add air to the flour. Stir in the sugar. Make a well in the center of the mixture using your fingers.

3 In a small bowl, beat the eggs with the sour cream, milk, and oil with the fork, then stir into the well in the dry ingredients. Beat well, gradually incorporating all the surrounding flour mixture to make a thick and creamy batter.

4 Stir the white and semisweet chocolate pieces into the batter.

5 Spoon the mixture into the liners with two metal spoons, filling them almost to the top. Bake for 25–30 minutes, until well risen and firm to the touch.

6 Ask an adult to remove from the oven and cool in the pan slightly before moving to a wire rack to cool completely. Dust with cocoa powder to serve, if you like.

COOK'S TIP

▶ If you don't have sour cream, you can use plain yogurt instead. Alternatively, you can use heavy cream or extra milk.

sour cream

Banana gingerbread

This sticky treat improves with keeping.
You can store it in a container for up to two
months—if you can bear to leave it that long.

makes **12** squares

ingredients

- **ripe bananas**, 3
- **all-purpose flour**, 1¾ cups
- **baking soda**, 2 teaspoons
- **ground ginger**, 2 teaspoon
- **rolled oats**, 1¼ cups
- **dark Barbados** or **brown sugar**, ¼ cup
- **butter**, 6 tablespoons, plus extra for greasing
- **light corn syrup**, ⅔ cup
- **egg**, 1, beaten
- **confectioners' sugar**, ¼ cup
- **preserved ginger**, chopped, to decorate (optional)

preserved ginger

tools

- ✳ 7 x 11-inch cake pan
- ✳ 2 small mixing bowls
- ✳ Fork
- ✳ Large mixing bowl
- ✳ Strainer or sifter
- ✳ Wooden spoon
- ✳ Small heavy pan
- ✳ Skewer
- ✳ Oven mitts
- ✳ Medium sharp knife
- ✳ Cutting board

1 Preheat the oven to 325°F. Lightly grease and line a 7 x 11-inch cake pan.

2 Put the bananas in a small mixing bowl and mash with the fork. Sift the flour, baking soda, and ground ginger into the large bowl. Stir in the oats.

3 Put the sugar, butter and syrup in a pan. Heat gently for a few minutes, stirring occasionally, until the ingredients are melted and well combined. Adult supervision is required.

4 Stir into the flour mixture. Beat in the egg and mashed bananas.

5 Spoon into the pan, level the surface, and bake for about 1 hour, or until a skewer comes out clean when it is inserted. Adult supervision is required.

6 Remove from the oven, cool in the pan, and turn out. Cut into squares. Adult supervision is required.

7 Meanwhile, sift the confectioners' sugar into the remaining bowl. Stir in just enough water to make a smooth, runny glaze.

8 Drizzle the glaze over each square of gingerbread and top with pieces of chopped ginger, if desired.

Bilberry bread

This wonderful, cakelike "quick" bread has a crumbly topping. Serve it cold for picnics or warm with a hot drink.

makes *8* pieces

ingredients

- **butter**, 4 tablespoons, plus extra for greasing
- **superfine sugar**, scant 1 cup
- **egg**, 1, at room temperature
- **milk**, ½ cup
- **all-purpose flour**, 2 cups
- **baking powder**, 2 teaspoons
- **salt**, ½ teaspoon
- **fresh bilberries** or **blueberries**, 2½ cups

for the topping

- **superfine sugar**, generous ½ cup
- **all-purpose flour**, ⅓ cup
- **ground cinnamon**, ½ teaspoon
- **butter**, 4 tablespoons, cut into pieces

tools

- ✳ **9-inch shallow casserole or baking pan**
- ✳ **2 large mixing bowls**
- ✳ **Electric mixer or wooden spoon**
- ✳ **Wooden spoon**
- ✳ **Strainer or sifter**
- ✳ **Skewer**
- ✳ **Oven mitts**
- ✳ **Large sharp knife**
- ✳ **Cutting board**

1 Preheat the oven to 375°F. Lightly grease a 9-inch shallow casserole or baking pan.

3 Add the egg and beat to combine, then mix in the milk until combined.

5 Transfer the mixture to the casserole or pan.

2 Put the butter and sugar in a bowl and beat together with an electric mixer or wooden spoon until pale and creamy. Adult supervision is required.

4 Sift over the flour, baking powder, and salt, and stir with a wooden spoon just enough to blend the ingredients. Add the bilberries or blueberries and stir gently.

6 **To make the topping,** place the sugar, flour, cinnamon, and butter in a mixing bowl. Using your fingertips, rub in the butter until the mixture resembles bread crumbs. Sprinkle over the batter mixture.

7 Bake the quick bread in the oven for about 45 minutes, or until a skewer inserted in the center comes out clean.

8 Ask an adult to remove from the oven and let cool slightly in the bowl or pan. Turn out and cut into squares. Serve warm or cold.

Carrot cake

It may seem funny adding vegetables to a cake but some, such as carrots, add a great taste.

serves **10–12**

ingredients
- **self-rising flour**, 2 cups
- **baking powder**, 2 teaspoons
- **brown sugar**, 1 scant cup
- **plumped dried figs**, 4 ounces, roughly chopped
- **carrots**, 4 medium (about 8 ounces), grated
- **ripe bananas**, 2 small, mashed
- **eggs**, 2
- **sunflower oil**, ⅔ cup, plus extra for greasing

for the topping
- **cream cheese**, ¾ cup (6 ounces)
- **confectioners' sugar**, 1½ cups, sifted
- **small, soft candies, chopped nuts, or grated chocolate**, to decorate

carrots

COOK'S TIPS
▶ Because this cake contains moist vegetables and fruit and is topped with a cream cheese frosting, it will not keep longer than a week and is best stored in an airtight container in the refrigerator—but it is so tasty it probably won't last that long!
▶ Dried figs add a wonderful chewy texture to the cake, as well as making it healthier by adding fiber, which is very good for you. Figs are sold in most supermarkets and specialty dried fruit stores.

dried figs

tools
- ✳ 7-inch round, loose-bottom cake pan
- ✳ Pencil
- ✳ Parchment paper
- ✳ Scissors
- ✳ Strainer or sifter
- ✳ 2 large mixing bowls
- ✳ 2 wooden spoons
- ✳ Small mixing bowl
- ✳ Fork
- ✳ Palette knife
- ✳ Skewer
- ✳ Oven mitts
- ✳ Wire rack

1 Lightly grease a 7-inch cake pan with butter or vegetable oil. Draw around the bottom of the pan onto parchment paper. Cut out the circle and use to line the bottom of the pan.

2 Preheat the oven to 350°F. Sift the flour, baking powder, and sugar into a large bowl. Mix together well with a wooden spoon, then stir in the figs.

3 Using your hands, squeeze as much liquid out of the grated carrots as you can and add to the flour mixture. Add the mashed bananas and stir to combine.

4 Lightly beat the eggs and oil together in a small mixing bowl with a fork, then pour them into the flour mixture. Beat everything together well with a wooden spoon.

 = Watch out! Sharp or electrical tool in use. = Watch out! Heat is involved.

7 Once the cake has completely cooled, spread the frosting over the top. Use small colorful candies, chopped nuts, or grated chocolate to decorate the frosting.

5 Transfer to the pan and level it with a palette knife. Cook for 1–1¼ hours, until a skewer pushed into the center comes out clean. Ask an adult to remove from the pan. Cool on a wire rack.

6 **To make the topping,** put the cream cheese and sugar in a large mixing bowl. Beat together with a clean wooden spoon, to make a thick frosting. This may take a few minutes.

8 Transfer to a serving dish, cut into small wedges, and serve immediately.

Simple chocolate cake

Every chef needs a good chocolate cake recipe, and this can be yours. For special occasions, top with whipped cream.

serves 6–8

ingredients
- **butter** or **oil**, for greasing
- **semisweet chocolate**, 4 ounces, broken into squares
- **milk**, 3 tablespoons
- **unsalted butter**, 6 tablespoons
- **light brown sugar**, scant 1 cup
- **eggs**, 3
- **self-rising flour**, 1¾ cups
- **cocoa powder**, 1 tablespoon

for the buttercream and topping
- **unsalted butter**, 6 tablespoons
- **confectioners' sugar**, 1½ cups, plus extra for dusting, plus extra for dusting
- **cocoa powder**, 1 tablespoon
- **vanilla extract**, ½ teaspoon

tools
- ✳ two 7-inch, round cake pans
- ✳ Parchment paper
- ✳ Heatproof bowl
- ✳ Medium pan
- ✳ 2 mixing bowls
- ✳ Electric mixer or wooden spoon
- ✳ Strainer or sifter
- ✳ Large metal spoon
- ✳ Skewer
- ✳ Oven mitts
- ✳ Wire rack
- ✳ Mixing bowl
- ✳ Wooden spoon

1 Preheat the oven to 350°F. Grease two 7-inch cake pans with butter and line with parchment paper.

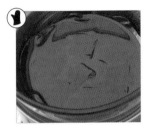

2 Melt the chocolate with the milk in a heatproof bowl set over a pan of barely simmering water. Cool. Adult supervision is required.

3 Put the butter and sugar in a mixing bowl and beat together until pale and creamy with an electric mixer (adult supervision is required) or wooden spoon. Add the eggs, one at a time, beating well after each addition. Stir in the chocolate mixture.

4 Sift the flour and cocoa over the mixture and fold in with a metal spoon until evenly mixed. Transfer the mixture to the pans and level the surface. Bake for 35–40 minutes, until a skewer pushed into the middle of the cake comes out clean.

5 Ask an adult to remove from the oven. Cool slightly in the pans before turning out onto a wire rack to cool completely.

6 **To make the buttercream**, beat the butter, sugar, cocoa powder, and vanilla extract together in a clean bowl until the mixture is smooth.

7 Sandwich the cake layers together with the buttercream. Dust the top with a mixture of sifted confectioners' sugar and cocoa before serving.

(!) = Watch out! Sharp or electrical tool in use.　 = Watch out! Heat is involved.

Luscious lemon cake

This sugar-crusted cake is soaked in a lemon syrup, so it stays moist and delicious.

serves 10

Ingredients

- **butter**, generous 1 cup, plus extra for greasing
- **superfine sugar**, generous 1 cup
- **eggs**, 5
- **all-purpose flour**, 2½ cups, sifted
- **baking powder**, 2 teaspoons
- **salt**, a pinch

for the sugar crust
- **lemon juice**, 4 tablespoons
- **light corn syrup**, 1 tablespoon
- **sugar**, 2 tablespoons

flour

lemons

tools

✳ 9 x 5 x 3-inch loaf pan	✳ Electric mixer or wooden spoon	✳ Skewer
✳ Parchment paper	✳ Strainer or sifter	✳ Oven mitts
✳ Large mixing bowl	✳ 2 metal spoons	✳ Small heavy pan

1 Preheat the oven to 350°F. Grease and line a 9 x 5 x 3-inch loaf pan.

2 Beat the butter and sugar using an electric mixer (adult supervision is required) or wooden spoon, until pale and creamy. Gradually beat in the eggs.

3 Sift the flour, baking powder, and salt into the bowl and fold in.

4 Spoon into the pan, level the surface, and bake for 40–50 minutes, until a skewer pushed into the center comes out clean. Adult supervision is required.

5 Ask an adult to remove from the oven. Stab a skewer right the way through in several places.

6 Put the lemon juice and syrup in a small, heavy pan and heat gently, stirring, until the syrup melts. Adult supervision is required.

7 Add the sugar to the pan and immediately spoon over the cake, so the syrup soaks through but leaves some sugar crystals on the top.

8 Let cool before removing from the pan and serving.

Lemon meringue cakes

Everyone, especially grown-ups, are impressed by people who can make a good meringue, and this easy recipe reveals exactly how to do it.

makes **18**

ingredients
- **butter**, ½ cup
- **superfine sugar**, scant 1 cup
- **eggs**, 2
- **self-rising flour**, 1 cup
- **baking powder**, 1 teaspoon
- **lemons**, 2, grated rind
- **lemon juice**, 2 tablespoons
- **egg whites**, 2

tools
- ✳ two 9-hole muffin pans
- ✳ 18 paper cupcake liners
- ✳ 2 large mixing bowls
- ✳ Electric mixer or wooden spoon
- ✳ 3 metal spoons
- ✳ Balloon whisk (optional)
- ✳ Oven mitts
- ✳ Wire rack

eggs

VARIATION
• Use a mixture of oranges and lemons for a sweeter taste, or use only oranges.

1 Preheat the oven to 375°F. Stand the paper liners in the muffin pans.

2 Put the butter in a bowl and beat with an electric mixer (adult supervision is required) or wooden spoon until soft. Add ½ cup of the sugar and continue to beat until smooth and creamy.

3 Beat in the eggs, flour, baking powder, half the lemon rind, and all the lemon juice. Mix well to combine thoroughly.

4 Divide the cake mixture between the paper liners using two metal spoons. Fill the liners to near the top of the paper.

5 Put the egg whites in a clean mixing bowl and whisk with a balloon whisk or clean electric mixer until soft peaks form when the whisk or beaters are lifted. Adult supervision is required.

6 Stir in the remaining superfine sugar and lemon rind with a spoon.

7 Put a spoonful of the meringue mixture on top of each cake. Cook for 20–25 minutes, until the meringue is crisp and brown.

8 Ask an adult to remove from the oven and cool in the pan slightly before cooling completely on a wire rack. Serve hot or cold.

(!) = Watch out! Sharp or electrical tool in use.   (🔥) = Watch out! Heat is involved.

Orange and apple rockies

A mixture of cake and cookie, these fruit-filled "rock" cakes are a fantastic afternoon treat to throw together at a moment's notice.

makes **24**

ingredients
- **self-rising flour**, 2 cups
- **margarine**, ½ cup
- **oil**, for greasing
- **apple**, 1 large
- **plumped dried apricots**, ⅓ cup
- **golden raisins**, ⅓ cup
- **orange**, 1 small, grated rind
- **raw sugar**, ¼ cup
- **egg**, 1
- **milk**, 1 tablespoon

tools
- ✳ **Large mixing bowl**
- ✳ **2 nonstick baking sheets**
- ✳ **Pastry brush**
- ✳ **Peeler**
- ✳ **Cutting board**
- ✳ **Small sharp knife**
- ✳ **Small bowl**
- ✳ **Fork**
- ✳ **Wooden spoon**
- ✳ **Wire rack**

3 Peel the apple, then cut it into quarters. Remove the core. Chop the apricots. Adult supervision is required.

5 Beat the egg and milk in a small bowl with a fork. Stir into the flour mixture with a wooden spoon until just beginning to bind together.

VARIATION
• Try replacing the apricots with other dried fruit, such as prunes, figs, or mango or banana chips, or add chocolate chips.

1 Put the flour into a large mixing bowl and rub in the margarine with your fingertips until the mixture resembles bread crumbs. Set aside.

2 Preheat the oven to 375°F. Brush two baking sheets with a little oil.

4 Stir the apple and apricots into the flour mixture with the golden raisins and orange rind. Reserving 2 tablespoons of the sugar, stir the rest into the mixture.

6 Drop spoonfuls, well spaced apart, onto the baking sheets. Sprinkle with the reserved sugar.

7 Bake for 12–15 minutes, until golden and firm. Ask an adult to remove from the oven and transfer to a wire rack to cool. Serve warm or cold with butter.

Pecan squares

Halved pecan nuts are mixed with sugar and honey and baked in a pastry crust in this sweet treat. Serve on its own or with cream.

makes **36**

ingredients

- **butter** or **oil** for greasing
- **all-purpose flour**, 2 cups
- **salt**, a pinch
- **sugar**, ½ cup
- **cold butter** or **margarine**, 1 cup, cubed
- **egg**, 1, lightly beaten
- **lemon**, 1, finely grated rind

for the topping

- **butter**, ¾ cup
- **honey**, ⅓ cup
- **sugar**, ¼ cup
- **dark brown sugar**, ½ cup
- **whipping cream**, 5 tablespoons
- **pecan halves**, 4 cups

tools

- ✳ 14½ x 10½ x 1-inch jelly roll pan
- ✳ Strainer or sifter
- ✳ Large mixing bowl
- ✳ Wooden spoon
- ✳ Fork or palette knife
- ✳ Oven mitts
- ✳ Small heavy pan
- ✳ 2 baking sheets
- ✳ Large sharp knife

1 Preheat the oven to 375°F. Lightly grease the pan.

2 Sift the flour and salt into a large mixing bowl. Stir in the sugar. Add the butter or margarine and rub into the flour and sugar with your fingertips until the mixture resembles chunky bread crumbs.

3 Add the egg and lemon rind and blend well with a fork or palette knife until the mixture just holds together.

4 Spoon the mixture into the pan. With floured fingertips, press into an even layer. Prick the pastry all over with a fork, cover, and chill for 10 minutes.

5 Bake for 15 minutes. Ask an adult to remove from the oven.

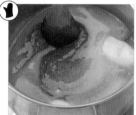

6 **To make the topping,** put the butter, honey, and both kinds of sugar in a small heavy pan. Melt over a low heat, stirring frequently. Increase the heat and boil, without stirring, for 2 minutes. Adult supervision is required.

7 Remove from the heat and stir in the cream and pecans. Pour over the pastry crust. Ask an adult to return to the oven. Bake for 25 minutes, until set. Ask an adult to remove from the oven and let cool.

8 Invert onto a baking sheet, place another baking sheet on top, and invert again. Cut into squares.

 ⚠ = Watch out! Sharp or electrical tool in use. ✊ = Watch out! Heat is involved.

Rich chocolate cookie slice

Refigerator cookies are cool! Simply mix all the ingredients together, then let them chill while you do something else.

makes about **10**

ingredients
- **semisweet chocolate**, 5 ounces
- **milk chocolate**, 5 ounces
- **unsalted butter**, ½ cup, plus extra for greasing
- **plain cookies**, 3½ ounces
- **white chocolate**, 3½ ounces

semisweet, milk, and white chocolates

tools
- ✳ 8 x 4 x 2-inch loaf pan
- ✳ Parchment paper
- ✳ Heatproof bowl
- ✳ Cutting board
- ✳ Large sharp knife
- ✳ Medium heavy pan
- ✳ Wooden spoon
- ✳ Plastic wrap

1 Lightly grease the loaf pan and line the bottom and sides with parchment paper, making sure it comes up over the top.

2 Break the semisweet and milk chocolates into small pieces and place in a heatproof bowl. With adult supervision, chop the butter and add to the bowl.

3 Set the bowl over a pan of simmering water (be careful not to let the water touch the bottom of the bowl) and stir with a until melted. Cool for 20 minutes. Adult supervision is required.

4 Meanwhile, break up the plain cookies into very small pieces with your fingers.

(!)

5 Finely chop the white chocolate. Adult supervision is required. Stir into the melted chocolate with the cookies.

6 Turn into the pan and pack down gently. Cover with plastic wrap and chill for 2 hours, or until set. Turn out, remove the paper, and cut into slices.

VARIATION
- There are a lot of ways you can vary this recipe. Try different kinds of chocolate, such as ginger, hazelnut, honey and almond, peanut, or mocha; add chopped dried fruit, such as apricots, mangoes, cranberries, or dried blueberries; or vary the cookies, using gingersnaps, graham crackers, chocolate chip cookies, or macaroons.

Chewy oat bars

Not only are these scrumptous treats easy to make, but they will also give you energy to keep going through the busiest of days!

makes **18**

ingredients
- **unsalted butter**, generous 1 cup
- **orange**, 1 large, finely grated rind
- **light corn syrup**, ⅔ cup
- **light Barbados** or **brown sugar**, ⅓ cup
- **rolled oats**, 3¾ cups

orange rind

tools
- ✴ **11 x 8-inch, shallow baking pan**
- ✴ **Parchment paper**
- ✴ **Large heavy pan**
- ✴ **Wooden spoon**
- ✴ **Oven mitts**
- ✴ **Cutting board**
- ✴ **Medium sharp knife**

1 Preheat the oven to 350°F. Line the bottom and sides of the pan with parchment paper.

2 Put the butter, orange rind, syrup, and sugar in a large heavy pan and heat gently, stirring occasionally, until the butter has melted. Adult supervision is required.

3 Add the oats to the pan and stir to mix thoroughly. Pour the mixture into the pan and spread into the corners in an even layer.

4 Bake for 15–20 minutes, until just beginning to color around the edges. (The mixture will still be soft but will harden as it cools).

5 Ask an adult to remove the pan from the oven and let the mixture cool in the pan for a few minutes before marking the mixture into squares or bars.

6 Let cool completely, then turn out onto a board and cut along the scored lines.

COOK'S TIPS
▶ Avoid overcooking these bars or they will turn crispy and dry and lose their chewy texture.

▶ It is important to score the bars while they are still warm, or they may be hard to cut later.

(!) = Watch out! Sharp or electrical tool in use.   (🖑) = Watch out! Heat is involved.

Peanut and jelly cookies

These nutty jelly cookies are a twist on the original American peanut butter cookie and are a real hit with kids and adults alike at any time of the day.

makes 20–22

ingredients
- **crunchy peanut butter** (with no added sugar), 8 ounces
- **unsalted butter**, 6 tablespoons, at room temperature, diced
- **golden superfine sugar**, ½ cup
- **light Barbados** or **brown sugar**, ¼ cup
- **large egg**, 1, beaten
- **self-rising flour**, 1¼ cups
- **seedless raspberry jelly**, scant 1 cup

tools
- ✳ 3–4 baking sheets
- ✳ Parchment paper
- ✳ Large mixing bowl
- ✳ Electric mixer or wooden spoon
- ✳ Strainer or sifter
- ✳ Fork
- ✳ Oven mitts
- ✳ Palette knife
- ✳ Wire rack
- ✳ Teaspoon

1 Preheat the oven to 350°F. Line three or four baking sheets with parchment paper.

2 Put the peanut butter and unsalted butter in a large mixing bowl and beat together with a wooden spoon or electric mixer (adult supervision is required) until well combined and creamy.

3 Add the superfine and Barbados or brown sugars and mix well. Add the egg and blend. Sift in the flour and mix to a stiff dough.

4 Roll the dough into walnut-size balls between the palms of your hands. Place the balls on the prepared baking sheets and gently flatten each one with a fork to make a rough-textured cookie with a ridged surface. (Don't worry if the dough cracks slightly.)

5 Bake for 10–12 minutes, or until cooked but not browned. Using a palette knife, transfer to a wire rack to cool.

6 Spoon jelly onto one cookie and top with a second. Continue to sandwich the rest in this way.

VARIATION
- If you don't like raspberry jelly, you can use another flavor, such as strawberry, grape, or apricot. Alternatively, leave out the jelly altogether and simply serve the cookies on their own.

Triple chocolate cookies

You'll find these chocolatey treats so hard to resist you will want to eat them as soon as they come out of the oven—just be careful to avoid burning your fingers!

makes **12** large cookies

- **milk chocolate**, 3½ ounces
- **white chocolate**, 3½ ounces
- **semisweet chocolate**, 11 ounces
- **unsalted butter**, 7 tablespoons, at room temperature, diced
- **vanilla extract**, 1 teaspoon
- **light Barbados** or **brown sugar**, ¾ cup
- **self-rising flour**, 1¼ cups
- **macadamia nut halves**, scant 1 cup

macadamia nuts

tools
- ✳ Cutting board
- ✳ Large sharp knife
- ✳ 2 baking sheets
- ✳ Parchment paper
- ✳ Large heatproof bowl
- ✳ Medium pan
- ✳ Wooden spoon
- ✳ 2 tablespoons
- ✳ Oven mitts
- ✳ Palette knife
- ✳ Wire rack

1 On a cutting board, roughly chop the milk and white chocolates into small pieces and set aside. Adult supervision is required.

2 Preheat the oven to 350°F. Grease the baking sheets and line with parchment paper.

3 Chop two-thirds of the semisweet chocolate into chunks. Set aside.

4 Break up the remaining semisweet chocolate. Place in a heatproof bowl set over a pan of simmering water. Stir until melted. Adult supervision is required.

5 Remove from the heat and stir in the butter, then the vanilla extract and Barbados sugar. Add the flour and mix gently.

6 Add half the semisweet chocolate chunks, all the milk and white chocolates, and the nuts and mix well.

7 Using two tablespoons, spoon 12 dollops of the mixture onto the baking sheets, spaced well apart to leave room for spreading. Press the remaining semi-sweet chocolate chunks into the top of each cookie.

8 Bake the cookies for about 12 minutes, until just beginning to color. Ask an adult to remove from the oven and let the cookies cool on the baking sheets. Using the palette knife, lift the cookies onto a wire rack to cool completely before serving.

(!) = Watch out! Sharp or electrical tool in use. (✋) = Watch out! Heat is involved.

Chocolate caramel nuggets

Inside each of these crumbly, buttery cookies lies a soft-centered, chocolate-coated caramel, which softens during cooking and makes an oozy surprise filling.

makes **12**

ingredients
- **self-rising flour**, 1¼ cups
- **unsalted butter**, 7 tablespoons, chilled and diced, plus extra for greasing
- **golden superfine sugar**, ¼ cup
- **egg yolk**, 1
- **vanilla extract**, 1 teaspoon
- **soft-centered chocolate caramels**, 14
- **confectioners' sugar** and **cocoa powder**, for dusting

tools
- ✳ **Food processor**
- ✳ **Plastic wrap**
- ✳ **Large baking sheet**
- ✳ **Rolling pin**
- ✳ **2-inch round cookie cutter**
- ✳ **Oven mitts**
- ✳ **Palette knife**
- ✳ **Wire rack**

VARIATION
• You can use pieces of fudge instead of chocolate caramels, if desired.

1 Put the flour and butter in a food processor and process until the mixture resembles fine bread crumbs. Adult supervision is required.

3 Wrap the dough in plastic wrap and chill for 30 minutes. Preheat the oven to 400°F. Grease a baking sheet.

5 Place one chocolate caramel on a dough circle, then lay a second circle on top. Pinch the edges of the dough together so that the caramel is completely enclosed, then place on the baking sheet. Make the remaining cookies in the same way.

6 Bake the cookies for about 10 minutes, until pale golden.

7 Ask an adult to remove the tray from the oven, transfer the cookies to a wire rack with a palette knife, and let cool. Serve dusted with confectioners' sugar and cocoa powder.

2 Add the sugar, egg yolk, and vanilla extract to the food processor and process to a smooth dough.

4 Roll out the dough thinly on a floured surface and cut out 28 circles using a 2-inch cutter.

Party food

It's party time! Whether it's your birthday, Easter, Christmas, or you simply have something special to celebrate, it's always fun to rustle up some scrummy treats for all your friends. Better still, get a couple of them over to help you make it—just make sure you don't eat it all before the others arrive!

Crazy rainbow popcorn

Before you start, you'll need to take a trip to a good kitchen store to get special colorings. Once you have them, you will have loads of fun making crazy popcorn!

serves **10–15**

ingredients
- **vegetable oil**, 1 tablespoon
- **popcorn kernels**, 6 ounces (see Fact File)
- **green, red**, and **blue powdered food colorings** (see Cook's Tip)
- **red cheese**, such as **red Leicester** or **American**, grated, ½ cup
- **green** or **blue cheese**, such as **sage Derby**, grated, ½ cup

red Leceister cheese

FACT FILE
POPCORN
Completely natural and good for you, popcorn is the ideal snack food. It is also inexpensive and loads of fun to cook because it pops in the pan. The kernels of the corn are naturally hard and come in two main varieties: yellow and white. The yellow type tends to pop to a larger size than the white kind, and that is why it is often used in movies, but the white kernels tend to have more flavor. Either can be used in this colorful recipe.

popcorn kernels

tools
- ✳ **Large heavy pan**
- ✳ **Wooden spoon**
- ✳ **3 or 4 plastic sandwich or freezer bags**
- ✳ **Small spoon or knife**
- ✳ **Large mixing bowl**
- ✳ **Grater**

1 Put the oil and popcorn kernels in a pan and stir to coat the kernels in oil. Cover with a lid and cook for about 5 minutes, until you hear the corn starting to pop. Do not remove the lid. Shake the pan a few times. Adult supervision is required.

2 When you hardly hear any popping at all, ask an adult to remove the pan from the heat and remove the lid. Put small amounts of popcorn in a few plastic sandwich or freezer bags (use as many bags as there are different colorings).

3 Use a tiny spoon or the tip of a knife to add a small amount of food coloring to each of the bags of popcorn. You can choose what colors you use and how much popcorn you want to make a particular color.

4 Close the bags and hold each in turn in one hand. Shake and tap with the other hand, tossing the popcorn inside the bag to coat it evenly in the coloring. As you color each batch, put it into a large serving bowl.

 = Watch out! Sharp or electrical tool in use. 🖐 = Watch out! Heat is involved.

5 When all the popcorn is colored, transfer it all to a large mixing bowl. Add both types of grated cheese to the colored corn. Carefully toss the mixture together with your hands and serve the popcorn immediately.

COOK'S TIP
► Use powdered food coloring because the liquid type will turn the popcorn soggy. You will find the powdered kind in specialty cake decorating stores.

Cheese and potato twists

If you like cheese sandwiches, then you'll love these delicious cheesy twists. They are great served warm or cold at any party, so make plenty to avoid running out!

makes **8**

ingredients
- **potatoes**, 2 medium (about 8 ounces), peeled, diced, and boiled
- **white bread flour**, 2 cups
- **easy-blend dried yeast**, 1 teaspoon
- **salt**, a pinch
- **lukewarm water**, ⅔ cup
- **red Leicester cheese**, finely grated, 1½ cups
- **olive oil**, 2 teaspoons, for greasing

tools
* Potato masher
* Strainer or sifter
* Large mixing bowl
* Large cutting board or tray
* Nonstick baking sheet
* Oven mitts

3 Knead for 5 minutes on a floured counter. Return to the bowl, cover with a damp cloth, and let rise in a warm place for 1 hour, until doubled in size.

5 Scatter the cheese over a clean surface, such as a large cutting board or tray. Roll each ball of dough in the cheese.

COOK'S TIP
▶ You can't beat making your own bread, but you can also try using a bread mix and adding mashed potato.

1 Mash the potatoes and set aside. Sift the flour into a bowl and add the yeast and a pinch of salt. Stir in the potatoes and rub with your fingers until it resembles bread crumbs.

2 Make a well in the center and pour in the water. Bring the mixture together with your hands.

4 Turn out on to the counter and reknead the dough for a few seconds. Divide into 12 pieces and shape into balls.

6 Roll each roll on a dry surface to form a long sausage shape. Fold the two ends together and twist the bread. Lay these on a baking sheet.

7 Cover with a damp cloth and let rise in a warm place for 30 minutes.

8 Preheat the oven to 425°F. Bake for 10–15 minutes, until risen and golden. Ask an adult to remove from the oven and serve.

(!) = Watch out! Sharp or electrical tool in use.   (🔥) = Watch out! Heat is involved.

Sandwich shapes

Try using a selection of different shaped cutters to make these sandwiches. You can also use different-color breads to make a white layer topped with a brown layer.

ham

mayonnaise

serves **4–6**

ingredients
- **medium white bread**, 8 slices
- **medium whole-wheat bread**, 8 slices
- **butter** or **margarine**, for spreading
- **shredded lettuce**, **radishes**, and **cress**, to garnish

ham and cheese filling
- **ham**, 4 thin slices
- **Cheddar cheese**, 8 thin slices

chicken and mayonnaise filling
- **roast chicken breast**, 4 thin slices
- **mayonnaise**, for spreading

tools
✷ **Butter knife**
✷ **A selection of different-shape cookie cutters**

1 Lay the slices of bread out on a counter and lightly spread one side with softened butter or margarine with a knife.

2 To make the ham and cheese sandwiches, put a slice of ham on four slices of the bread, then put two slices of cheese on top of the ham.

3 For the chicken and mayonnaise sandwiches, put a slice of chicken on four of the remaining slices of bread and spread a little mayonnaise on top.

4 Use the remaining eight slices of bread to make the sandwich lids. Press down lightly on the top pieces to secure.

5 Using a selection of different-shape cookie cutters, such as fish, rabbits, teddy bears, stars, or hearts, stamp out shapes from the sandwiches by placing the cutter on the sandwich and pushing down. Try to stamp out two or more shapes from each to avoid any waste. (You can eat the leftovers!)

VARIATION
- You can make tasty sandwich shapes with any favorite fillings. Try chopped egg, tuna, or cheese and tomato.

6 Arrange the sandwiches on a serving plate and garnish with a little shredded lettuce, radishes, and cress around the edges, if desired. Serve the sandwiches immediately or cover well with plastic wrap and chill for 2–3 hours, until needed.

Mini burgers 'n' rolls

Instead of serving these burgers with French fries, go for the healthier option of cucumber strips. You can also try carrot and pepper strips for colorful burgers.

makes 8

ingredients
- **onion**, 1 small
- **ground beef**, 8 ounces
- **egg**, 1
- **fresh bread crumbs**, ½ cup (*see* Cook's Tips)
- **tomato paste**, 1 tablespoon
- **small soft bread rolls**, 8
- **Cheddar cheese**, 4 slices
- **ketchup**, to serve
- **lettuce** and **cherry tomatoes**, to garnish

for the cucumber strips
- **cucumber**, 1

cucumber

COOK'S TIPS
▶ To make fresh breadcrumbs, take a chunk of stale bread and grate it with a coarse grater. Alternatively, blend in a blender or food processor for a few seconds. Adult supervision is required. For crisp crumbs, spread the fresh ones out on a baking sheet and grill for about 2 minutes, shaking the sheet halfway through. Adult supervision is required.

bread

▶ Instead of using a round cutter, you can make funny shapes out of the cheese with novelty cutters for themed parties, such as Easter, Halloween, or Christmas.

▶ Although mini burgers are ideal for parties, you can make four larger burgers for a family meal using this recipe.

tools
- ✳ Aluminum foil
- ✳ 2 cutting boards
- ✳ Medium sharp knife
- ✳ Large mixing bowl
- ✳ Wooden spoon
- ✳ Tongs
- ✳ Small round cutter
- ✳ Large serrated knife

1 Ask an adult to preheat the broiler to medium-hot. Line a broiler pan with foil. Meanwhile, peel the onion and chop it finely on a cutting board. Adult supervision is required.

2 Put the meat in a bowl and add the egg, onion, bread crumbs, and tomato paste. Using a wooden spoon, mix all the ingredients together until they are evenly combined.

3 Wet your hands. Take a small handful of the mixture, shape it into a ball, and flatten it slightly. Do this until all the mixture is used up. Place the burgers on the broiler pan.

4 Cook for 5 minutes. Carefully turn over with a pair of tongs and put them back under the broiler for another 5–8 minutes, until cooked through. Adult supervision is required.

(!) = Watch out! Sharp or electrical tool in use.　 = Watch out! Heat is involved.

7 Place the bottom halves of the rolls on serving plates and place a cheese circle on top. Add a dollop a little ketchup on top.

5 Meanwhile, **make the cucumber strips**. Cut the cucumber in half lengthwise, then slice into two or three pieces. Cut these pieces into thin strips. Adult supervision is required.

6 Stamp out four cheese circles using a round cutter on a cutting board. With adult supervision, use a serrated knife to carefully cut open the bread rolls on the same board.

8 Put the burgers on top of the ketchup and place the lids on top. Serve with the cucumber strips, lettuce, and cherry tomatoes.

Mini ciabatta pizzas

These tasty little pizzas are perfect for any party. Experiment with different types of bread and toppings to discover your favorite combinations.

serves 8

ingredients
- red bell peppers, 2
- yellow bell peppers, 2
- ciabatta bread, 1 loaf
- prosciutto, 8 slices
- mozzarella cheese, 5 ounces
- ground black pepper
- tiny basil leaves, to garnish

Prosciutto

tools
- ✳ **Cutting board**
- ✳ **Medium sharp knife**
- ✳ **Large bowl**
- ✳ **Large serrated knife**
- ✳ **Oven mitts**

VARIATION
▶ There are an almost endless number of different toppings you can use. These may include replacing the bell peppers with sliced fresh tomatoes or whole roasted tomatoes or, for a spicy kick, adding some pepperoni or chopped, drained jalepeño peppers.

pepperoni

1 Ask an adult to preheat a broiler. Cut the bell peppers in half.

2 Remove the seeds. Place on a broiler rack. Broil until they turn black. Place in the bowl, cover, and let stand for 10 minutes. Peel off the skins. Adult supervision is required.

3 Cut the bread into eight thick slices and toast both sides until golden. (Leave the broiler on.) Adult supervision is required.

4 Cut both the bell peppers and prosciutto into thick strips and arrange on the toast. Adult supervision is required.

5 Thinly slice the mozzarella cheese and arrange on top. Grind over plenty of black pepper. Broil for 2–3 minutes, until the cheese is bubbling.

6 Ask an adult to remove from the broiler. Arrange the fresh basil leaves on top and serve.

 = Watch out! Sharp or electrical tool in use.   = Watch out! Heat is involved.

Tortilla squares

A Spanish omelet makes a great supper, but if you cut it into small squares, you can also enjoy it as a "nibble" at parties. Try serving the pieces on toothpicks.

serves **6–8**

ingredients
- **olive oil**, 3 tablespoons
- **Bermuda onions**, 2, thinly sliced
- **waxy potatoes**, 3 medium (about 11 ounces), cut into ½-inch dice
- **shelled fava beans**, 1¾ cups
- **chopped fresh thyme**, 1 teaspoon
- **large eggs**, 6
- **mixed chopped fresh chives** and **Italian parsley**, 3 tablespoons
- **salt** and **ground black pepper**

tools
- ✳ **9-inch, deep nonstick skillet with lid**
- ✳ **Wooden spoon**
- ✳ **Medium pan**
- ✳ **Colander or strainer**
- ✳ **Large mixing bowl**
- ✳ **Small mixing bowl**
- ✳ **Fork**
- ✳ **Spatula**
- ✳ **Plate**
- ✳ **Large knife**

1 Heat 2 tablespoons of the oil in a 9-inch, deep nonstick skillet. Add the onions and potatoes and stir to coat. Cover and cook, stirring frequently, for 20–25 minutes, until the potatoes are cooked and the onions are very soft. Adult supervision is required.

2 Meanwhile, fill two-thirds of a medium pan with cold water. Add a little salt and bring to a boil. Add the beans and cook for 5 minutes, until tender. Ask an adult to drain them well and put in the large bowl to cool.

3 When the beans are cool enough to handle, peel off the gray outer skins and throw them away. This is fussy work, but fun.

4 Add the beans to the pan, together with the thyme. Season, stir well to mix, then cook for another 2–3 minutes.

5 Beat the eggs and herbs in a bowl. Add to the pan and increase the heat.

6 Cook until the egg browns underneath, pulling it away from the sides of the pan and tilting it to let the uncooked egg run underneath. Adult supervision is required.

7 With adult supervision, cover the pan with an upside-down plate and invert the tortilla onto it. Heat the remaining oil in the pan. Slip the tortilla into the pan, uncooked-side down, and cook for 3–5 minutes, until brown. Slide onto a serving plate. Cut into squares and serve.

Chicken mini rolls

These small, crispy rolls can be served warm as part of a party buffet or as nibbles. If you want to get ahead, make them the day before, then reheat in the oven.

serves **4**

ingredients
- **phyllo pastry**, 10 ounces, thawed if frozen
- **olive oil**, 3 tablespoons, plus extra for greasing
- **fresh Italian parsley**, to garnish

for the filling
- **ground chicken**, 12 ounces
- **egg**, 1, beaten
- **ground cinnamon**, ½ teaspoon
- **ground ginger**, ½ teaspoon
- **raisins**, 2 tablespoons
- **salt** and **ground black pepper**
- **olive oil**, 1 tablespoon
- **onion**, 1 small, finely chopped

tools
- ✳ **Large mixing bowl**
- ✳ **Large skillet**
- ✳ **Wooden spoon**
- ✳ **Baking sheet**
- ✳ **Cutting board**
- ✳ **Small sharp knife**
- ✳ **Pastry brush**
- ✳ **Oven mitts**
- ✳ **Palette knife**
- ✳ **Wire rack**

1 First, **make the filling**. Put the chicken, egg, cinnamon, ginger, and raisins in a large mixing bowl and season well.

2 Gently heat the oil in a skillet, add the onion, and cook over a low heat, stirring occasionally, for 5 minutes, until tender. Let cool, then add to the bowl. Adult supervision is required.

3 Preheat the oven to 350°F. Grease the baking sheet. Open the phyllo pastry and carefully unravel. Cut the pastry into 4 x 10-inch strips. Adult supervision is required.

4 Take one strip, keeping the remainder covered, and brush with oil. Place a small spoonful of the filling about ½ inch from the end.

5 Fold the sides inward to a width of 2 inches and roll into a roll shape. Place on the baking tray and brush with oil. Repeat with the remaining ingredients.

6 Bake for 20–25 minutes, until golden brown and crisp. Ask an adult to remove from the oven and transfer to a wire rack. Serve garnished with parsley.

COOK'S TIP
► Once phyllo pastry is exposed to the air, it dries out really fast, so it is important to work quickly once the pastry is opened and always keep the pastry you are not using covered with with plastic wrap.

 (!) = Watch out! Sharp or electrical tool in use.   🔥 = Watch out! Heat is involved.

Falafel

Sesame seeds are used to create a crunchy coating on these tasty chickpea patties. Serve on toothpicks with hummus.

serves 4

ingredients
- **canned chickpeas**, 14 ounces, drained
- **garlic**, 1 clove, crushed
- **ground coriander**, 1 teaspoon
- **ground cumin**, 1 teaspoon
- **chopped fresh mint**, 1 tablespoon
- **chopped fresh parsley**, 1 tablespoon
- **scallions**, 2, finely chopped
- **salt** and **ground black pepper**
- **large egg**, 1, beaten
- **sesame seeds**, for coating
- **sunflower oil**, for frying
- **hummus**, to serve

canned chickpeas

parsley

tools
- ✳ Large mixing bowl
- ✳ Wooden spoon
- ✳ Food processor
- ✳ Plate or small mixing bowl
- ✳ Large skillet
- ✳ Metal spatula
- ✳ 12–14 toothpicks

1 Put the chickpeas, garlic, ground spices, herbs, scallions, salt, and pepper in a large mixing bowl. Add the egg and mix well with a wooden spoon.

2 Place the mixture in a food processor and blend until it forms a coarse paste. Adult supervision is required. If the paste seems too soft, chill for 30 minutes.

3 Wet your hands slightly. Form the chilled chickpea paste into 12–14 balls with your hands, making them about the same size as a walnut.

4 Put the sesame seeds on a plate or in a small bowl, then roll each chickpea ball in turn in the sesame seeds to coat the outsides thoroughly.

5 Heat enough oil to cover the bottom of a large skillet. Fry the falafel, in batches if necessary, for 6 minutes, turning once with a spatula. Adult supervision is required.

6 Transfer to a plate lined with paper towels to drain and cool slightly. Spear each ball with a toothpick and serve with hummus.

VARIATION
- If you don't want to fry the falafel, you can bake them instead. Simply preheat the oven to 350°F, place the balls on a greased baking sheet, and cook for about 30 minutes, until crispy on the outside.

Mini muffins

Mini mouthfuls of delicious treats are bound to win over party guests. Look out for mini muffin pans in good kitchen stores and department stores.

makes **24**

ingredients
- **butter**, 4 tablespoons
- **candied cherries**, ¼ cup
- **plumped dried apricots**, ⅓ cup
- **all-purpose flour**, 1½ cups
- **baking powder**, 2 teaspoons
- **light brown sugar**, ¼ cup
- **milk**, ⅔ cup
- **egg**, 1, beaten
- **vanilla extract**, ½ teaspoon

tools
- ✳ 2 mini muffin pans
- ✳ 24 petits fours paper liners
- ✳ Small pan
- ✳ Cutting board
- ✳ Medium sharp knife
- ✳ Large mixing bowl
- ✳ Wooden spoon
- ✳ 2 metal teaspoons
- ✳ Oven mitts
- ✳ Wire rack

1 Preheat the oven to 425°F. Place the liners in the mini muffin pans.

(!) 2 Put the butter in a small pan and heat until melted. Let cool. Meanwhile, chop the cherries and apricots into small pieces. Adult supervision is required.

3 Put the flour, baking powder, and sugar in a large mixing bowl and add the milk, egg, and melted butter. Stir thoroughly with a wooden spoon until the mixture is smooth and well combined. Add the chopped fruit and the vanilla extract and stir to combine thoroughly.

4 Spoon the mixture into the paper liners, using two teaspoons, so they are about three-quarters full.

5 Bake for 10–12 minutes, until well risen and browned. Ask an adult to remove from the oven, cool slightly in the pan then transfer to a wire rack.

VARIATION
- To make orange and banana muffins, substitute 2 small mashed bananas for ¼ cup of the milk. Omit the chopped cherries and apricots and the vanilla extract, and add 1 tablespoon of grated orange rind.

(!) = Watch out! Sharp or electrical tool in use. = Watch out! Heat is involved.

Cupcake faces

Make happy, funny, laughing faces on yummy cakes with a selection of colorful candies.

makes 12

ingredients
- **margarine**, ⅔ cup
- **superfine sugar**, ⅔ cup
- **self-raising flour**, 1 cup
- **eggs**, 2

for the topping
- **butter**, 4 tablespoons, cubed
- **confectioners' sugar**, 1 cup
- **pink food coloring**
- **sugar-coated chocolate candies**, 4 ounces
- **red licorice shoelaces**, 2
- **licorice** and **gum drop mixture**, 12
- **semisweet chocolate**, 75g/3oz broken into pieces

sugar-coated chocolate candies

tools
- ✳ **12 paper cake liners**
- ✳ **12-hole muffin pan**
- ✳ **Large mixing bowl**
- ✳ **Electric mixer or wooden spoon**
- ✳ **2 metal spoons**
- ✳ **Oven mitts**
- ✳ **Wire rack**
- ✳ **Small mixing bowl**
- ✳ **Strainer or sifter**
- ✳ **Wooden spoon**
- ✳ **Palette knife**
- ✳ **Small heatproof bowl**
- ✳ **Small heavy pan**
- ✳ **Parchment paper**
- ✳ **Scissors**

3 Cook for 12–15 minutes, until the cakes are well risen and spring back when pressed with a fingertip. Ask an adult to remove from the oven. Let cool slightly in the pan, then transfer to wire rack.

1 Preheat the oven to 350°F. Place the paper liners in the muffin pan. Put all the cake ingredients in a bowl and beat with an electric mixer (adult supervision is required) or wooden spoon until smooth.

2 Divide the cake mixture among the liners.

4 Meanwhile, **make the topping**. Put the butter in a small mixing bowl. Sift over the confectioners' sugar and beat the mixture until smooth. Stir in a little pink food coloring.

5 Spread the frosting over the cakes with a palette knife.

6 Add sugar-coated chocolate candies for eyes, short pieces of licorice for mouths, and other candies for noses.

7 Put the chocolate in a heatproof bowl. Set over a pan of simmering water. Heat until melted. Adult supervision is required.

8 Remove the pan from the heat and stir the melted chocolate. Spoon into a parchment paper piping bag (see page 33).

9 Snip off the tip of the piping bag and draw hair, eye balls, glasses, and moustaches on the top of the cakes.

Puppy faces

These lightly spiced cookies decorated with cute puppy faces are sure to be a huge hit at any birthday party or special occasion, and are a lot of fun to make.

makes **10**

ingredients

- **all-purpose flour**, scant 1 cup
- **rolled oats**, ½ cup
- **allspice**, ½ teaspoon
- **unsalted butter**, ¼ cup, chilled and diced, plus extra for greasing
- **superfine sugar**, ½ cup
- **egg yolk**, 1

for the decoration
- **apricot jam**, 4 tablespoons
- **white rolled fondant icing**, 9 ounces
- **soft colored candies**, 10
- **black** and **red writing icing tubes**
- **confectioners' sugar**, for dusting

COOK'S TIPS

▶ You can make your own icing instead of using store-bought rolled icing. This type of icing turns hard to create a solid finish, so is perfect for creating designs for cookies. To make your own, beat 1 egg white for a few seconds with a fork in a large bowl. Mix in ⅔ cup sifted confectioners' sugar, a little at a time, until the mixture stands in soft peaks and is thick enough to spread. You can then roll it out and use as in the recipe. This makes enough to cover about 10 cookies, but you can just multiply the quantities if you make more cookies.

▶ Spreading the cookies with strained apricot jam helps the icing to stick to the cookie.

apricot jelly

tools

- ✳ Food processor or blender
- ✳ Plastic wrap
- ✳ 1 large nonstick baking sheet
- ✳ Rolling pin
- ✳ 2½-inch cutter
- ✳ Oven mitts
- ✳ Palette knife
- ✳ Wire rack
- ✳ Strainer or sifter
- ✳ Small bowl

1 Put the flour, rolled oats, allspice, and butter into a food processor or blender. Blend until it resembles fine bread crumbs. Add the sugar, egg yolk, and 1 teaspoon of water and blend until the mixture begins to form a ball. Adult supervision is required.

2 Knead on a floured counter for 5 minutes, until smooth. Shape into a ball, wrap in plastic wrap, and chill for 30 minutes.

3 Preheat the oven to 400°F. Grease a baking sheet.

4 Roll out the dough on a floured counter. Stamp out 10 circles using a cookie cutter. Transfer to the baking sheet, spacing slightly apart.

5 Bake for 12 minutes, until pale golden.

6 Ask an adult to remove from the oven and transfer to a wire rack with a palette knife. Let cool.

7 Press the jam through a strainer into a small bowl. Spread a little jam over each cookie to within ¼ inch of the edge. Let stand until cold.

8 Roll out half the icing very thinly on a surface dusted with confectioners' sugar. Cut out 10 circles using a 2½-inch cutter and lay one over each cookie.

9 **To make the eyes,** halve the colored candies, brush the icing lightly with water, and press the candies into the cookies. Use the black writing icing tube to pipe the noses and mouths, finishing with red tongues.

10 **To make the ears,** divide the remaining icing into 20 pieces. Roll each piece into a ball and flatten to make a flat pear shape. Brush with water and stick on either side of the cookies. Arrange in a single layer and let dry.

Gingerbread people

With this easy gingerbread recipe, there are no end of possibilities for the different-shape cookies you can make.

makes about **24**

ingredients
- **oil**, for greasing
- **all-purpose flour**, 2 cups
- **ground ginger**, 1 teaspoon
- **ground cinnamon**, ¼ teaspoon
- **baking soda**, 1½ teaspoons
- **margarine**, 4 tablespoons
- **light brown sugar**, ⅔ cup
- **light corn syrup**, 3 tablespoons
- **milk**, 2 tablespoons
- **semisweet chocolate**, 3 ounces
- **sugar-coated chocolate candies, thin candy shoelaces, sprinkles**, or **any other candies you like**
- **colored icing pens**

colored sprinkles

ground ginger

COOK'S TIPS
▶ Chocolate decorations soften cookies, so you need to eat them on the day you make them or decorate as many cookies as you will eat and store the rest in an airtight container for up to four days.

▶ As an alternative, why not use animal-shape cutters and make a gingerbread farm.

tools
- ✳ 2 baking sheets
- ✳ Pastry brush
- ✳ Strainer or sifter
- ✳ Large mixing bowl
- ✳ Medium heavy pan
- ✳ Wooden spoon
- ✳ Rolling pin
- ✳ Gingerbread men and women cutters
- ✳ Oven mitts
- ✳ Palette knife
- ✳ Wire rack
- ✳ Medium pan
- ✳ Medium heatproof bowl
- ✳ Piping bag fitted with a fine plain nozzle or parchment paper piping bag

1 Brush two baking sheets with a little oil. Sift the flour, spices, and baking soda into a mixing bowl.

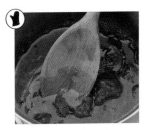

2 Place the margarine, sugar, and syrup in a pan and heat gently until the margarine has melted. Adult supervision is required.

3 Ask an adult to remove from the heat and pour the mixture into the mixing bowl containing the flour. Add the milk and mix to a firm dough with a wooden spoon. Chill for 30 minutes.

4 Preheat the oven to 325°F.

5 Lightly knead the dough for 1 minute on a lightly floured counter, until it is pliable. Roll out the cookie dough to about ¼ inch in thickness with the rolling pin. Carefully stamp out gingerbread men and women with cookie cutters.

6 Carefully transfer the cookies to the oiled baking sheets with a palette knife. Bring the dough trimmings together into a ball and roll out again. Stamp out as many more people as you can until all the dough is used.

7 Cook for 10 minutes, until golden. Ask an adult to remove from the oven and loosen with a palette knife. Set aside to cool and harden a little on the baking sheets. Transfer to the wire rack once cool with the palette knife.

8 Break the chocolate into pieces and put in a heatproof bowl. Set over a pan of simmering water. Heat until melted. Adult supervision is required.

9 Use some of the chocolate to make clothes. Let stand to set.

10 Spoon the remaining chocolate into a piping bag fitted with a small nozzle and pipe faces on all the cookies. Decorate the cookies as you like, using any of the candies and chocolates and piping colorful hair on the heads, if you want.

party food   227

Jelly sandwich cookies

These buttery cookies are absolutely wonderful. Sandwiched with buttercream and a spoonful of strawberry jelly, they are perfect for birthday parties.

serves **4**

ingredients
- **all-purpose flour**, 2 cups
- **unsalted butter**, ¾ cup, chilled and diced
- **superfine sugar**, ⅔ cup
- **egg yolk**, 1
- **strawberry jelly**, 4–5 tablespoons

for the buttercream
- **unsalted butter**, 4 tablespoons, at room temperature, diced
- **confectioners' sugar**, scant 1 cup

tools
- ✳ Food processor
- ✳ Plastic wrap
- ✳ 2 baking sheets
- ✳ Rolling pin
- ✳ 2½-inch fluted cookie cutter
- ✳ Heart-shaped cookie cutter, ¾ inch in diameter
- ✳ Oven mitts
- ✳ Palette knife
- ✳ Wire rack
- ✳ Medium mixing bowl
- ✳ Wooden spoon
- ✳ Metal spoon

1 Put the flour and butter in a food processor and blend until it resembles bread crumbs. Add the sugar and egg yolk and blend until it starts to form a dough. Adult supervision is required.

2 Knead on a floured counter until smooth. Shape into a ball, wrap in plastic wrap, and chill for 30 minutes. Preheat the oven to 350°F.

3 Roll out the dough and cut out circles with the cookie cutter.

4 Reroll the trimmings and cut out more circles until you have 40 in total. Place half the circles on a baking sheet. Using the heart-shaped cutter, cut out the centers of the remaining circles. Place the circles on the other baking sheet.

5 Bake for 12 minutes, until pale golden. Ask an adult to transfer to a wire rack. Let cool completely.

6 To make the buttercream, beat together the butter and sugar in a medium bowl.

7 Using a palette knife, spread a little buttercream onto each whole cookie. Spoon a little jelly onto the buttercream, then gently press the cut-out cookies on top, so that the jelly fills the heart-shaped hole.

 = Watch out! Sharp or electrical tool in use. = Watch out! Heat is involved.

Chocolate cookies on sticks

makes 12

Let your imagination run wild when decorating these chocolaty treats. The only hard part about this recipe is not eating all the decorations!

ingredients
- **milk chocolate**, 4¼ ounces
- **white chocolate**, 3 ounces
- **oatmeal cookies** or **other cookies of your choice**, 2 ounces, crumbled into chunks
- **small soft candies**, **chocolate chips**, or **chocolate-coated raisins**, to decorate

chocolate chips

tools
- ✳ 2 medium heatproof bowls
- ✳ 2 medium pans
- ✳ Metal spoon
- ✳ Parchment paper
- ✳ Pencil
- ✳ Large baking sheet
- ✳ 12 wooden popsicle sticks
- ✳ Piping bag

1 Break the milk and white chocolates into pieces and put in separate heatproof bowls. Place each over a pan of simmering water and heat, stirring frequently, until melted. Do not let the bowl touch the water. Adult supervision is required.

2 Meanwhile, carefully draw six 2¾-inch circles and six 3½ x 2¾-inch rectangles on the parchment paper. Invert the paper onto the large baking sheet.

3 Spoon most of the milk chocolate into the outlines on the paper, reserving one or two spoonfuls for attaching the sticks. Using the back of the teaspoon, carefully spread the chocolate to the edges of the pencil outlines to make neat shapes.

4 Press the end of a wooden popsicle stick into each of the shapes, and spoon over a little more melted milk chocolate to cover the top of the sticks. Sprinkle the shapes with the crumbled cookies while the chocolate is still warm.

5 Pipe over white chocolate squiggles with the piping bag or a spoon, then decorate with colored candies, chocolate chips, or chocolate-coated raisins. Chill for 1 hour, until set, then carefully peel away the parchment paper.

Wobbly gelatin

Gelatin is a classic party favorite, and these fun fruity faces make a great alternative to the normal way of serving it.

serves 4

ingredients

- **strawberry gelatin**, 5 ounces
- **ripe plums**, 2
- **fromage frais** or **strained plain yogurt**, ⅔ cup
- **licorice** or **gum drop mixture**, 4, cut in half
- **sugar** or **chocolate strands**, 2 teaspoons

plums   fromage frais

tools

- ✳ Small sharp knife or scissors
- ✳ Large, heatproof mixing bowl
- ✳ Wooden spoon
- ✳ Cutting board
- ✳ Medium sharp knife
- ✳ Teaspoon
- ✳ 4 small bowls or individual ramekins

1 Place the gelatin in a heatproof bowl and ask an adult to pour over boiling water, following the instructions on the package. Stir with a wooden spoon until the gelatin has dissolved, then set aside to cool.

2 On a cutting board, cut the plums in half with a sharp knife. Remove the pits with a teaspoon, then cut four slices for a garnish; reserve the slices. Chop the remaining fruit into pieces. Adult supervision is required.

3 Stir the fromage frais or yogurt into the gelatin.

4 Divide the fruit among four small bowls or ramekins. Pour over the gelatin mixture and chill for 2 hours, until set.

5 Carefully dip the bottoms of the bowls or ramekins in a bowl of hot water and turn out onto plates. Decorate with plums for mouths. Push in licorice or gum drops for eyes and sugar or chocolate strands for hair.

(!) = Watch out! Sharp or electrical tool in use.   (✊) = Watch out! Heat is involved.

Yogurt popsicles

These supercool popsicles are perfect for summer parties. Make plenty in advance, because these are so delicious you will probably quickly run out!

makes **6**

ingredients
- **strawberry yogurt**, ½ cup
- **milk**, ⅔ cup
- **strawberry milkshake powder**, 2 teaspoons

tools
- ✳ **Measuring pitcher**
- ✳ **Wooden spoon**
- ✳ **6 popsicle molds**
- ✳ **6 popsicle sticks**
- ✳ **Large heatproof bowl**

1 In a pitcher, mix together the strawberry yogurt, milk, and strawberry milkshake powder with a wooden spoon. Beat well to blend completely and ensure there are no lumps of milkshake powder.

2 Carefully pour the yogurt mixture into six small plastic popsicle molds, filling them to the top. Insert six popsicle sticks in the center of each, then freeze for 6 hours or overnight, until firm.

3 Fill the large heatproof bowl halfway with hot, not boiling, water. Ask an adult to dip the molds into the hot water, count to 15, then flex the handles and lift out the popsicles. Serve immediately.

COOK'S TIPS
▶ You can store these popsicles for a few weeks in the freezer. Make sure they are tightly covered.

▶ Try freezing the mixture in an ice-cube tray. Then simply pop out a mouthful of frozen yogurt when you feel like it.

▶ You can make these popsicles with any of your favorite flavors. Try banana yogurt with banana milkshake powder or raspberry yogurt with strawberry milkshake powder.

Chocolate fudge sundaes

Who needs to go to an ice cream parlor when you can make our very own extra fudgy chocolate sundaes at home! These are perfect for any special occasion.

serves **4**

ingredients
- **vanilla** and **coffee** or **chocolate ice cream**, 4 scoops each
- **small bananas**, 2, peeled and sliced
- **toasted sliced almonds**, to serve

for the chocolate fudge sauce
- **semisweet chocolate**, 5 ounces
- **light brown sugar**, ¼ cup
- **light corn syrup**, ½ cup
- **strong black coffee** or **water**, 3 tablespoons
- **ground cinnamon**, 1 teaspoon (optional)
- **whipping cream**, scant 1 cup

tools
- ✳ **Cutting board**
- ✳ **Large sharp knife**
- ✳ **Small heavy pan**
- ✳ **Wooden spoon**
- ✳ **4 tall sundae glasses**
- ✳ **Ice cream scoop**
- ✳ **Mixing bowl**
- ✳ **Whisk**

1 On a cutting board, chop the chocolate. Adult supervision is required.

2 **To make the chocolate fudge sauce**, put the sugar, syrup, coffee or water, and cinnamon in a heavy pan. Simmer for 5 minutes, stirring often. Adult supervision is required.

3 Turn off the heat and stir in the chopped chocolate. When melted and smooth, stir in ⅓ cup of the cream.

4 Place one scoop of vanilla ice cream into each of four sundae glasses. Top with a scoop of coffee or chocolate ice cream.

5 Whip the remaining cream. Arrange the bananas over the ice cream. Pour a drizzle of fudge sauce over the bananas, then top each with a spoonful of cream.

6 Sprinkle almonds over the cream and serve the sundaes immediately.

VARIATION
- You can use pistachio ice cream instead of vanilla ice cream, white or milk chocolate instead of semisweet chocolate, and toasted chopped pistachios instead of almonds.

(!) = Watch out! Sharp or electrical tool in use.   (✊) = Watch out! Heat is involved.

Strawberry ice cream

Making your own ice cream is cool! This foolproof recipe is easier than a "classic" one, where you have to make your own custard.

makes 3¾ cups

ingredients
- **heavy cream**, 1¼ cups
- **custard**, 1 package, prepared following the package directions
- **strawberries**, 1 pound, plus extra to decorate
- **wafers**, to decorate

strawberries

tools
- ✳ **Large mixing bowl**
- ✳ **Whisk**
- ✳ **Large metal spoon**
- ✳ **Strainer**
- ✳ **Blender or food processor**
- ✳ **Large sealable plastic container**
- ✳ **Fork**

1 Put the cream in a mixing bowl and whisk until soft peaks form. Using a large metal spoon, fold in the custard.

2 Pull and twist the stalks from the strawberries (known as hulling). Rinse the strawberries in a strainer and pat dry on paper towels.

3 Place the strawberries in the blender or food processor and blend until smooth. Adult supervision is required. Pass through the strainer into the cream.

4 Pour the mixture into the sealable container and freeze for 6–7 hours, until semi-frozen.

5 Beat with a fork or blend in a blender or food processor until smooth. Return to the freezer and freeze until solid.

6 Remove from the freezer 10 minutes before serving so that it can soften slightly. Serve with wafers and extra strawberries.

VARIATION
- To make strawberry ripple ice cream, purée and strain an extra 9 ounces of strawberries into a separate small bowl in Step 3. Stir in 2 tablespoons of confectioners' sugar. Swirl this puree into the half-frozen ice cream in Step 4, then freeze until solid and serve. You can make the puree from raspberries instead.

Balloon cake

Whether it's for a family birthday or a gift for a friend, this impressive cake will make a wonderful centerpiece for any party. Plan plenty of time to make it.

serves **10–12**

ingredients

for the cake
- **butter** or **oil**, for greasing
- **self-rising flour**, 2 cups
- **baking powder**, 2 teaspoons
- **soft butter**, 1 cup
- **superfine sugar**, 1 cup
- **eggs**, 4

for the decoration
- **buttercream**, ½ cup (see page 228)
- **apricot jelly** 3 tablespoons, warmed
- **confectioners' sugar**, for dusting
- **marzipan**, 1 pound
- **rolled fondant icing**, 3 cups
- **red, blue, green,** and **yellow food coloring paste** (see Cook's Tips)
- **royal icing**, ¾ cup

tools
- ✳ **8-inch, round, loose-bottom cake pan**
- ✳ **Parchment paper**
- ✳ **Pencil**
- ✳ **Scissors**
- ✳ **Strainer or sifter**
- ✳ **Large mixing bowl**
- ✳ **Wooden spoon or electric mixer**
- ✳ **Skewer**
- ✳ **Oven mitts**
- ✳ **Wire rack**
- ✳ **Large serrated knife**
- ✳ **Sharp knife**
- ✳ **Pastry brush**
- ✳ **Rolling pin**
- ✳ **Piping bag fitted with a small star nozzle**
- ✳ **Ribbon and candles**

1 Preheat the oven to 325°F. Lightly grease an 8-inch cake pan. Place the pan on the parchment paper and draw around the bottom with a pencil. Cut out the circle with scissors and use to line the bottom of the pan.

2 Sift the flour and baking powder into a large mixing bowl. Add the butter, sugar, and eggs. Beat with a wooden spoon or an electric mixer (adult supervision is required) for 2–3 minutes, until pale, creamy and glossy.

3 Spoon the mixture into the cake pan and level the surface with the back of a spoon. Bake for 30–40 minutes, or until a skewer inserted into the center of the cake comes out clean. Ask an adult to remove from the oven and turn out onto a wire rack. Cool.

4 Ask an adult to cut the cake in half and spread one half with the buttercream. Sandwich the other half on top and place the cake on a cake board. Brush all over with apricot jelly.

5 On a counter dusted with confectioners' sugar, roll out the marzipan and use to cover the cake. Smooth over the surface and down the sides with your hands. Trim the edges. Adult supervision is required. Brush with water.

! = Watch out! Sharp or electrical tool in use.   = Watch out! Heat is involved.

8 Color the royal icing yellow. Place some in a piping bag and pipe balloon strings or numbers onto the top of the cake.

9 Place the remaining yellow icing in a piping bag fitted with a small star nozzle and pipe a border around the bottom. Tie the ribbon around the side of the cake and add the candles.

6 Roll out the fondant icing and use most of it to cover the cake. Trim the edges with the knife, reserving the trimmings. Add the trimmings to the reserved fondant icing, then divide into three. Color them pink, blue, and green.

7 Draw the outlines of nine balloons on parchment paper. Roll out the colored fondant icing and cut out three balloons from each color. Brush one side with water and carefully place on the cake, overlapping the balloons.

Spooky cookies

If you're really lucky, these dramatic cookies might scare away guests, leaving all the more for you!

makes **28**

ingredients

- **all-purpose flour**, 2 cups
- **unsalted butter**, ¾ cup, chilled and diced
- **orange**, 1, finely grated rind
- **light Barbados** or **brown sugar**, ⅔ cup
- **egg yolk**, 1

for the decoration

- **orange juice**, 2 tablespoons
- **confectioners' sugar**, 1¾ cups, sifted
- **orange** and **green food coloring pastes**
- **red** and **black writing icing pens**
- **assorted soft candies**

tools

- ✳ Food processor
- ✳ Plastic wrap
- ✳ Rolling pin
- ✳ 2½-inch round cookie cutter
- ✳ 2 nonstick baking sheets
- ✳ Oven mitts
- ✳ Palette knife
- ✳ Wire rack
- ✳ Large mixing bowl
- ✳ Wooden spoon
- ✳ 3 small mixing bowls
- ✳ Small butter knife

1 Put the flour, butter, and orange rind into a food processor. Blend until the mixture resembles bread crumbs. Add the sugar and egg yolk and blend until it starts to bind together. Adult supervision is required.

2 Turn out onto a lightly floured counter and knead until it forms a dough.

3 Shape the dough into a ball and wrap in plastic wrap. Chill for 30 minutes.

4 Preheat the oven to 350°F. Roll out the dough on a floured counter and stamp out circles using a 2½-inch round cookie cutter. Reroll the trimmings and repeat the process.

5 Transfer the circles to the baking sheets, spacing them slightly apart. Bake for 12–15 minutes, until pale golden. Ask an adult to remove from the oven and transfer to a wire rack with the palette knife to cool.

6 To decorate the cookies, put the orange juice in a large mixing bowl and gradually stir in the confectioners' sugar until the mixture is about the consistency of heavy cream. Divide the mixture among three small bowls. Keeping one batch white, color one orange and the third green with the coloring paste.

7 Spread the cookies with the different colored icings using a butter knife. Using the red and black writing icing pens and various candies, make vampire faces on the white cookies, witchy faces and hair on the green cookies, and pumpkin faces on the orange cookies. Let stand to set for 30 minutes.

Chocolate witchy apples

You won't want to give these away to the trick-or-treaters! Better than toffee apples, you can get all your friends at the party to decorate their own.

makes 6

ingredients
- **oil** or **butter**, for greasing
- **apples**, 6 small
- **milk chocolate**, 8 ounces
- **round candies**, 12
- **candy shoelaces**
- **ice cream cones**, 6
- **jewel-colored candies** (optional)

apples

tools
* **Baking sheet**
* **Parchment papers**
* **Vegetable peeler**
* **6 wooden skewers** or popsicle sticks
* **Heatproof bowl**
* **Medium pan**
* **Wooden spoon**

1 Lightly grease a baking sheet with oil or butter and line with a piece of parchment paper.

2 Peel the apples with a vegetable peeler and thoroughly dry them on paper towels. Press a wooden skewer or popsicle stick into the core of each one. Adult supervision is required.

3 Put the chocolate in a heatproof bowl set over a pan of barely simmering water (being careful to not let the water touch the bottom of the bowl). Let the chocolate melt for about 5 minutes. Remove the bowl from the pan and stir the chocolate gently with a wooden spoon. Adult supervision is required.

4 Tilt the bowl to collect a deep pool of chocolate on one side of the bowl. Dip each apple in the chocolate, coating the outside completely (reserve any leftover chocolate in the bowl). Place each apple on the lined baking sheet. Let stand for 30 minutes, until the chocolate is almost set.

5 One at a time, hold the apples by the sticks. Press two round candies into the chocolate on each apple to make the witch's eyes. Use a small piece of a candy shoelace to make a smile, and attach longer pieces to the top of the apple to make hair. Repeat with the other apples.

6 Use a little of the remaining melted chocolate to attach the cone to the top of the apple for a hat. If you like, use a little more melted chocolate to attach jewel-colored candies to the cone for decoration.

Jack-o'-lantern cake

This spooky cake is guaranteed to be popular at your next Halloween party. Cook it the day before so you don't need to rush and the icing will have time to dry.

COOK'S TIP

▶ Liquid glucose is sometimes referred to as glucose syrup. It is a thick, clear liquid used for sweetening a number of desserts, cakes, and candies. It differs from sugar in that it does not form sugar crystals when it is used, producing a smoother result. This is especially important when you want a nice smooth icing, or when you are making ice cream. To make it easier to measure, warm the syrup or the spoon slightly before measuring, so it doesn't stick.

serves **8–10**

ingredients
- **all-purpose flour**, ½ cups
- **baking powder**, 2½ teaspoons
- **salt**, a pinch
- **butter**, ½ cup, at room temperature, plus extra for greasing
- **superfine sugar**, generous 1 cup
- **egg yolks**, 3, at room temperature, well beaten
- **grated lemon rind**, 1 teaspoon
- **milk**, ¾ cup

for the cake covering
- **confectioners' sugar**, 5 cups, plus extra for dusting
- **egg white**, 1
- **liquid glucose**, 2 tablespoons (see Cook's Tip)
- **orange** and **black food coloring pastes**

flour, sugar, and butter

tools
- ✳ 8-inch round, loose-bottom cake pan
- ✳ Pencil
- ✳ Parchment paper
- ✳ Scissors
- ✳ Strainer or sifter
- ✳ 2 large mixing bowls
- ✳ Electric mixer or wooden spoon
- ✳ 2 metal spoons
- ✳ Skewer
- ✳ Oven mitts
- ✳ Wire rack
- ✳ Rolling pin
- ✳ Small sharp knife
- ✳ Pastry brush

1 Preheat the oven to 375°F. Grease the cake pan. Using a pencil draw around the pan onto parchment paper. Cut out the circle and use it to line the bottom of the pan.

2 Sift together the flour, baking powder, and salt into a large bowl.

3 Using an electric mixer (adult supervision is required) or wooden spoon, beat the butter and sugar until pale and creamy.

4 Gradually beat in the egg yolks, then add the lemon rind. Fold in the flour mixture in three batches, alternating with the milk, using a large metal spoon. Spoon into the prepared pan.

5 Bake for 35–40 minutes, until golden brown and a skewer comes out clean when inserted into the center. Ask an adult to remove from the oven. Cool in the pan for 5 minutes. Turn out onto a wire rack to cool completely.

6 For the cake covering, sift 5 cups of the confectioners' sugar into another bowl. Make a well in the center and add 1 egg white and the liquid glucose. Mix, add the food coloring, then mix to form a dough.

(!) = Watch out! Sharp or electrical tool in use.   = Watch out! Heat is involved.

7 Transfer the icing dough to a clean counter dusted generously with confectioners' sugar and knead briefly until pliable and the dough is an even shade of orange.

8 Add some more confectioners' sugar to the counter and use some more to dust a rolling pin, then roll out the icing to about ¼ inch in thickness and to form a circle large enough to cover the top and sides of the cake.

9 Drape the icing over the rolling pin, lift over the cake, and position. Smooth over the edges and sides with your hands. Trim around bottom, reserving the excess icing. Adult supervision is required.

10 Put the excess icing back in the bowl and add a small amount of black food coloring paste. Mix well until evenly colored, then transfer to the counter and roll out thinly. Cut two triangles for the eyes, a slightly smaller triangle for the nose, and a jagged shape for the teeth. Cut small shapes for the hair.

11 Brush the undersides of the shapes with a little water and arrange the icing on top of the cake.

party food   **239**

Creamy fudge

Fudge is an old-fashioned treat that makes a perfect gift for birthdays or celebrations, such as Christmas. You can make some decorative gift boxes to give it in.

makes **2** pounds

ingredients
- **unsalted butter**, 4 tablespoons, plus extra for greasing
- **white sugar**, 2 cups
- **heavy cream**, 1¼ cups
- **milk**, ⅔ cup
- **water**, 3 tablespoons

flavorings
- **semisweet** or **milk chocolate chips**, 1 cup
- **almonds**, **hazelnuts**, **walnuts**, or **brazil nuts**, 1 cup, chopped
- **candied cherries**, **dates**, or **dried apricots**, ½ cup, chopped

candied cherries

tools
- ✳ 8-inch shallow square pan
- ✳ Large heavy pan
- ✳ Cup
- ✳ Wooden spoon
- ✳ Large sharp knife

1 Grease the pan. Put the butter, sugar, cream, milk, and water into a pan. Heat very gently, until the sugar has dissolved. Fill a cup with cold water. Bring the mixture to a rolling boil. Spoon a small amount into the water. If you can roll it into a soft ball, then it is ready. If not, boil and test again in a few minutes. Adult supervision is required.

2 If you are making chocolate-flavored fudge, add the chocolate chips to the mixture at this stage. Stir well.

3 Remove the pan from the heat and beat with a wooden spoon until the mixture starts to thicken and become opaque. Adult supervision is required.

4 Just before this stage has been reached, add the nuts, cherries, or dried fruit. Beat well.

5 Carefully pour into the pan. Let stand until cool. Using the knife, score small squares and let stand in the pan until firm. Turn out and cut into squares. Adult supervision is required.

COOK'S TIP
▶ There are different stages when you are boiling sugar, depending on what you are making, that tell you when the mixture is ready. If you go beyond the required stage, the sugar will set too firmly. This recipe uses the "soft ball" method.

(!) = Watch out! Sharp or electrical tool in use.   = Watch out! Heat is involved.

Striped cookies

Try these attractive cookies with vanilla ice cream or chocolate mousse. You will have loads of fun molding them around a spoon handle to get the special shape.

makes **25**

ingredients
- **butter** or **oil**, for greasing
- **white chocolate**, 2 ounces, melted
- **red** and **green food coloring dusts** or **pastes**
- **egg whites**, 2
- **superfine sugar**, ⅓ cup
- **all-purpose flour**, ½ cup
- **unsalted butter**, 4 tablespoons, melted

tools
- ✳ **2 nonstick baking sheets**
- ✳ **Parchment paper**
- ✳ **2 small bowls**
- ✳ **2 piping bags fitted with plain nozzles**
- ✳ **Large mixing bowl**
- ✳ **Whisk**
- ✳ **Strainer or sifter**
- ✳ **Teaspoon**
- ✳ **Palette knife**
- ✳ **Oven mitts**
- ✳ **2–3 wooden spoons**
- ✳ **Wire rack**

white chocolate

1 Preheat the oven to 375°F. Grease and line two nonstick baking sheets.

2 Put half the chocolate in one bowl, and the other half in another. Add red food coloring to one and green to the other and mix. Fill two piping bags with each and fold down the tops.

3 Put the egg whites in a large mixing bowl and whisk until they form stiff peaks. Gradually add the sugar, whisking well after each addition, to make a thick meringue.

4 Sift in the flour and add the melted butter. Fold in until the mixture is smooth.

5 Drop teaspoonfuls of the mixture onto the baking sheets and spread into circles with a palette knife.

6 Pipe zigzags of green and red chocolate over each. Bake for 3–4 minutes, until pale golden. Loosen with the palette knife and ask an adult to return to the oven for a few seconds.

7 With adult supervision, carefully take a cookie out of the oven and roll it around a spoon handle. Let stand for a few seconds to set. Repeat to make the remaining cookies.

8 Remove the set cookies from the spoon handles and let cool completely on the wire rack.

Christmas tree angels

These edible tree decorations will make any Christmas party complete. Hang them on the tree before guests arrive and give them as "going home presents."

makes **20–30**

ingredients
- **raw sugar**, scant ½ cup
- **light corn syrup**, scant 1 cup
- **ground ginger**, 1 teaspoon
- **ground cinnamon**, 1 teaspoon
- **ground cloves**, ¼ teaspoon
- **unsalted butter**, ½ cup, cut into pieces, plus extra for greasing
- **baking soda**, 2 teaspoons

- **egg**, 1, beaten
- **all-purpose flour**, 4½ cups, sifted

for the decoration
- **egg white**, 1
- **confectioners' sugar**, 1½–2 cups, sifted
- **silver** and **gold balls**

cloves

tools
- ✳ 2 large baking sheets
- ✳ Parchment paper
- ✳ Large heavy pan
- ✳ Wooden spoon
- ✳ Large heatproof bowl
- ✳ Strainer or sifter
- ✳ Rolling pin
- ✳ Plain round cookie cutter
- ✳ Small sharp knife
- ✳ Drinking straw
- ✳ Oven mitts
- ✳ Wire rack
- ✳ Palette knife
- ✳ Fork
- ✳ Small mixing bowl
- ✳ Piping bag fitted with a plain nozzle
- ✳ Fine ribbon or thread

VARIATIONS
- You can use this lightly spiced cookie dough to make cookies of many different shapes, including stars, Christmas trees, teddy bears, elephants—the only limit is the shape of the cookie cutters you happen to have.
- Don't restrict yourself to gold and silver balls when decorating the cookies—you can add any small, soft candies you like, such as gum drops, or why not try sprinkling with colored or chocolate sprinkles.

1 Preheat the oven to 325°F. Grease and line two baking sheets. Put the sugar, syrup, ginger, cinnamon, and cloves in a pan and bring to a boil, stirring. Remove from the heat. Adult supervision is required.

2 Put the butter in a large heatproof bowl and pour over the sugar mixture. Add the baking soda and stir until the butter has melted. Beat in the egg, then the flour. Mix, then knead on a floured counter to form a smooth dough.

3 Divide the dough into four pieces and roll out one at a time, between sheets of parchment paper, to a thickness of about ⅛ inch. Keep the unrolled dough in a plastic bag until needed to prevent it from drying out.

4 Stamp out medium circles with the cutter. With adult supervision, cut off two segments from either side of the circle to make a body and two wings. Place the wings, round-side down, behind the body and press together with your fingers.

5 Roll a small piece of dough for the head, place at the top of the body, and flatten with your fingers. Using the end of the drinking straw, stamp out a hole through which ribbon can be threaded when they are cooked.

 = Watch out! Sharp or electrical tool in use. = Watch out! Heat is involved.

6 Place the cookies on the baking sheets. Bake for 10–15 minutes, until golden brown. Ask an adult to remove from the oven. Let cool slightly on the sheets, then transfer to a wire rack with the palette knife. Cool completely.

7 **For the decoration**, beat the egg white with a fork in a small mixing bowl. Whisk in enough confectioners' sugar to make an icing that forms soft peaks when you lift the fork from the mixture.

8 Put the icing in a piping bag fitted with a plain writing nozzle and decorate the cookies with simple designs, such as stripes on the dress or wings, hair, faces, zigzags on the wings, or whatever you like.

9 Press silver and gold balls into the icing, in whatever patterns you like, before the icing has set. Let stand to set for about 15 minutes.

10 Finally, thread loops of fine ribbon through the holes in the tops of the cookies, so they can be hung up on a tree.

Mince pies

Although you need to make mincemeat in advance, it is well worth using your own rather than store-bought varieties because it tastes so much better.

makes **12**

ingredients
- **butter**, for greasing
- **confectioners' sugar**, for dusting (optional)

for the mincemeat
- **tart cooking apples**, 1¼ pounds, peeled, cored, and finely diced
- **plumped dried apricots**, ½ cup, coarsely chopped
- **dried mixed fruit**, 5⅓ cups
- **whole blanched almonds**, 1 cup, chopped
- **beef** or **vegetarian suet**, 1 cup

- **dark Barbados** or **brown sugar**, generous 1 cup
- **orange**, 1, grated rind and juice
- **lemon**, 1, grated rind and juice
- **ground cinnamon**, 1 teaspoon
- **grated nutmeg**, ½ teaspoon
- **gound ginger**, ½ teaspoon
- **orange juice**, ½ cup

for the pastry
- **all-purpose flour**, 2 cups
- **salt**, ½ teaspoon
- **superfine sugar**, 1 tablespoon
- **butter**, ⅔ cup
- **egg yolk**, 1
- **grated orange rind**, 5ml/1 teaspoon

tools
- ✳ 2 large glass mixing bowls
- ✳ 2 metal spoons
- ✳ Sterilized glass jars
- ✳ 12-hole muffin pan
- ✳ Rolling pin
- ✳ 3-inch round cutter
- ✳ 2-inch round cutter
- ✳ Teaspoon
- ✳ Pastry brush
- ✳ Oven mitts
- ✳ Wire rack

COOK'S TIPS
▶ Once opened, store jars of mincemeat in the refrigerator and use within 4 weeks. Unopened, it will keep for 1 year.

▶ Before canning, you need to "sterilize" the jars. To do this, wash the jars in hot, soapy water, rinse, and turn upside-down to drain. Stand on a baking sheet lined with paper towels. Rest any lids on top. Place in a cold oven, then heat to 225°F and bake for 30 minutes. Let stand to cool slightly before filling the jars.

1 To make the mincemeat, put the apples, apricots, dried fruit, almonds, suet, and sugar in a large glass mixing bowl and stir together with a large spoon until everything is thoroughly combined.

2 Add the orange and lemon rinds and juices, cinnamon, nutmeg, ginger, and orange juice and mix well. Cover the bowl with a clean dish towel and let stand in a cool place for 2 days, stirring occasionally.

3 Spoon the mincemeat into cool sterilized jars, pressing down well, and being very careful not to trap any air bubbles. Cover and seal. Store the jars in a cool, dark place for at least 4 weeks before using.

4 To make the pastry, sift the flour and salt into a large bowl and stir in the sugar. Rub in the butter until the mixture resembles bread crumbs. Stir in the egg yolk and orange rind and form into a ball. Chill for 30 minutes.

5 Preheat the oven to 425°F. Grease the 12-hole muffin pan. Roll out the pastry on a lightly floured counter to about ⅛ inch thick and, using a 3-inch cutter, cut out 12 circles.

(!) = Watch out! Sharp or electrical tool in use. = Watch out! Heat is involved.

6 Press the circles into the prepared muffin pan, crinkling the edge, if desired. Gather up the pastry scraps, form into a ball, and roll out again, cutting slightly smaller circles to make 12 lids.

7 Spoon mincemeat into each shell, dampen the edges of the pastry, and top with a pastry lid. Gently push down on the lid to make a good seal. Make a small slit in each pie with a small sharp knife.

8 Bake in the oven for 15–20 minutes, until the tops are light golden brown. Ask an adult to remove from the oven. Transfer to a wire rack to cool slightly and serve dusted with sugar, if desired.

Easter cookies

These delicious spiced cookies will go down really well after Easter lunch. Yummy!

makes about 18

ingredients

- **unsalted butter**, ¾ cup, at room temperature, diced
- **superfine sugar**, generous ½ cup
- **lemon**, 1, finely grated rind
- **egg yolks**, 2
- **all-purpose flour**, 2 cups
- **currants**, ¼ cup

currants

for the topping

- **marzipan**, ¾ cup
- **confectioners' sugar**, 1¾ cups, sifted, plus a little extra for dusting
- **3 different-color food coloring pastes**
- **mini sugar-coated chocolate Easter eggs**

tools

- ✳ **Large mixing bowl**
- ✳ **Wooden spoon or electric mixer**
- ✳ **Rolling pin**
- ✳ **3½-inch round or fluted cookie cutter**
- ✳ **Palette knife**
- ✳ **2 large, nonstick baking sheets**
- ✳ **2½-inch round or fluted cookie cutter**
- ✳ **Oven mitts**
- ✳ **Wire rack**
- ✳ **Medium mixing bowl**
- ✳ **3 small bowls**
- ✳ **3 teaspoons**

1 Preheat the oven to 350°F. Put the butter, sugar, and lemon rind in a large mixing bowl and beat with a wooden spoon or electric mixer (adult supervision is required) until pale and creamy.

2 Beat in the egg yolks, then stir in the flour.

3 Add the currants and mix to a firm dough. If it is a little soft, chill in the refrigerator until firm.

4 Roll out the dough so it is just under ¼-inch thick. Using a 3½-inch cutter, stamp out circles in the dough. Place the circles on the baking sheets.

5 To make the topping, roll out the marzipan on a counter dusted with confectioners' sugar to just under ¼-inch thick.

6 Use a 2½-inch cutter to stamp out enough circles to cover the cookies. Place a marzipan circle on top of each cookie.

7 Ask an adult to put the cookies in the oven and bake for 12 minutes, until just golden. Ask an adult to remove from the oven. Let stand for 5 minutes to cool on the baking sheets, then transfer to a wire rack.

8 Put the sugar in a bowl and add enough water to mix to a spreadable consistency. Divide among three bowls and add food coloring to each.

9 Divide the cookies into three and spread with icing. Press eggs on top and let stand to set.

(!) = Watch out! Sharp or electrical tool in use.   (🔥) = Watch out! Heat is involved.

Chocolate birds' nests

These are a real delight to make and wonderful to give as Easter gifts or to serve at an Easter party. You can also rustle them up at other times of the year, too.

makes 12

ingredients
- **milk chocolate**, 7 ounces
- **unsalted butter**, 2 tablespoons, diced
- **shredded wheat breakfast cereal**, 3½–4 cups (about 3½ ounces, *see* Variation)
- **small pastel, sugar-coated chocolate eggs**, 36

tools
- ✳ **12-hole muffin pan**
- ✳ **12 paper cake liners**
- ✳ **Medium heatproof bowl**
- ✳ **Medium pan**
- ✳ **Wooden spoon**
- ✳ **Teaspoon**

1 Line the holes of a 12-hole muffin pan with 12 decorative paper cake liners.

2 Break the chocolate into pieces and put it in a heatproof bowl with the butter. With adult supervision, place the bowl over the pan of simmering water.

3 Stir occasionally until melted. Remove the bowl from the heat and let cool for a few minutes. Adult supervision is required.

4 Meanwhile, crumble the shredded wheat. Stir into the melted chocolate until the cereal is completely coated.

5 Divide the mixture evenly among the paper liners, pressing it down gently with the back of a metal spoon.

6 Make an indentation in the center. Put three eggs into each and let stand in the refrigerator to set for about 2 hours.

VARIATION
- Replace the shredded wheat cereal with any other favorite cereal, such as Rice Krispies, Cheerios, Corn Flakes, Bran Flakes, or Shreddies. If the cereal is small, leave as it is, otherwise crumble as in recipe.

Nutritional notes

p40 Hummus Energy 226Cal/940kJ; Protein 6.5g; Carbohydrate 11.6g, of which sugars 0.4g; Fat 17.4g, of which saturates 2.4g; Cholesterol 0mg; Calcium 81mg; Fiber 3.5g; Sodium 153mg.

p41 Speedy Sausage Rolls Energy 91Cal/378kJ; Protein 2.3g; Carbohydrate 7.1g, of which sugars 0.5g; Fat 6.1g, of which saturates 2.7g; Cholesterol 11mg; Calcium 19mg; Fiber 0.2g; Sodium 171mg.

p42 Eggstra Special Sandwich Selection— egg and watercress filling Energy 155Cal/649kJ; Protein 4.7g; Carbohydrate 13.4g, of which sugars 0.8g; Fat 9.6g, of which saturates 3.5g; Cholesterol 77mg; Calcium 54mg; Fiber 0.5g; Sodium 222mg.

p42 Eggstra Special Sandwich Selection— egg and tuna filling Energy 114Cal/484kJ; Protein 7.9g; Carbohydrate 13.7g, of which sugars 0.8g; Fat 3.6g, of which saturates 0.8g; Cholesterol 70mg; Calcium 43mg; Fiber 0.4g; Sodium 200mg.

p44 Ham and Mozzarella Calzone Energy 686Cal/ 2877kJ; Protein 34.8g; Carbohydrate 70.2g, of which sugars 3.5g; Fat 31.5g, of which saturates 15.6g; Cholesterol 183mg; Calcium 453mg; Fiber 2.7g; Sodium 769mg.

p45 Tomato and Cheese Pizza Energy 420Cal/1761kJ; Protein 7.6g; Carbohydrate 49.8g, of which sugars 7.8g; Fat 22.6g, of which saturates 2.2g; Cholesterol 2mg; Calcium 133mg; Fiber 3.4g; Sodium 130mg.

p46 Cheese and Ham Tarts Energy 100Cal/419kJ; Protein 3.2g; Carbohydrate 9.6g, of which sugars 1.3g; Fat 5.6g, of which saturates 1.2g; Cholesterol 21mg; Calcium 59mg; Fiber 0.4g; Sodium 101mg.

p47 Spicy Sausage Tortilla Energy 273Cal/1136kJ; Protein 9.9g; Carbohydrate 18.9g, of which sugars 4.5g; Fat 17.8g, of which saturates 6.4g; Cholesterol 105mg; Calcium 142mg; Fiber 1.8g; Sodium 292mg.

p48 Popeye's Pie Energy 611Cal/2544kJ; Protein 20.8g; Carbohydrate 46.8g, of which sugars 4.7g; Fat 38.7g, of which saturates 23.1g; Cholesterol 145mg; Calcium 667mg; Fiber 6.4g; Sodium 1054mg.

p50 Tomato and Pasta Salad Energy 309Cal/1303kJ; Protein 8.6g; Carbohydrate 45g, of which sugars 3.6g; Fat 11.8g, of which saturates 1.3g; Cholesterol 0mg; Calcium 23mg; Fiber 2.3g; Sodium 16mg.

p51 Chicken Pasta Salad Energy 373Cal/1575kJ; Protein 32g; Carbohydrate 44g, of which sugars 3.7g; Fat 8.9g, of which saturates 2.6g; Cholesterol 69mg; Calcium 138mg; Fiber 3.4g; Sodium 419mg.

p52 Mozzarella and Avocado Salad Energy 613Cal/ 2554kJ; Protein 18.8g; Carbohydrate 38.3g, of which sugars 6.7g; Fat 43.8g, of which saturates 12.7g; Cholesterol 33mg; Calcium 232mg; Fiber 4.6g; Sodium 240mg.

p53 Tuna and Bean Salad Energy 294Cal/1235kJ; Protein 27.4g; Carbohydrate 23.9g, of which sugars 4.9g; Fat 10.5g, of which saturates 1.7g; Cholesterol 33mg; Calcium 105mg; Fiber 8.4g; Sodium 714mg.

p54 Confetti Salad Energy 276Cal/1150kJ; Protein 4.6g; Carbohydrate 41.9g, of which sugars 5.2g; Fat 9.9g, of which saturates 1.4g; Cholesterol 0mg; Calcium 29mg; Fiber 1.7g; Sodium 8mg.

p55 Lemony Couscous Salad Energy 211Cal/879kJ; Protein 6g; Carbohydrate 38.4g, of which sugars 2.8g; Fat 4.5g, of which saturates 0.4g; Cholesterol 0mg; Calcium 42mg; Fiber 1.1g; Sodium 451mg.

p56 Fabulous Fruit Salad Energy 162Cal/692kJ; Protein 2.4g; Carbohydrate 38.8g, of which sugars 37.5g; Fat 0.8g, of which saturates 0.2g; Cholesterol 0mg; Calcium 42mg; Fiber 4.1g; Sodium 8mg.

p57 Yogurt Cups—raspberry and apple puree Energy 68Cal/291kJ; Protein 4.8g; Carbohydrate 11.3g, of which sugars 11.3g; Fat 1g, of which saturates 0.5g; Cholesterol 1mg; Calcium 158mg; Fiber 2g; Sodium 65mg.

p57 Yogurt Cups—apricot compote Energy 139Cal/ 592kJ; Protein 6.4g; Carbohydrate 28.2g, of which sugars 28.2g; Fat 1.1g, of which saturates 0.4g; Cholesterol 1mg; Calcium 176mg; Fiber 3.7g; Sodium 69mg.

p57 Yogurt Cups—granola Energy 758Cal/3169kJ; Protein 19.8g; Carbohydrate 74.9g, of which sugars 35.7g; Fat 44.3g, of which saturates 4.5g; Cholesterol 1mg; Calcium 328mg; Fiber 7.4g; Sodium 101mg.

p58 Apricot and Pecan Bars Energy 240Cal/ 1000kJ; Protein 3.2g; Carbohydrate 18.3g, of which sugars 3.7g; Fat 17.6g, of which saturates 8.1g; Cholesterol 32mg; Calcium 21mg; Fiber 1.9g; Sodium 98mg.

p59 Date Slices Energy 211Cal/893kJ; Protein 3.6g; Carbohydrate 43.6g, of which sugars 35.5g; Fat 3.6g, of which saturates 0.5g; Cholesterol 12mg; Calcium 56mg; Fiber 1.3g; Sodium 18mg.

p60 Butterscotch Brownies Energy 469Cal/1961kJ; Protein 8.1g; Carbohydrate 48.7g, of which sugars 37.7g; Fat 28.3g, of which saturates 11.4g; Cholesterol 61mg; Calcium 182mg; Fiber 1g; Sodium 151mg.

p61 Chocolate Thumbprint Cookies Energy 54Cal/ 227kJ; Protein 0.7g; Carbohydrate 6.4g, of which sugars 3.5g; Fat 3g, of which saturates 1.8g; Cholesterol 10mg; Calcium 19mg; Fiber 0.2g; Sodium 33mg.

p62 Peanut Butter Cookies Energy 154Cal/641kJ; Protein 3.4g; Carbohydrate 13.7g, of which sugars 8.3g; Fat 9.9g, of which saturates 4g; Cholesterol 18mg; Calcium 19mg; Fiber 0.8g; Sodium 71mg.

p63 Blueberry and Lemon Muffins Energy 131Cal/ 552kJ; Protein 3.1g; Carbohydrate 20.3g, of which sugars 8.7g; Fat 4.8g, of which saturates 2.7g; Cholesterol 42mg; Calcium 47mg; Fiber 0.7g; Sodium 52mg.

p66 Frankfurter Sandwich Energy 517Cal/2158kJ; Protein 13.7g; Carbohydrate 39.1g, of which sugars 4.1g; Fat 35.4g, of which saturates 13.1g; Cholesterol 75mg; Calcium 52mg; Fiber 4.8g; Sodium 927mg.

p67 Ciabatta Sandwich Energy 693Cal/2909kJ; Protein 30.4g; Carbohydrate 74.1g, of which sugars 8.8g; Fat 32.6g, of which saturates 10.7g; Cholesterol 62mg; Calcium 433mg; Fiber 4.4g; Sodium 1380mg.

p68 Toasted Bacon Sandwich Energy 587Kcal/2439kJ; Protein 17.5g; Carbohydrate 28.2g, of which sugars 3g; Fat 46.1g, of which saturates 8.5g; Cholesterol 414mg; Calcium 150mg; Fiber 2g; Sodium 587mg.

p69 Cheesy Treats—croque monsieur Energy 384Cal/1602kJ; Protein 18.5g; Carbohydrate 22.5g, of which sugars 1.8g; Fat 24.3g, of which saturates 15.4g; Cholesterol 80mg; Calcium 331mg; Fiber 1.8g; Sodium 935mg.

p69 Cheesy Treats—Welsh rarebit Energy 334Cal/ 1390kJ; Protein 15.4g; Carbohydrate 13.9g, of which sugars 1.2g; Fat 23.4g, of which saturates 15g; Cholesterol 66mg; Calcium 404mg; Fiber 0.4g; Sodium 706mg.

p70 Cheese Toasts Energy 429Cal/1788kJ; Protein 18.5g; Carbohydrate 24.7g, of which sugars 1.4g; Fat 28.3g, of which saturates 17.2g; Cholesterol 166mg; Calcium 395mg; Fiber 0.8g; Sodium 705mg.

p70 Striped Toast Energy 418Cal/1743kJ; Protein 17g; Carbohydrate 24.7g, of which sugars 1.4g; Fat 27.5g, of which saturates 17.8g; Cholesterol 77mg; Calcium 427mg; Fiber 0.8g; Sodium 715mg.

p72 Sweet Toast Toppers—jammy toast Energy 216Cal/ 900kJ; Protein 2.4g; Carbohydrate 17g, of which sugars 4.2g; Fat 15.9g, of which saturates 10.2g; Cholesterol 43mg; Calcium 34mg; Fiber 0.4g; Sodium 284mg.

p72 Sweet Toast Toppers—cinnamon toast Energy 240Cal/1000kJ; Protein 2.8g; Carbohydrate 22.3g, of which sugars 8.6g; Fat 16.2g, of which saturates 10.3g; Cholesterol 43mg; Calcium 42mg; Fiber 0.4g; Sodium 285mg.

p73 Eggtastic—dippy egg with toast sticks Energy 382Cal/1611kJ; Protein 14.7g; Carbohydrate 49.3g, of which sugars 2.6g; Fat 15.6g, of which saturates 7.4g; Cholesterol 213mg; Calcium 140mg; Fiber 1.5g; Sodium 665mg.

p73 Eggtastic—poached egg on toast Energy 348Cal/1456kJ; Protein 17.1g; Carbohydrate 26.6g, of which sugars 1.4g; Fat 20.3g, of which saturates 8.7g; Cholesterol 404mg; Calcium 118mg; Fiber 0.8g; Sodium 496mg.

p74 Egg-Stuffed Tomatoes Energy 398Cal/1644kJ; Protein 7.9g; Carbohydrate 4.3g, of which sugars 4g; Fat 39.1g, of which saturates 6.5g; Cholesterol 223mg; Calcium 69mg; Fiber 1.8g; Sodium 281mg.

p75 Ham and Tomato Scramble Energy 350Cal/ 1456kJ; Protein 14.1g; Carbohydrate 17.1g, of which sugars 4.4g; Fat 25.7g, of which saturates 14.3g; Cholesterol 257mg; Calcium 78mg; Fiber 1.3g; Sodium 689mg.

p76 Dunkin' Dippers Energy 221Cal/919kJ; Protein 4.4g; Carbohydrate 11.2g, of which sugars 4.6g; Fat 18g, of which saturates 6.3g; Cholesterol 21mg; Calcium 71mg; Fiber 2.7g; Sodium 230mg.

p78 Skinny Dips Energy 444Cal/1870kJ; Protein 33.4g; Carbohydrate 45.9g, of which sugars 10g; Fat 15.1g, of which saturates 8.2g; Cholesterol 99mg; Calcium 159mg; Fiber 3g; Sodium 771mg.

p79 Chile Cheese Nachos Energy 290Cal/1210kJ; Protein 9.6g; Carbohydrate 18.7g, of which sugars 1.4g; Fat 19.7g, of which saturates 7.6g; Cholesterol 24mg; Calcium 236mg; Fiber 2.5g; Sodium 430mg.

p80 Cheese and Basil Tortillas Energy 420Cal/1752kJ; Protein 18.2g; Carbohydrate 29.9g, of which sugars 0.6g; Fat 24.8g, of which saturates 13.3g; Cholesterol 56mg; Calcium 480mg; Fiber 1.2g; Sodium 556mg.

p81 Chicken Pita Pockets Energy 349Cal/1472kJ; Protein 20g; Carbohydrate 45.6g, of which sugars 3.9g; Fat 10.9g, of which saturates 1.9g; Cholesterol 22mg; Calcium 149mg; Fiber 3.3g; Sodium 436mg.

p82 Chunky Veggie Salad Energy 184Cal/765kJ; Protein 7.2g; Carbohydrate 12g, of which sugars 10.5g; Fat 12.2g, of which saturates 1.9g; Cholesterol 0mg; Calcium 82mg; Fiber 5.1g; Sodium 22mg.

p83 Chicken and Tomato Salad Energy 424Cal/ 1762kJ; Protein 26.9g; Carbohydrate 7.2g, of which sugars 7g; Fat 32.2g, of which saturates 5.2g; Cholesterol 43mg; Calcium 230mg; Fiber 4.4g; Sodium 245mg.

p84 Country Pasta Salad Energy 381Cal/1600kJ; Protein 13.3g; Carbohydrate 44.4g, of which sugars 3.8g; Fat 18g, of which saturates 5g; Cholesterol 15mg; Calcium 212mg; Fiber 2.9g; Sodium 341mg.

p85 **Tuna Pasta Salad** 441Cal/1862kJ; Protein 27.4g; Carbohydrate 60.2g, of which sugars 6g; Fat 11.7g, of which saturates 1.8g; Cholesterol 25mg; Calcium 104mg; Fiber 8.2g; Sodium 543mg.

p88 **Chilled Tomato Soup** Energy 218Cal/902kJ; Protein 4.8g; Carbohydrate 7.5g, of which sugars 7.2g; Fat 19g, of which saturates 3.6g; Cholesterol 6mg; Calcium 100mg; Fiber 2.2g; Sodium 104mg.

p89 **Chilled Avocado Soup** Energy 242Cal/1001kJ; Protein 2.8g; Carbohydrate 3g, of which sugars 1.3g; Fat 24.2g, of which saturates 5.2g; Cholesterol 0mg; Calcium 22mg; Fiber 4.6g; Sodium 9mg.

p90 **Broccoli Soup** Energy 100Cal/423kJ; Protein 7.6g; Carbohydrate 14.6g, of which sugars 2.5g; Fat 1.6g, of which saturates 0.3g; Cholesterol 0mg; Calcium 98mg; Fiber 3.6g; Sodium 140mg.

p91 **Chinese Soup** Energy 176Cal/748kJ; Protein 6.3g; Carbohydrate 37.5g, of which sugars 5.6g; Fat 1.2g, of which saturates 0.1g; Cholesterol 0mg; Calcium 66mg; Fiber 3.4g; Sodium 39mg.

p92 **Potato and Pepper Frittata** Energy 374Cal/1563kJ; Protein 16.7g; Carbohydrate 34.9g, of which sugars 11.3g; Fat 19.4g, of which saturates 4.5g; Cholesterol 381mg; Calcium 87mg; Fiber 3.9g; Sodium 162mg.

p93 **Tomato Omelet Envelopes** Energy 488Cal/2027kJ; Protein 26g; Carbohydrate 8.6g, of which sugars 7.9g; Fat 38.2g, of which saturates 15.1g; Cholesterol 434mg; Calcium 226mg; Fiber 2.4g; Sodium 479mg.

p94 **Fiorentina Pizza** Energy 515Cal/2150kJ; Protein 20.9g; Carbohydrate 40.8g, of which sugars 5.2g; Fat 30.8g, of which saturates 11.4g; Cholesterol 104mg; Calcium 415mg; Fiber 3.2g; Sodium 634mg.

p95 **Ham and Pineapple Pizza** Energy 310Cal/1304kJ; Protein 14.4g; Carbohydrate 39.2g, of which sugars 12g; Fat 11.3g, of which saturates 5.1g; Cholesterol 29mg; Calcium 223mg; Fiber 2.7g; Sodium 666mg.

p96 **Mexican Tomato Rice** Energy 552Cal/2305kJ; Protein 12.7g; Carbohydrate 108.3g, of which sugars 4.8g; Fat 7g, of which saturates 1g; Cholesterol 0mg; Calcium 42mg; Fiber 3g; Sodium 10mg.

p97 **Quick and Easy Risotto** Energy 405Cal/1692kJ; Protein 18.3g; Carbohydrate 55.1g, of which sugars 0.2g; Fat 12g, of which saturates 6.5g; Cholesterol 136mg; Calcium 221mg; Fiber 0g; Sodium 425mg.

p98 **Presto Pasta Sauces—basic tomato** Energy 75Cal/313kJ; Protein 0.9g; Carbohydrate 4.4g, of which sugars 4g; Fat 6.2g, of which saturates 2.5g; Cholesterol 9mg; Calcium 15mg; Fiber 1.3g; Sodium 42mg.

p98 **Presto Pasta Sauces—roasted vegetable** Energy 79Cal/329kJ; Protein 1.5g; Carbohydrate 7.5g, of which sugars 7g; Fat 5g, of which saturates 0.8g; Cholesterol 0mg; Calcium 15mg; Fiber 2.5g; Sodium 8mg.

p98 **Presto Pasta Sauces—pesto** Energy 286Cal/1179kJ; Protein 5.8g; Carbohydrate 1.5g, of which sugars 0.7g; Fat 28.6g, of which saturates 5.2g; Cholesterol 10mg; Calcium 147mg; Fiber 1g; Sodium 114mg.

p98 **Presto Pasta Sauces—cream and Parmesan** Energy 283Cal/1169kJ; Protein 5.5g; Carbohydrate 0.8g, of which sugars 0.8g; Fat 30.4g, of which saturates 18.3g; Cholesterol 80mg; Calcium 167mg; Fiber 0g; Sodium 241mg.

p100 **Baked Macaroni Cheese** Energy 523Cal/2202kJ; Protein 20.6g; Carbohydrate 69.7g, of which sugars 6.6g; Fat 19.3g, of which saturates 11.7g; Cholesterol 51mg; Calcium 349mg; Fiber 2.5g; Sodium 349mg.

p101 **Farfalle with Tuna** Energy 459Cal/1949kJ; Protein 25.2g; Carbohydrate 78.6g, of which sugars 7.8g; Fat 7.1g, of which saturates 1.1g; Cholesterol 22mg; Calcium 53mg; Fiber 4.2g; Sodium 756mg.

p102 **Tortellini with Ham** Energy 509Cal/2118kJ; Protein 19.9g; Carbohydrate 26.2g, of which sugars 4.1g; Fat 36.8g, of which saturates 17.5g; Cholesterol 85mg; Calcium 353mg; Fiber 1.9g; Sodium 696mg.

p103 **Spaghetti Carbonara** Energy 707Cal/2964kJ; Protein 32.1g; Carbohydrate 66.4g, of which sugars 4.1g; Fat 36.8g, of which saturates 14.3g; Cholesterol 259mg; Calcium 246mg; Fiber 2.8g; Sodium 949mg.

p104 **Cabbage and Potatoes** Energy 219Cal/908kJ; Protein 2.5g; Carbohydrate 17.2g, of which sugars 2.5g; Fat 15.9g, of which saturates 1.9g; Cholesterol 0mg; Calcium 33mg; Fiber 2.6g; Sodium 14mg.

p105 **Bean and Tomato Chile** Energy 309Cal/1302kJ; Protein 16.7g; Carbohydrate 43.7g, of which sugars 14.1g; Fat 8.7g, of which saturates 4.2g; Cholesterol 18mg; Calcium 193mg; Fiber 12.4g; Sodium 1202mg.

p106 **Tuna and Corn Fish Cakes** Energy 329Cal/1382kJ; Protein 17g; Carbohydrate 30.7g, of which sugars 3.9g; Fat 16.3g, of which saturates 2.2g; Cholesterol 25mg; Calcium 27mg; Fiber 1.5g; Sodium 324mg.

p107 **Fast Fishes** Energy 268Cal/1124kJ; Protein 16.4g; Carbohydrate 27.1g, of which sugars 3.8g; Fat 11.2g, of which saturates 1.6g; Cholesterol 48mg; Calcium 99mg; Fiber 2.3g; Sodium 306mg.

p108 **Colorful Chicken Kebabs** Energy 229Cal/951kJ; Protein 18.2g; Carbohydrate 1g, of which sugars 0.7g; Fat 17g, of which saturates 4.4g; Cholesterol 81mg; Calcium 11mg; Fiber 0.2g; Sodium 69mg.

p109 **Sticky Chicken** Energy 109Cal/458kJ; Protein 14.7g; Carbohydrate 1.2g, of which sugars 1.1g; Fat 5.1g, of which saturates 1.4g; Cholesterol 77mg; Calcium 9mg; Fiber 0g; Sodium 222mg.

p110 **Honey Mustard Chicken** Energy 287Cal/1205kJ; Protein 33.9g; Carbohydrate 12.1g, of which sugars 12.1g; Fat 11.8g, of which saturates 3g; Cholesterol 174mg; Calcium 30mg; Fiber 0.7g; Sodium 386mg.

p111 **Yellow Bean Chicken** Energy 327Cal/1367kJ; Protein 30.8g; Carbohydrate 9g, of which sugars 2.5g; Fat 18.9g, of which saturates 3.7g; Cholesterol 48mg; Calcium 40mg; Fiber 2.3g; Sodium 272mg.

p112 **Turkey Burgers** Energy 141Cal/596kJ; Protein 24.8g; Carbohydrate 0.8g, of which sugars 0.6g; Fat 4.4g, of which saturates 1.1g; Cholesterol 69mg; Calcium 15mg; Fiber 0.2g; Sodium 62mg.

p113 **Pitas with Lamb Koftas** Energy 609Cal/2568kJ; Protein 35.3g; Carbohydrate 83.8g, of which sugars 5.4g; Fat 17g, of which saturates 7.3g; Cholesterol 87mg; Calcium 230mg; Fiber 3.8g; Sodium 737mg.

p114 **Mexican Tacos** Energy 559Cal/2325kJ; Protein 24.6g; Carbohydrate 26g, of which sugars 3.2g; Fat 39.6g, of which saturates 16g; Cholesterol 77mg; Calcium 322mg; Fiber 3.8g; Sodium 610mg.

p115 **Meatballs in Tomato Sauce** Energy 475Cal/1972kJ; Protein 28.5g; Carbohydrate 15.8g, of which sugars 5.1g; Fat 33.2g, of which saturates 10.7g; Cholesterol 123mg; Calcium 58mg; Fiber 2g; Sodium 131mg.

p116 **Pork Satay** Energy 103Cal/432kJ; Protein 13.1g; Carbohydrate 5.2g, of which sugars 4.4g; Fat 3.5g, of which saturates 0.8g; Cholesterol 33mg; Calcium 20mg; Fiber 0.5g; Sodium 54mg.

p117 **Honey Chops** Energy 550Cal/2278kJ; Protein 17.6g; Carbohydrate 19.1g, of which sugars 18.5g; Fat 45.3g, of which saturates 20.1g; Cholesterol 109mg; Calcium 68mg; Fiber 3.1g; Sodium 217mg.

p120 **Corn and Potato Chowder** Energy 251Cal/1052kJ; Protein 9.7g; Carbohydrate 25.9g, of which sugars 9.3g; Fat 12.9g, of which saturates 4.9g; Cholesterol 18mg; Calcium 128mg; Fiber 5.5g; Sodium 1154mg.

p121 **Carrot Soup** Energy 209Cal/865kJ; Protein 5.6g; Carbohydrate 14.1g, of which sugars 12.5g; Fat 15.2g, of which saturates 8.7g; Cholesterol 27mg; Calcium 123mg; Fiber 6g; Sodium 134mg.

p122 **Super-duper Soup** Energy 131Cal/553kJ; Protein 4.4g; Carbohydrate 23.3g, of which sugars 6.2g; Fat 2.8g, of which saturates 0.5g; Cholesterol 0mg; Calcium 38mg; Fiber 3.3g; Sodium 26mg.

p123 **Tomato and Bread Soup** Energy 285Cal/1194kJ; Protein 5g; Carbohydrate 28g, of which sugars 7.2g; Fat 17.9g, of which saturates 2.5g; Cholesterol 0mg; Calcium 64mg; Fiber 2.6g; Sodium 243mg.

p124 **Boston Baked Beans** Energy 235Cal/997kJ; Protein 19.1g; Carbohydrate 37.4g, of which sugars 13g; Fat 2g, of which saturates 0.5g; Cholesterol 18mg; Calcium 92mg; Fiber 9.5g; Sodium 221mg.

p125 **Zucchini and Potato Bake** Energy 248Cal/1032kJ; Protein 4.2g; Carbohydrate 19.1g, of which sugars 7.6g; Fat 17.7g, of which saturates 2.6g; Cholesterol 0mg; Calcium 43mg; Fiber 3.1g; Sodium 18mg.

p126 **Creamy Coconut Noodles** Energy 181Cal/766kJ; Protein 7.2g; Carbohydrate 30.4g, of which sugars 12.3g; Fat 4.3g, of which saturates 1.1g; Cholesterol 8mg; Calcium 115mg; Fiber 3.6g; Sodium 559mg.

p127 **Crunchy Summer Rolls** 106Kcal/445kJ; Protein 3.5g; Carbohydrate 21.2g, of which sugars 4.7g; Fat 0.7g, of which saturates 0.2g; Cholesterol 0mg; Calcium 44mg; Fiber 2.2g; Sodium 10mg.

p128 **Chinese Omelet Parcels** Energy 148Cal/614kJ; Protein 10.4g; Carbohydrate 6.2g, of which sugars 5.4g; Fat 9.3g, of which saturates 2.2g; Cholesterol 190mg; Calcium 152mg; Fiber 3g; Sodium 323mg.

p130 **Raving Ravioli** Energy 710Cal/2962kJ; Protein 19.7g; Carbohydrate 56.1g, of which sugars 3.7g; Fat 51.1g, of which saturates 25.3g; Cholesterol 245mg; Calcium 190mg; Fiber 2.5g; Sodium 125mg.

p132 **Fantastic Potatoes—stir-fried vegetables** Energy 328Cal/1380kJ; Protein 8.5g; Carbohydrate 46.3g, of which sugars 7.6g; Fat 12.5g, of which saturates 1.8g; Cholesterol 0mg; Calcium 53mg; Fiber 5.4g; Sodium 1009mg.

p132 **Fantastic Potatoes—red bean chiles** Energy 500Cal/2094kJ; Protein 13.1g; Carbohydrate 59g, of which sugars 7.8g; Fat 25.1g, of which saturates 1 5.2g; Cholesterol 48mg; Calcium 139mg; Fiber 8.9g; Sodium 586mg.

p132 **Fantastic Potatoes—cheese and creamy corn** Energy 417Cal/1760kJ; Protein 14.5g; Carbohydrate 66.9g, of which sugars 12.9g; Fat 11.4g, of which saturates 6.7g; Cholesterol 28mg; Calcium 232mg; Fiber 3.9g; Sodium 505mg.

p134 **Vegetable Paella** Energy 388Cal/1646kJ; Protein 13.5g; Carbohydrate 78.8g, of which sugars 7.5g; Fat 3.6g, of which saturates 0.9g; Cholesterol 0mg; Calcium 57mg; Fiber 8.5g; Sodium 299mg.

p135 **Fish and Rice Paella** Energy 585Cal/2445kJ; Protein 36.1g; Carbohydrate 60.9g, of which sugars 10.1g; Fat 20.4g, of which saturates 5.6g; Cholesterol 268mg; Calcium 132mg; Fiber 4.2g; Sodium 1055mg.

p136 **Flounder with Tomato Sauce** Energy 334Cal/1391kJ; Protein 22.5g; Carbohydrate 14.2g, of which sugars 4g; Fat 21.1g, of which saturates 2.5g; Cholesterol 0mg; Calcium 90mg; Fiber 1.3g; Sodium 279mg.

p137 **Fish and Cheese Pies** Energy 300Cal/1252kJ; Protein 19.7g; Carbohydrate 18.6g, of which sugars 5.4g; Fat 16.6g, of which saturates 8.3g; Cholesterol 60mg; Calcium 260mg; Fiber 1.8g; Sodium 373mg.

p138 **Tandoori-Style Chicken** Energy 202Cal/847kJ; Protein 19.4g; Carbohydrate 11.4g, of which sugars 2.8g; Fat 9g, of which saturates 2.2g; Cholesterol 87mg; Calcium 67mg; Fiber 0.8g; Sodium 63mg.

p140 **Chicken Fajitas** Energy 485Cal/2044kJ; Protein 26g; Carbohydrate 67.4g, of which sugars 15.3g; Fat 14.2g, of which saturates 3.8g; Cholesterol 60mg; Calcium 118mg; Fiber 4g; Sodium 53mg.

p142 **Turkey Croquettes** Energy 404Cal/1698kJ; Protein 19.4g; Carbohydrate 47g, of which sugars 7.7g; Fat 16.7g, of which saturates 2.4g; Cholesterol 73mg; Calcium 93mg; Fiber 3.3g; Sodium 315mg.

p143 **Turkey Surprise Packages** Energy 236Cal/988kJ; Protein 39.2g; Carbohydrate 2.4g, of which sugars 2.3g; Fat 7.7g, of which saturates 2.5g; Cholesterol 90mg; Calcium 25mg; Fiber 1.1g; Sodium 392mg.

p144 **Pork and Pineapple Curry** Energy 187Cal/790kJ; Protein 22.2g; Carbohydrate 15.3g, of which sugars 15.3g; Fat 4.5g, of which saturates 1.6g; Cholesterol 63mg; Calcium 55mg; Fiber 1.2g; Sodium 449mg.

p145 **Thai Pork Burgers** Energy 235Cal/976kJ; Protein 21.7g; Carbohydrate 0.1g, of which sugars 0.1g; Fat 16.4g, of which saturates 4.7g; Cholesterol 74mg; Calcium 11mg; Fiber 0.1g; Sodium 79mg.

p146 **Sausage Casserole** Energy 414Cal/1736kJ; Protein 14.2g; Carbohydrate 45.4g, of which sugars 11.4g; Fat 20.8g, of which saturates 7.9g; Cholesterol 30mg; Calcium 107mg; Fiber 6.7g; Sodium 894mg.

p147 **Mini Toads-In-the-Hole** Energy 282Cal/1183kJ; Protein 11.5g; Carbohydrate 28.3g, of which sugars 2.9g; Fat 14.6g, of which saturates 4.8g; Cholesterol 119mg; Calcium 131mg; Fiber 1.3g; Sodium 372mg.

p148 **Lamb and Potato Pies** Energy 784Cal/3275kJ; Protein 25.1g; Carbohydrate 74.6g, of which sugars 5.2g; Fat 44.9g, of which saturates 26.1g; Cholesterol 178mg; Calcium 155mg; Fiber 4g; Sodium 345mg

p149 **Shepherd's Pie** Energy 487Cal/2045kJ; Protein 29.4g; Carbohydrate 50.1g, of which sugars 15.2g; Fat 20.2g, of which saturates 8.4g; Cholesterol 69mg; Calcium 55mg; Fiber 5.3g; Sodium 379mg.

p150 **Crown Roast** Energy 479Cal/1988kJ; Protein 21.4g; Carbohydrate 28.5g, of which sugars 5.5g; Fat 31g, of which saturates 15.9g; Cholesterol 95mg; Calcium 28mg; Fiber 1.1g; Sodium 114mg.

p151 **Lamb Stew** Energy 152Cal/635kJ; Protein 12.3g; Carbohydrate 7.5g, of which sugars 5g; Fat 8.4g, of which saturates 3.3g; Cholesterol 44mg; Calcium 29mg; Fiber 2.2g; Sodium 59mg.

p152 **Steak with Tomato Salsa** Energy 291Cal/1215kJ; Protein 35.3g; Carbohydrate 5g, of which sugars 5g; Fat 14.5g, of which saturates 5.9g; Cholesterol 87mg; Calcium 22mg; Fiber 1.7g; Sodium 110mg.

p153 **Cheesy Burgers** Energy 288Cal/1206kJ; Protein 29.9g; Carbohydrate 8.9g, of which sugars 2.6g; Fat 15.1g, of which saturates 6.9g; Cholesterol 118mg; Calcium 83mg; Fiber 0.4g; Sodium 246mg.

p156 **Magic Chocolate Pudding** Energy 480Cal/2025kJ; Protein 10g; Carbohydrate 77.6g, of which sugars 58.3g; Fat 16.7g, of which saturates 10.2g; Cholesterol 34mg; Calcium 227mg; Fiber 3g; Sodium 309mg.

p157 **Rice Pudding** Energy 325Cal/1365kJ; Protein 6.7g; Carbohydrate 56.2g, of which sugars 38.2g; Fat 6.3g, of which saturates 1.9g; Cholesterol 1mg; Calcium 44mg; Fiber 0.5g; Sodium 171mg.

p158 **Lazy Fruit Pastry** Energy 462Cal/1940kJ; Protein 5.4g; Carbohydrate 64.8g, of which sugars 36.2g; Fat 22g, of which saturates 13.8g; Cholesterol 89mg; Calcium 81mg; Fiber 2.8g; Sodium 214mg.

p159 **Plum Crumble** Energy 569Cal/2390kJ; Protein 8.2g; Carbohydrate 80.1g, of which sugars 50.6g; Fat 25.7g, of which saturates 11.3g; Cholesterol 44mg; Calcium 126mg; Fiber 4.8g; Sodium 157mg.

p160 **Lemon Surprise Pudding** Energy 319Cal/1341kJ; Protein 7g; Carbohydrate 43.1g, of which sugars 33.8g; Fat 14.5g, of which saturates 8.1g; Cholesterol 126mg; Calcium 166mg; Fiber 0.4g; Sodium 190mg.

p161 **Baked Bananas** Energy 416Cal/1740kJ; Protein 6.3g; Carbohydrate 50.7g, of which sugars 47.2g; Fat 21.1g, of which saturates 9.5g; Cholesterol 35mg; Calcium 117mg; Fiber 1.9g; Sodium 124mg.

p162 **Banana and Toffee Ice Cream** Energy 455Cal/1909kJ; Protein 6.9g; Carbohydrate 63.2g, of which sugars 56.6g; Fat 21.1g, of which saturates 12.6g; Cholesterol 53mg; Calcium 215mg; Fiber 0.6g; Sodium 178mg.

p163 **Pineapple Sorbet on Sticks** Energy 79Cal/337kJ; Protein 0.5g; Carbohydrate 20.1g, of which sugars 20.1g; Fat 0.2g, of which saturates 0g; Cholesterol 0mg; Calcium 23mg; Fiber 1.2g; Sodium 3mg.

p164 **Strawberry Mousse** Energy 492Cal/2037kJ; Protein 1.8g; Carbohydrate 29.1g, of which sugars 29.1g; Fat 40.3g, of which saturates 25.1g; Cholesterol 103mg; Calcium 61mg; Fiber 0.7g; Sodium 24mg.

p165 **Strawberries and Meringue** Energy 526Cal/2182kJ; Protein 3.5g; Carbohydrate 32.8g, of which sugars 32.8g; Fat 40.4g, of which saturates 25.1g; Cholesterol 103mg; Calcium 60mg; Fiber 1.4g; Sodium 53mg.

p166 **Chocolate Banana Fools** Energy 268Cal/1127kJ; Protein 4.1g; Carbohydrate 42.1g, of which sugars 38.1g; Fat 9.6g, of which saturates 4.9g; Cholesterol 3mg; Calcium 81mg; Fiber 1.4g; Sodium 33mg.

p167 **Banana and Apricot Trifle** Energy 452Cal/1893kJ; Protein 4.8g; Carbohydrate 53.8g, of which sugars 44.1g; Fat 25.7g, of which saturates 13.6g; Cholesterol 129mg; Calcium 104mg; Fiber 0.7g; Sodium 77mg.

p168 **Very Berry Cheesecake** Energy 472Cal/1969kJ; Protein 11.2g; Carbohydrate 41.3g, of which sugars 29g; Fat 30.1g, of which saturates 18.3g; Cholesterol 85mg; Calcium 188mg; Fiber 1.3g; Sodium 477mg.

p170 **Fruit Fondue** Energy 197Cal/833kJ; Protein 3.8g; Carbohydrate 33.7g, of which sugars 30.2g; Fat 5.4g, of which saturates 2.3g; Cholesterol 4mg; Calcium 107mg; Fiber 1.5g; Sodium 44mg.

p171 **Cantaloupe Melon Salad** Energy 34Cal/144kJ; Protein 0.7g; Carbohydrate 8g, of which sugars 8g; Fat 0.1g, of which saturates 0g; Cholesterol 0mg; Calcium 21mg; Fiber 1.1g; Sodium 8mg.

p172 **Chocolate Puffs** Energy 403Cal/1687kJ; Protein 4.2g; Carbohydrate 48.4g, of which sugars 39.8g; Fat 22.8g, of which saturates 13.6g; Cholesterol 115mg; Calcium 62mg; Fiber 0.6g; Sodium 106mg.

p174 **Chocolate Heaven** Energy 1388Cal/5814kJ; Protein 21.2g; Carbohydrate 171.6g, of which sugars 110.8g; Fat 73.2g, of which saturates 15.3g; Cholesterol 45mg; Calcium 502mg; Fiber 2.4g; Sodium 746mg.

p176 **Fresh Orange Fizz** Energy 181Cal/773kJ; Protein 2.9g; Carbohydrate 44.8g, of which sugars 44.8g; Fat 0.3g, of which saturates 0g; Cholesterol 0mg; Calcium 130mg; Fiber 4.3g; Sodium 14mg.

p177 **Ruby Red Soda** Energy 119Cal/503kJ; Protein 0.7g; Carbohydrate 30.8g, of which sugars 28.5g; Fat 0g, of which saturates 0g; Cholesterol 0mg; Calcium 12mg; Fiber 1.2g; Sodium 1mg.

p178 **Totally Tropical** Energy 162Cal/692kJ; Protein 2.4g; Carbohydrate 38.9g, of which sugars 37.5g; Fat 0.8g, of which saturates 0.2g; Cholesterol 0mg; Calcium 42mg; Fiber 4.1g; Sodium 8mg.

p179 **Fruit Punch** Energy 111Cal/473kJ; Protein 0.9g; Carbohydrate 27.7g, of which sugars 27.7g; Fat 0.4g, of which saturates 0g; Cholesterol 0mg; Calcium 37mg; Fiber 1.7g; Sodium 17mg.

p180 **What a Smoothie** Energy 94Cal/401kJ; Protein 5.1g; Carbohydrate 17.6g, of which sugars 17.6g; Fat 1g, of which saturates 0.4g; Cholesterol 1mg; Calcium 158mg; Fiber 2.2g; Sodium 68mg.

p181 **Strawberry and Apple Cooler** Energy 78Cal/331kJ; Protein 1.4g; Carbohydrate 18.8g, of which sugars 18.8g; Fat 0.2g, of which saturates 0g; Cholesterol 0mg; Calcium 28mg; Fiber 2.7g; Sodium 24mg.

p182 **Rainbow Juice** Energy 78Cal/332kJ; Protein 1.5g; Carbohydrate 17.8g, of which sugars 17.6g; Fat 0.6g, of which saturates 0g; Cholesterol 0mg; Calcium 39mg; Fiber 2.8g; Sodium 7mg.

p182 **Fruit Slush** Energy 75Cal/319kJ; Protein 1g; Carbohydrate 18.8g, of which sugars 17.1g; Fat 0.1g, of which saturates 0g; Cholesterol 0mg; Calcium 28mg; Fiber 1.7g; Sodium 3mg.

p184 **Vanilla Milkshake** Energy 648Cal/2687kJ; Protein 15.8g; Carbohydrate 36.4g, of which sugars 36.3g; Fat 49.6g, of which saturates 30.8g; Cholesterol 83mg; Calcium 475mg; Fiber 0g; Sodium 205mg.

p185 **Strawberry Shake** Energy 286Cal/1195kJ; Protein 9.1g; Carbohydrate 30.4g, of which sugars 30.4g; Fat 16.2g, of which saturates 8.9g; Cholesterol 17mg; Calcium 217mg; Fiber 2.2g; Sodium 93mg.

p186 **Candy Stripe** Energy 349Cal/1467kJ; Protein 6.8g; Carbohydrate 54.2g, of which sugars 47.2g; Fat 13.1g, of which saturates 8.2g; Cholesterol 38mg; Calcium 176mg; Fiber 1.3g; Sodium 79mg.

p187 **Banana High** Energy 469Cal/1958kJ; Protein 6.9g; Carbohydrate 54.1g, of which sugars 51.8g; Fat 26.3g, of which saturates 16.4g; Cholesterol 72mg; Calcium 213mg; Fiber 1.1g; Sodium 75mg.

p190 **Griddle Cakes** Energy 60Cal/252kJ; Protein 2g; Carbohydrate 11.1g, of which sugars 1.8g; Fat 1.1g, of which saturates 0.2g; Cholesterol 11mg; Calcium 66mg; Fiber 0.4g; Sodium 56mg.

p191 **Buttermilk Biscuits** Energy 74Cal/311kJ; Protein 1.7g; Carbohydrate 10.9g, of which sugars 0.7g; Fat 3g, of which saturates 1.8g; Cholesterol 8mg; Calcium 34mg; Fiber 0.4g; Sodium 26mg.

p192 **Buttermilk Pancakes** Energy 90Cal/380kJ; Protein 3.2g; Carbohydrate 18.7g, of which sugars 4.4g; Fat 0.8g, of which saturates 0.2g; Cholesterol 17mg; Calcium 61mg; Fiber 0.6g; Sodium 18mg.

p193 **French Toast** Energy 494Cal/2060kJ; Protein 8.6g; Carbohydrate 44.7g, of which sugars 17.7g; Fat 32.5g, of which saturates 15g; Cholesterol 148mg; Calcium 111mg; Fiber 1.3g; Sodium 287mg.

p194 **Banana Muffins** Energy 152Cal/642kJ; Protein 2.8g; Carbohydrate 29g, of which sugars 13.9g; Fat 3.6g, of which saturates 0.5g; Cholesterol 16mg; Calcium 34mg; Fiber 1g; Sodium 9mg.

p195 **Double Choc Chip Muffins** Energy 281Cal/1183kJ; Protein 4.7g; Carbohydrate 41.3g, of which sugars 21.9g; Fat 11.9g, of which saturates 5.7g; Cholesterol 7mg; Calcium 94mg; Fiber 1.3g; Sodium 40mg.

p196 **Banana Gingerbread** Energy 133Cal/563kJ; Protein 2.3g; Carbohydrate 25.9g, of which sugars 15.2g; Fat 3g, of which saturates 0.5g; Cholesterol 19mg; Calcium 37mg; Fiber 0.7g; Sodium 18mg.

p197 **Bilberry Bread** Energy 374Cal/1575kJ; Protein 5g; Carbohydrate 66.2g, of which sugars 40.9g; Fat 11.7g, of which saturates 6.9g; Cholesterol 51mg; Calcium 104mg; Fiber 2.1g; Sodium 95mg.

p198 **Carrot Cake** Energy 331Cal/1387kJ; Protein 6.4g; Carbohydrate 41g, of which sugars 24.6g; Fat 16.9g, of which saturates 7g; Cholesterol 73mg; Calcium 63mg; Fiber 1.5g; Sodium 83mg.

p200 **Simple Chocolate Cake** Energy 427Cal/1776kJ; Protein 6.1g; Carbohydrate 29.2g, of which sugars 9.8g; Fat 32.6g, of which saturates 19.6g; Cholesterol 139mg; Calcium 65mg; Fiber 1.4g; Sodium 238mg.

p201 **Luscious Lemon Cake** Energy 420Cal/1757kJ; Protein 6g; Carbohydrate 49.2g, of which sugars 28.3g; Fat 23.6g, of which saturates 14.3g; Cholesterol 153mg; Calcium 70mg; Fiber 0.9g; Sodium 229mg.

p202 **Lemon Meringue Cakes** Energy 123Cal/514kJ; Protein 1.7g; Carbohydrate 16.6g, of which sugars 11.7g; Fat 6g, of which saturates 3.5g; Cholesterol 35mg; Calcium 19mg; Fiber 0.2g; Sodium 54mg.

p203 **Orange and Apple Rockies** Energy 87Cal/366kJ; Protein 1.3g; Carbohydrate 11.6g, of which sugars 4.5g; Fat 4.3g, of which saturates 0.9g; Cholesterol 8mg; Calcium 19mg; Fiber 0.5g; Sodium 42mg.

p204 **Pecan Squares** Energy 245Cal/1016kJ; Protein 2.1g; Carbohydrate 15.5g, of which sugars 10.5g; Fat 19.8g, of which saturates 7.6g; Cholesterol 33mg; Calcium 26mg; Fiber 0.8g; Sodium 71mg.

p205 **Rich Chocolate Cookie Slice** Energy 326Cal/1361kJ; Protein 2.7g; Carbohydrate 29g, of which sugars 23.8g; Fat 23g, of which saturates 13.9g; Cholesterol 33mg; Calcium 44mg; Fiber 0.9g; Sodium 144mg.

p206 **Chewy Oat Bars** Energy 241Cal/1007kJ; Protein 2.7g; Carbohydrate 29.5g, of which sugars 14.3g; Fat 13.2g, of which saturates 7.2g; Cholesterol 30mg; Calcium 18mg; Fiber 1.4g; Sodium 125mg.

p207 **Peanut and Jelly Cookies** Energy 170Cal/713kJ; Protein 3.3g; Carbohydrate 21g, of which sugars 15.3g; Fat 8.5g, of which saturates 3.1g; Cholesterol 16mg; Calcium 36mg; Fiber 0.8g; Sodium 92mg.

p208 **Triple Chocolate Cookies** Energy 416Cal/1738kJ; Protein 4.3g; Carbohydrate 47.6g, of which sugars 37.8g; Fat 24.4g, of which saturates 11.8g; Cholesterol 21mg; Calcium 71mg; Fiber 1.6g; Sodium 84mg.

p209 **Chocolate Caramel Nuggets** Energy 149Cal/625kJ; Protein 1.8g; Carbohydrate 18.7g, of which sugars 9.5g; Fat 8g, of which saturates 4.6g; Cholesterol 30mg;Calcium 34mg; Fiber 0.3g; Sodium 58mg.

p212 **Crazy Rainbow Popcorn** Energy 103Cal/430kJ; Protein 2.4g; Carbohydrate 5.7g, of which sugars 0.1g; Fat 7.9g, of which saturates 2g; Cholesterol 6mg; Calcium 50mg; Fiber 0g; Sodium 49mg.

p214 **Cheese and Potato Twists** Energy 231Cal/971kJ; Protein 8.7g; Carbohydrate 26.4g, of which sugars 0.8g; Fat 10.4g, of which saturates 5.2g; Cholesterol 21mg; Calcium 203mg; Fiber 1.2g; Sodium 162mg..

p215 **Sandwich Shapes** Energy 342Cal/1433kJ; Protein 14.6g; Carbohydrate 31.5g, of which sugars 2.2g; Fat 18.2g, of which saturates 7.9g; Cholesterol 50mg; Calcium 136mg; Fiber 1.7g; Sodium 726mg.

p216 **Mini Burgers 'n' Rolls** Energy 229Cal/960kJ; Protein 12.9g; Carbohydrate 20.7g, of which sugars 1.5g; Fat 10.8g, of which saturates 5.2g; Cholesterol 54mg; Calcium 148mg; Fiber 0.7g; Sodium 341mg.

p218 **Mini Ciabatta Pizzas** Energy 154Cal/647kJ; Protein 8.6g; Carbohydrate 18.7g, of which sugars 6.2g; Fat 5.4g, of which saturates 2.9g; Cholesterol 16mg; Calcium 106mg; Fiber 2g; Sodium 325mg.

p219 **Tortilla Squares** Energy 177Cal/738kJ; Protein 9.2g; Carbohydrate 15.5g, of which sugars 4.8g; Fat 9.2g, of which saturates 1.9g; Cholesterol 150mg; Calcium 71mg; Fiber 3.7g; Sodium 66mg.

p220 **Chicken Mini Rolls** Energy 467Cal/1963kJ; Protein 27.9g; Carbohydrate 49.6g, of which sugars 6.9g; Fat 19g, of which saturates 3.5g; Cholesterol 132mg; Calcium 109mg; Fiber 2.1g; Sodium 105mg.

p221 **Falafel** Energy 372Cal/1557kJ; Protein 19.3g; Carbohydrate 35.3g, of which sugars 5.8g; Fat 18.1g, of which saturates 2.6g; Cholesterol 48mg; Calcium 280mg; Fiber 8g; Sodium 89mg.

p222 **Mini Muffins** Energy 67Cal/281kJ; Protein 1.4g; Carbohydrate 11.1g, of which sugars 4.8g; Fat 2.2g, of which saturates 1.2g; Cholesterol 13mg; Calcium 25mg; Fiber 0.4g; Sodium 19mg.

p223 **Cupcake Faces** Energy 328Cal/1374kJ; Protein 3.2g; Carbohydrate 42.5g, of which sugars 33.1g; Fat 17.3g, of which saturates 5.4g; Cholesterol 43mg; Calcium 53mg; Fiber 0.6g; Sodium 127mg.

p224 **Puppy Faces** Energy 251Cal/1063kJ; Protein 2.1g; Carbohydrate 52.2g, of which sugars 40.9g; Fat 5.2g, of which saturates 2.8g; Cholesterol 31mg; Calcium 37mg; Fiber 0.7g; Sodium 38mg.

p226 **Gingerbread People** Energy 94Cal/395kJ; Protein 1.2g; Carbohydrate 16.5g, of which sugars 9.3g; Fat 3g, of which saturates 0.7g; Cholesterol 0mg; Calcium 19mg; Fiber 0.4g; Sodium 23mg.

p228 **Jelly Sandwich Cookies** Energy 831Cal/3480kJ; Protein 6.4g; Carbohydrate 104.6g, of which sugars 63.9g; Fat 45.9g, of which saturates 28.3g; Cholesterol 162mg; Calcium 119mg; Fiber 1.7g; Sodium 334mg.

p229 **Chocolate Cookies on Sticks** Energy 107Cal/448kJ; Protein 1.5g; Carbohydrate 12.3g, of which sugars 10.9g; Fat 6.1g, of which saturates 3.5g; Cholesterol 2mg; Calcium 43mg; Fiber 0.2g; Sodium 30mg.

p230 **Wobbly Gelatin** Energy 195Cal/824kJ; Protein 4.9g; Carbohydrate 39.2g, of which sugars 38.9g; Fat 3.2g, of which saturates 2g; Cholesterol 9mg; Calcium 55mg; Fiber 0.3g; Sodium 26mg.

p231 **Yogurt Popsicles** Energy 41Cal/172kJ; Protein 1.9g; Carbohydrate 7.3g, of which sugars 7.3g; Fat 0.6g, of which saturates 0.4g; Cholesterol 2mg; Calcium 68mg; Fiber 0g; Sodium 27mg.

p232 **Chocolate Fudge Sundaes** Energy 595Cal/2498kJ; Protein 6.3g; Carbohydrate 88.1g, of which sugars 85.3g; Fat 26.5g, of which saturates 14.1g; Cholesterol 26mg; Calcium 139mg; Fiber 1.8g; Sodium 144mg.

p233 **Strawberry Ice Cream** Energy 2198Cal/9105kJ; Protein 21.6g; Carbohydrate 110g, of which sugars 93.9g; Fat 183.6g, of which saturates 108.7g; Cholesterol 456mg; Calcium 657mg; Fiber 5.8g; Sodium 290mg.

p234 **Balloon Cake** Energy 574Cal/2413kJ; Protein 5.9g; Carbohydrate 89g, of which sugars 76.2g; Fat 24.1g, of which saturates 5.9g; Cholesterol 74mg; Calcium 82mg; Fiber 1.2g; Sodium 226mg.

p236 **Spooky Cookies** Energy 122Cal/515kJ; Protein 1g; Carbohydrate 18.7g, of which sugars 12.5g; Fat 5.4g, of which saturates 3.4g; Cholesterol 22mg; Calcium 19mg; Fiber 0.3g; Sodium 48mg.

p237 **Chocolate Witchy Apples** Energy 348Cal/1467kJ; Protein 4.3g; Carbohydrate 54.8g, of which sugars 49.9g; Fat 13.8g, of which saturates 8g; Cholesterol 13mg; Calcium 107mg; Fiber 1.7g; Sodium 84mg.

p238 **Jack-o'-Lantern Cake** cake Energy 458Cal/1936kJ; Protein 3.8g; Carbohydrate 90.2g, of which sugars 76.9g; Fat 11.6g, of which saturates 6.9g; Cholesterol 88mg; Calcium 93mg; Fiber 0.5g; Sodium 110mg.

p240 **Creamy Fudge** Energy 5886Cal/24635kJ; Protein 40.4g; Carbohydrate 708.8g, of which sugars 704.5g; Fat 340.8g, of which saturates 171g; Cholesterol 540mg; Calcium 874mg; Fiber 14.1g; Sodium 512mg.

p241 **Striped Cookies** Energy 47Cal/198kJ; Protein 0.6g; Carbohydrate 6.5g, of which sugars 5g; Fat 2.3g, of which saturates 1.4g; Cholesterol 5mg; Calcium 11mg; Fiber 0.1g; Sodium 22mg.

p242 **Christmas Tree Angels** Energy 147Cal/622kJ; Protein 1.9g; Carbohydrate 28.7g, of which sugars 16g; Fat 3.6g, of which saturates 2.1g; Cholesterol 15mg; Calcium 31mg; Fiber 0.5g; Sodium 45mg.

p244 **Mince Pies** Energy 236Cal/993kJ; Protein 2.5g; Carbohydrate 36.7g, of which sugars 22.4g; Fat 9.8g, of which saturates 5.2g; Cholesterol 37mg; Calcium 43mg; Fiber 1g; Sodium 70mg.

p246 **Easter Cookies** Energy 285Cal/1197kJ; Protein 2.9g; Carbohydrate 45g, of which sugars 35.4g; Fat 11.6g, of which saturates 5.5g; Cholesterol 43mg; Calcium 48mg; Fiber 0.9g; Sodium 66mg.

p247 **Chocolate Birds' Nests** Energy 214Cal/896kJ; Protein 3.4g; Carbohydrate 24.4g, of which sugars 19g; Fat 12.1g, of which saturates 7.2g; Cholesterol 12mg; Calcium 77mg; Fiber 1g; Sodium 42mg.

Index

A

apples 20
  Chocolate Witchy Apples 237
  Lazy Fruit Pastry 158
  Orange and Apple Rockies 203
  peeling and coring 20
  Strawberry and Apple Cooler 181
  Yogurt Cups 57
apricot conserve: Banana and
    Apricot Trifle 167
apricots 21
  Apricot and Pecan Bars 58
  Yogurt Cups 57
arugula: Chilled Tomato Soup 88
avocados 52
  Chilled Avocado Soup 89
  Chile Cheese Nachos 79
  Mozzarella and Avocado Salad 52

B

bacon: Spaghetti Carbonara 103
  Toasted Bacon Sandwich 68
  Turkey Surprise Packages 143
balloon whisk 18
bananas 20
  Baked Bananas 161
  Banana and Apricot Trifle 167
  Banana and Toffee Ice
    Cream 162
  Banana Gingerbread 196
  Banana Muffins 194
  Banana High 187
  Carrot Cake 198
  Chocolate Banana Fools 166
  Chocolate Fudge
    Sundaes 232
baking soda 26
  Bilberry Bread
    197

bars: Apricot and Pecan Bars 58
  Chewy Oat Bars 206
basic techniques 28–33
basil 24
  Cheese and Basil Tortillas 80
beans 23
  Bean and Tomato Chile 105
  Boston Baked Beans 124
  Country Pasta Salad 84
  Potato and Pepper Frittata 92
  Tortilla Squares 219
  Tuna and Bean Salad 53
  Tuna Pasta Salad 85
bean sprouts: Crunchy Summer
    Rolls 127
beef: Cheesy Burgers 153
  Meatballs in Tomato Sauce 115
  Mexican Tacos 112
  Mini Burgers 'n' Rolls 216–17
  Sausage Casserole 146
  Shepherd's Pie 149
  Steak with Tomato Salsa 152
bell peppers 23
  Confetti Salad 54
  Dunkin' Dippers 76–77
  Potato and Pepper Frittata 92
  Roasted Vegetable Sauce 98
biscuits: Buttermilk Biscuits 191
blackberries: Ruby Red Soda 177
blenders 9, 19
blueberries: Bilberry Bread 197
  Blueberry and Lemon Muffins 63
  Ruby Red Soda 177
bread 216
  Cheese Toasts 70–71
  Cheesy Treats 69
  Chicken Pita Pockets 81
  Ciabatta Sandwich 67
  Eggstra Special Sandwich
    Selection 42
  Eggtastic 73
  Frankfurter Sandwich 66
  French Toast 193
  Ham and Pineapple Pizza 95
  Ham and Tomato Scramble 75
  Mini Ciabatta Pizzas 218
  Pitas with Lamb Koftas 113

  Sandwich Shapes 215
  Speedy Sausage Rolls 41
  Sweet Toast Toppers 72
  Toasted Bacon Sandwich 68
  Tomato and Bread Soup 123
broccoli 23
  Broccoli Soup 90
brownies: Butterscotch Brownies 60
Brussels sprouts 23
  Cabbage and Potatoes 104
burgers: Cheesy Burgers 153
  Mini Burgers 'n' Rolls 216–17
  Thai Pork Burgers 145
  Turkey Burgers 112
butter 25
  creaming butter and sugar 30
  rubbing in flour and butter 30
buttermilk 192
  Buttermilk Pancakes 192
  Buttermilk Biscuits 191

C

cabbage 23
  Cabbage and Potatoes 104
cake pans 19
cakes: all-in-one 30
  Balloon Cake 234–35
  Carrot Cake 198–99
  Chocolate Birds' Nests 247
  Cupcake Faces 223
  Jack-o'-Lantern Cake 238–39
  Lemon Meringue Cakes 202
  Luscious Lemon Cake 201
  Orange and Apple Rockies 203
  Simple Chocolate Cake 200
carrots 23
  Carrot Cake 198–99
  Carrot Soup 121
  Crunchy Summer Rolls 127
celery 23

cheese 25, 153
  Baked Macaroni Cheese 100
  Cheese and Basil Tortillas 80
  Cheese and Ham Tarts 46
  Cheese and Potato Twists 214
  Cheese Toasts 70–71
  Cheesy Burgers 153
  Cheesy Treats 69
  Chile Cheese Nachos 79
  Cream and Parmesan Sauce 98
  Dunkin' Dippers 76–77
  Fiorentina Pizza 94
  Fish and Cheese Pies 137
  grating 25
  Ham and Mozzarella Calzone 44
  Mozzarella and Avocado Salad 52
  Quick and Easy Risotto 97
  Sandwich Shapes 215
  Tomato and Cheese Pizza 45
  Tomato Omelet Envelopes 93
cheesecake: Summer Fruit
    Cheesecake 168–69
chicken 24
  Chicken and Tomato Salad 83
  Chicken Mini Rolls 220
  Chicken Fajitas 140–41
  Chicken Pasta Salad 51
  Chicken Pita Pockets 81
  Chinese Soup 91
  Colorful Chicken Kebabs 108
  Honey Mustard Chicken 110
  Sandwich Shapes 215
  Sticky Chicken 109
  Tandoori-Style Chicken 138–39
  Yellow Bean Chicken 111
chickpeas: Falafel 221
  Hummus 40
chiles 96, 105
  Bean and Tomato Chile 105
  Chile Cheese Nachos 79
  Mexican Tomato Rice 96
chocolate 27
  Butterscotch Brownies 60
  Chocolate Banana Fools 166
  Chocolate Birds' Nests 247
  Chocolate Cookies on Sticks 229
  Chocolate Cups 172
  Chocolate Fudge Sundaes 232
  Chocolate Heaven 174–75
  Chocolate Puffs 173
  Chocolate Thumbprint Cookies 61

  Chocolate Witchy Apples 237
  Cupcake Faces 223
  Double Choc Chip Muffins 195
  Fruit Fondue 170
  Gingerbread People 226
  Magic Chocolate Pudding 156
  melting 27
  Rich Chocolate Cookie Slice 205
  Simple Chocolate Cake 200
  Triple Chocolate Cookies 208
  Chocolate Caramel Nuggets 209
chorizo sausages 116
  Sausage and Spring Onion Hash 116
  Spicy Sausage Tortilla 47
cilantro 128
cinnamon 24
  Sweet Toast Toppers 72
citrus juicers 18
coconut milk: Creamy Coconut
    Noodles 126
  Pork and Pineapple Curry 144
  Pork Satay 116
cod: Fish and Cheese Pies 137
  Fast Fishes 107
colander 17
cooking terms 14–15
cookie cutters 17, 32
cookies: Chocolate Caramel
    Nuggets 209
  Chocolate Cookies on Sticks 229
  Chocolate Heaven 174–75
  Chocolate Thumbprint Cookies 61
  Christmas Tree Angels 242–43
  Easter Cookies 246
  Gingerbread People 226–27
  Jelly Sandwich Cookies 228
  Peanut and Jelly Cookies 207
  Peanut Butter Cookies 62
  Puppy Faces 224–25
  Rich Chocolate Cookie Slice 205
  Spooky Cookies 236
  Striped Cookies 241
  Triple Chocolate Cookies 208
cooling rack 18
coriander 128
  Zucchini and Potato Bake 125
corn: Corn and Potato Chowder 120
  Dunkin' Dippers 76–77
  Tuna and Corn Fish Cakes 106
corn syrup 27
couscous: Lemony Couscous Salad 55

cream 25
  Cream and Parmesan Sauce 98
  whipping 29
cucumbers: Dunkin' Dippers 76–77
  Mini Burgers 'n' Rolls 216–17
cutting boards 8, 17

D
dairy produce 10, 11, 25
dates: Date Slices 59
dips: Dunkin' Dippers 76–77
  Skinny Dips 78
drinks: Banana High 187
  Candystripe 186
  Fresh Orange Fizz 176
  Fruit Punch 179
  fruit smoothies 13
  Rainbow Juice and Fruit
    Slush 182–83
  Ruby Red Soda 177
  Strawberry and Apple Cooler 181
  Strawberry Shake 185
  Totally Tropical 178
  Vanilla Milkshake 184
  What a Smoothie 180

E
eggplants 23
  Roasted Vegetable Sauce 98
eggs 11
  breaking 29
  Chinese Omelet Parcels 128–29
  Egg-Stuffed Tomatoes 74
  Eggstra Special Sandwich
    Selection 42–43
  Eggtastic 73
  Fiorentina Pizza 94
  French Toast 193
  Ham and Tomato Scramble 75
  separating 29
  Spicy Sausage Tortilla 47
  Tomato Omelet
    Envelopes 93

Tortilla Squares 219
  whisking egg whites 29
electric mixers 9, 19
equipment 8, 9, 16–17

F
Falafel 221
Farfalle with Tuna 101
figs 198
  Carrot Cake 198
fish: Fish and Rice Paella 135
  see also fish names
Flounder with Tomato Sauce 136
flour 26
food allergies and intolerance 12
food processors 9, 19
food wheel 10, 11
fruit 10, 11, 12, 20–22
  Fabulous Fruit Salad 56
  Fruit Fondue 170
  Rainbow Juice and Fruit Slush 182–83
  see also the names of fruits
fruit juice: Fruit Punch 179
fudge: Chocolate Fudge Sundaes 232
  Creamy Fudge 240

G
garlic 22, 90
garlic press 17
gelatin 168
getting started 6–7
gingerbread: Banana
    Gingerbread 196
  Gingerbread People 226–27
grapes: Totally Tropical 178
graters, grating 9, 15, 16, 17

Griddle Cakes 190
grill irons/pans 19
ground allspice 24
guacamole: Dunkin' Dippers 76–77

H
ham: Cheese and Ham Tarts 46
  Cheesy Treats 69
  Ciabatta Sandwich 67
  Ham and Mozzarella Calzone 44
  Ham and Pineapple Pizza 95
  Ham and Tomato Scramble 75
  Mini Ciabatta Pizzas 218
  Quick and Easy Risotto 97
  Sandwich Shapes 215
  Tortellini with Ham 102
harissa paste 117
hazelnuts 25
healthy eating 10–13
herbs 24
hoki: Fish and Cheese Pies 137
  Fast Fishes 107
honey 27, 27
  Honey Chops 117
Hummus 40

I
ice cream: Baked Bananas 161
  Banana and Toffee Ice Cream 162
  Chocolate Fudge Sundaes 232
  Strawberry Ice Cream 233

J
jelly: Banana and Apricot Trifle 167
  Jelly Sandwich Cookies 228
  Peanut and Jelly Cookies 207
  Sweet Toast Toppers 72
  Wobbly Gelatin 230

K
kebabs: Colorful Chicken Kebabs 108
  Pork Satay 116
kiwis 21
  Fabulous Fruit Salad 56
  Rainbow Juice 182–83
knives 8, 17

L
ladle 18
lamb 24, 150
  Crown Roast 150

Lamb Stew 151
  Pitas with Lamb Koftas 113
  Sausage Casserole 146
lemongrass 145
lemons 21
  Blueberry and Lemon Muffins 63
  Lemon Meringue Cakes 202
  Lemon Surprise Pudding 160
  Luscious Lemon Cake 201
  Summer Fruit Cheesecake 168–69
  zesting 39
lettuce: Crunchy Summer Rolls 127
limes 21

M
macaroni: Baked Macaroni
    Cheese 100
  Tuna Pasta Salad 85
mangoes 21
  Fabulous Fruit Salad 56
  Totally Tropical 178
marshmallows: Candy Stripe 186
mayonnaise: Sandwich Shapes 215
measurements 4, 7
measuring cups 16
measuring spoons 16, 28
meat 24
  see meat names
melons: Cantaloupe Melon Salad 171
menu ideas 34–35
meringues: Lemon Meringue Cakes
    202
  Strawberries and Meringue 165
milk 13, 25
  milkshakes: Banana High 187
  Candy Stripe 186
  Vanilla Milkshake 184
Mince Pies 244–5
mozzarella cheese: Ham and
    Mozzarella Calzone 44
  Mozzarella and Avocado
    Salad 52

muffins: Banana Muffins 194
  Blueberry and Lemon Muffins 63
  Double Choc Chip Muffins 195
  Mini Muffins 222

N
nectarines 21
  Yogurt Cups 57
noodles 25
  Chinese Soup 91
  Creamy Coconut Noodles 126
nuts 12, 25

O
oats: Yogurt Cups 57
oils 27, 83
olive oil 27
olives 101
omelets: Chinese Omelet
    Parcels 128–29
  Potato and Pepper Frittata 92
  Spicy Sausage Tortilla 47
  Tomato Omelet Envelopes 93
  Tortilla Squares 219
onions 22
  chopping an onion 22
  Lamb and Potato Pies 148
orange juice: What a Smoothie 180
oranges: Fresh Orange Squash 176
  Orange and Apple Rockies 203
  zesting 30
oven mitts 9

P
pancakes: Buttermilk Pancakes 192
pancetta: Spaghetti Carbonara 103
  Tortellini with Ham 102
pans 19
paper piping bag 33
Parmesan cheese 25, 130
  Cream and Parmesan Sauce 98
party ideas 36–37
passata 101
passion fruits 22
pasta 26, 122
  Baked Macaroni Cheese 100
  Chicken Pasta Salad 51
  Country Pasta Salad 84
  Farfalle with Tuna 101
  Raving Ravioli 130–31
  Spaghetti Carbonara 103

Tomato and Pasta Salad 50
  Tortellini with Ham 102
  Tuna Pasta Salad 85
pasta sauces: Basic Tomato Sauce 98
  Cream and Parmesan Sauce 98
  Pesto Sauce 98
  Roasted Vegetable Sauce 98
pastry, stamping out 32
pastry dish, lining a 32
peaches 21
peanut butter: Hummus 40
  Peanut and Jelly Cookies 207
  Peanut Butter Cookies 62
peas 23
  Mexican Tomato Rice 96
pecan nuts: Apricot and Pecan
    Bars 58
  Pecan Squares 204
peeler 17
pestle and mortar 29, 88
phyllo pastry 220
pies: Fish and Cheese Pies 137
  Popeye's Pie 48–49
  Shepherd's Pie 149
pine nuts 25
pineapples 22, 182
  Ham and Pineapple Pizza 95
  Pineapple Sorbet on Sticks 163
  Pork and Pineapple Curry 144
  Totally Tropical 178
pita breads: Chicken Pita Pockets 81
  Pitas with Lamb Koftas 113
pizzas: Fiorentina Pizza 94
  Ham and Mozzarella Calzone 44
  Ham and Pineapple Pizza 95
  Mini Ciabatta Pizzas 218
  Tomato and Cheese Pizza 45
plums 21
  Wobbly Gelatin 230
  Plum Crumble 159
popcorn: Crazy Rainbow
    Popcorn 212–13
pork: Boston Baked Beans 124
  Honey Chops 117
  Meatballs in Tomato Sauce 115
  Pork and Pineapple Curry 144
  Pork Satay 116
  Sausage Casserole 146
  Thai Pork Burgers 145
potatoes 22, 132
  Cabbage and Potatoes 104

Cheese and Potato Twists 214
  Corn and Potato Chowder 120
  Country Pasta Salad 84
  Fantastic potatoes! 132–33
  mashing 23
  Potato and Pepper Frittata 92
  Sausage and Scallion Hash 116
  Shepherd's Pie 149
  Skinny Dips 78
  Tortilla Squares 219
  Tuna and Corn Fish Cakes 106
  Turkey Croquettes 142
  Zucchini and Potato Bake 125
pumpkins 22

R
raspberries: Very Berry
    Cheesecake 168–69
  What a Smoothie 180
  Yogurt Cups 57
rice 26
  Colorful Chicken Kebabs 108
  Confetti Salad 54
  Fish and Rice Paella 135
  Mexican Tomato Rice 96
  Quick and Easy Risotto 97
  Rice Pudding 157
  Vegetable Paella 134
rice papers: Crunchy Summer Rolls 127
rising agents 26
rolling pin 18

S
safety in the kitchen 8–9
salad greens 24
salads 10, 11

Cantaloupe Melon Salad 171
Chicken and Tomato Salad 83
Chicken Pasta Salad 51
Chunky Veggie Salad 82
Confetti Salad 54
Country Pasta Salad 84
Fabulous Fruit Salad 56
Lemony Couscous Salad 55
Mozzarella and Avocado
    Salad 52
Tomato and Pasta Salad 50
Tuna and Bean Salad 53
Tuna Pasta Salad 85
sandwiches see bread
sausages 24
    Frankfurter Sandwich 66
    Meatballs in Tomato Sauce 115
    Mini Toads-in-the-Hole 147
    Lamb and Potato Pies 148
    Sausage Casserole 146
    Speedy Sausage Rolls 41
    see also chorizo sausages
scales 28
scallions: Sausage and Scallion
    Hash 116
seeds 25
    sprouted 82
shrimp: Fish and Rice Paella 135
skillets 19
soda: Ruby Red Soda 177
soups: Broccoli Soup 90
    Carrot Soup 121
    Chilled Avocado Soup 89
    Chilled Tomato Soup 88
    Chinese Soup 91
    Corn and Potato Chowder 120
    Super Duper Soup 122
    Tomato and Bread Soup 123
    Spaghetti Carbonara 103
spatulas 18
spices 24
spinach 24, 48
    Fiorentina Pizza 94
    Popeye's Pie 48–49
    Raving Ravioli 130–31
spoons 18
squashes 22
star ratings 6
steak: Mini Burgers 'n'
    Rolls 216–17
    Steak with Tomato Salsa 152

strainers 15, 16
strawberries: Candy Stripe 186
    Cantaloupe Melon Salad 171
    Strawberries and Meringue 165
    Strawberry and Apple
        Cooler 181
    Strawberry Ice Cream 233
    Strawberry Mousse 164
    Strawberry Shake 185
    Very Berry Cheesecake 168–69
sugar 26

T
tacos: Mexican Tacos 114
timers 18
toffees: Banana and Toffee Ice
    Cream 162
tomatoes 24, 113
    Basic Tomato Sauce 98
    Bean and Tomato Chile 105
    Chicken and Tomato Salad 83
    Chilled Tomato Soup 88
    Chile Cheese Nachos 79
    Confetti Salad 54
    Country Pasta Salad 84
    Dunkin' Dippers 76–77
    Egg-Stuffed Tomatoes 74
    Flounder with Tomato
        Sauce 136
    Ham and Tomato Scramble 75
    Meatballs in Tomato Sauce 115
    Mexican Tomato Rice 96
    peeling 24
    Roasted Vegetable Sauce 98
    Steak with Tomato Salsa 152
    Tomato and Bread Soup 123
    Tomato and Cheese Pizza 45
    Tomato and Pasta Salad 50
    Tomato Omelet Envelopes 93
tongs 18
tortilla chips: Chile Cheese
    Nachos 79
    Dunkin' Dippers 76–77
tortillas: Cheese and Basil
    Tortillas 80
    Chicken Fajitas 140–41
trout: Raving Ravioli 130–31
tuna: Eggstra Special Sandwich
    Selection 42–43
    Farfalle with Tuna 101
    Tuna and Bean Salad 53

Tuna and Corn Fish Cakes 106
Tuna Pasta Salad 85
turkey: Mexican Tacos 114
    Turkey Croquettes 142
    Turkey Burgers 112
    Turkey Surprise Packages 143
V
Vanilla Milkshake 184
vegetables 10, 11, 12, 22–24
    Chinese Omelet Parcels 128–29
    Chunky Veggie Salad 82
    Creamy Coconut Noodles 126
    Fantastic Potatoes! 132–33
    Super-duper Soup 122
    Vegetable Paella 134

W, Y
whisks, wire 18
woks 19
yellow bean sauce: Yellow Bean
    Chicken 111
yogurt 25
    Strawberry Shake 185
    What a Smoothie 180
    Yogurt Popsicles 231
    Yogurt Cups 57

Picture credits
The publishers would like to thank
the following for permission to
reproduce their images:
iStock Images: 6t (Thomas Perkins); 7bl
(Ekaterina Monakhova); 7t (Margarita
Borodina); 8br (Rich Yasick); 8c (Daniel
Loiselle); 12bl (Arne Trautmann);
13br (Carrie Bottomley); 17tr (Edd
Westmacott); 19cl (Bojan Pavlukovic);
22tl (Daniel Kirkegaard Mouritsen);
p184m and 185m (Joao Virissimo).
Corbis: 7br (Ingolf Hatz/zefa/Corbis).